New Perspectives on

The Internet Using
Netscape Communicator™
Software

INTRODUCTORY

The New Perspectives Series

The New Perspectives Series consists of texts and technology that teach computer concepts and microcomputer applications (listed below). You can order these New Perspectives texts in many different lengths, software releases, custom-bound combinations, CourseKits™ and Custom Editions®. Contact your Course Technology sales representative or customer service representative for the most up-to-date details.

The New Perspectives Series

Computer Concepts

Borland® dBASE®

Borland® Paradox®

Corel® Presentations™

Corel® Quattro Pro®

Corel® WordPerfect®

DOS

HTML

Lotus® 1-2-3®

Microsoft® Access

Microsoft® Excel

Microsoft® Internet Explorer

Microsoft® Office Professional

Microsoft® PowerPoint®

Microsoft® Windows® 3.1

Microsoft® Windows® 95

Microsoft® Windows NT® Server 4.0

Microsoft® Windows NT® Workstation 4.0

Microsoft® Word

Microsoft® Works

Netscape Communicator

Netscape Navigator™

Netscape Navigator™ Gold

Microsoft® Visual Basic® 4 and 5

New Perspectives on

The Internet Using
Netscape Communicator™
Software

Sandra E. Poindexter
Northern Michigan University

Joan and Patrick Carey
Carey Associates, Inc.

COURSE
TECHNOLOGY

ONE MAIN STREET, CAMBRIDGE, MA 02142

an International Thomson Publishing company I(T)P®

Cambridge • Albany • Bonn • Boston • Cincinnati • London • Madrid • Melbourne • Mexico City
New York • Paris • San Francisco • Singapore • Tokyo • Toronto • Washington

New Perspectives on the Internet Using Netscape Communicator™ Software—Introductory is published by Course Technology.

Associate Publisher	Mac Mendelsohn
Series Consulting Editor	Susan Solomon
Product Manager	Donna Gridley
Associate Product Manager	Rachel Crapser
Developmental Editor	Joan Carey
Production Editor	Seth Andrews
Text and Cover Designer	Ella Hanna
Cover Illustrator	Douglas Goodman

© 1998 by Course Technology—I(T)P®

For more information contact:

Course Technology
One Main Street
Cambridge, MA 02142

ITP Europe
Berkshire House 168-173
High Holborn
London WCIV 7AA
England

Nelson ITP, Australia
102 Dodds Street
South Melbourne, 3205
Victoria, Australia

ITP Nelson Canada
1120 Birchmount Road
Scarborough, Ontario
Canada M1K 5G4

International Thomson Editores
Seneca, 53
Colonia Polanco
11560 Mexico D.F. Mexico

ITP GmbH
Königswinterer Strasse 418
53227 Bonn
Germany

ITP Asia
60 Albert Street, #15-01
Albert Complex
Singapore 189969

ITP Japan
Hirakawacho Kyowa Building, 3F
2-2-1 Hirakawacho
Chiyoda-ku, Tokyo 102
Japan

ISBN 0-7600-5764-8

Printed in the United States of America

5 6 7 8 9 BM 02 01 00 99

At Course Technology we have one foot in education and the other in technology. We believe that technology is transforming the way people teach and learn, and we are excited about providing instructors and students with materials that use technology to teach about technology.

Our development process is unparalleled in the higher education publishing industry. Every product we create goes through an exacting process of design, development, review, and testing.

Reviewers give us direction and insight that shape our manuscripts and bring them up to the latest standards. Every manuscript is quality tested. Students whose backgrounds match the intended audience work through every keystroke, carefully checking for clarity and pointing out errors in logic and sequence. Together with our own technical reviewers, these testers help us ensure that everything that carries our name is error-free and easy to use.

We show both how and why technology is critical to solving problems in college and in whatever field you choose to teach or pursue. Our time-tested, step-by-step instructions provide unparalleled clarity. Examples and applications are chosen and crafted to motivate students.

As the New Perspectives Series team at Course Technology, our goal is to produce the most timely, accurate, creative, and technologically sound product in the entire college publishing industry. We strive for consistent high quality. This takes a lot of communication, coordination, and hard work. But we love what we do. We are determined to be the best. Write to us and let us know what you think. You can also e-mail us at NewPerspectives@course.com.

The New Perspectives Series Team

Joseph J. Adamski	Jessica Evans	Mac Mendelsohn
Judy Adamski	Marilyn Freedman	William Newman
Roy Ageloff	Kathy Finnegan	Dan Oja
Tim Ashe	Robin Geller	David Paradice
David Auer	Donna Gridley	June Parsons
Daphne Barbas	Kate Habib	Harry Phillips
Dirk Baldwin	Roger Hayen	Sandra Poindexter
Rachel Bunin	Charles Hommel	Mark Reimold
Joan Carey	Cindy Johnson	Ann Shaffer
Patrick Carey	Janice Jutras	Karen Shortill
Sharon Caswell	Chris Kelly	Susan Solomon
Barbara Clemens	Mary Kemper	Susanne Walker
Rachel Crapser	Stacy Klein	John Zeanchock
Kim Crowley	Terry Ann Kremer	Beverly Zimmerman
Melissa Dezotell	John Leschke	Scott Zimmerman
Michael Ekedahl		

What is the New Perspectives Series?

Course Technology's **New Perspectives Series** is an integrated system of instruction that combines text and technology products to teach computer concepts and microcomputer applications. Users consistently praise this series for innovative pedagogy, creativity, supportive and engaging style, accuracy, and use of interactive technology. The first New Perspectives text was published in January of 1993. Since then, the series has grown to more than 100 titles and has become the best-selling series on computer concepts and microcomputer applications. Others have imitated the New Perspectives features, design, and technologies, but none have replicated its quality and its ability to consistently anticipate and meet the needs of instructors and students.

What is the Integrated System of Instruction?

New Perspectives textbooks are part of a truly Integrated System of Instruction: text, graphics, video, sound, animation, and simulations that are linked and that provide a flexible, unified, and interactive system to help you teach and help your students learn. Specifically, the *New Perspectives Integrated System of Instruction* includes a Course Technology textbook in addition to some or all of the following items: Course Labs, Course Test Manager, Online Companions, and Course Presenter. These components—shown in the graphic on the back cover of this book—have been developed to work together to provide a complete, integrative teaching and learning experience.

How is the New Perspectives Series different from other microcomputer concepts and applications series?

The **New Perspectives Series** distinguishes itself from other series in at least four substantial ways: sound instructional design, consistent quality, innovative technology, and proven pedagogy. The applications texts in this series consist of two or more tutorials, which are based on sound instructional design. Each tutorial is motivated by a realistic case that is meaningful to students. Rather than learn a laundry list of features, students learn the features in the context of solving a problem. This process motivates all concepts and skills by demonstrating to students *why* they would want to know them.

Instructors and students have come to rely on the high quality of the **New Perspectives Series** and to consistently praise its accuracy. This accuracy is a result of Course Technology's unique multi-step quality assurance process that incorporates student testing at at least two stages of development, using hardware and software configurations appropriate to the product. All solutions, test questions, and other supplements are tested using similar procedures. Instructors who adopt this series report that students can work through the tutorials independently with minimum intervention or "damage control" by instructors or staff. This consistent quality has meant that if instructors are pleased with one product from the series, they can rely on the same quality with any other New Perspectives product.

The **New Perspectives Series** also distinguishes itself by its innovative technology. This series innovated Course Labs, truly *interactive* learning applications. These have set the standard for interactive learning.

How do I know that the New Perspectives Series will work?

Some instructors who use this series report a significant difference between how much their students learn and retain with this series as compared to other series. With other series, instructors often find that students can work through the book and do well on homework and tests, but still not demonstrate competency when asked to perform particular tasks outside the context of the text's sample case or project. With the **New Perspectives Series**, however, instructors report that students have a complete, integrative learning experience that stays with them. They credit this high retention and competency to the fact that this series incorporates critical thinking and problem-solving with computer skills mastery.

How does this book I'm holding fit into the New Perspectives Series?

New Perspectives applications books are available in the following categories:

Brief books are typically about 150 pages long, contain two to four tutorials, and are intended to teach the basics of an application.

Introductory books are typically about 300 pages long and consist of four to seven tutorials that go beyond the basics. These books often build out of the Brief editions by providing two or three additional tutorials. The book you are holding is an Introductory book.

Comprehensive books are typically about 600 pages long and consist of all of the tutorials in the Introductory books, plus a few more tutorials covering higher-level topics. Comprehensive books typically also include two Windows tutorials and three or four Additional Cases.

Advanced books cover topics similar to those in the Comprehensive books, but go into more depth. Advanced books present the most high-level coverage in the series.

Custom Books The New Perspectives Series offers you two ways to customize a New Perspectives text to fit your course exactly: *CourseKits*™, two or more texts packaged together in a box, and *Custom Editions*®, your choice of books bound together. Custom Editions offer you unparalleled flexibility in designing your concepts and applications courses. You can build your own book by ordering a combination of titles bound together to cover only the topics you want. Your students save because they buy only the materials they need. There is no minimum order, and books are spiral bound. Both CourseKits and Custom Editions offer significant price discounts. Contact your Course Technology sales representative for more information.

New Perspectives Series Microcomputer Applications

■ Brief Titles or Modules	■ Introductory Titles or Modules	■ Intermediate Tutorials	■ Advanced Titles or Modules	▢ Other Modules
Brief	**Introductory**	**Comprehensive**	**Advanced**	**Custom Editions**
2 to 4 tutorials	6 or 7 tutorials, or Brief + 2 or 3 more tutorials	Introductory + 3 to 6 more tutorials. Includes Brief Windows tutorials and Additional Cases	Quick Review of basics + in-depth, high-level coverage	Choose from any of the above to build your own Custom Editions® or CourseKits™

In what kind of course could I use this book?

This book can be used in any course in which you want students to learn all the most important topics of Netscape Communicator, including browsing with Navigator, e-mail management with Messenger, newsgroup management with Collabra, and Web page composition with Composer. It is ideal for a short course on Netscape Communicator or as part of a full-semester course on the Internet. This book assumes that students have learned basic Windows 95 or NT navigation and file management skills from Course Technology's *New Perspectives on Microsoft Windows 95—Brief*, *New Perspectives on Microsoft Windows NT—Introductory* or an *equivalent* book.

How do the Windows 95 or NT editions differ from the Windows 3.1 editions?

Sessions We've divided the tutorials into sessions. Each session is designed to be completed in about 45 minutes to an hour (depending, of course, upon student needs and the speed of your lab equipment). With sessions, learning is broken up into more easily assimilated portions. You can more accurately allocate time in your syllabus, and students can better manage the available lab time. Each session begins with a "session box," which quickly describes the skills students will learn in the session. Furthermore, each session is numbered, which makes it easier for you and your students to navigate and communicate about the tutorial. Look on page NC 1.5 for the session box that opens Session 1.1.

Quick Checks Each session concludes with meaningful, conceptual Quick Check questions that test students' understanding of what they learned in the session. Answers to the Quick Check questions in this book are provided on pages NC 3.50 through NC 3.52 and NC 5.38 through NC 5.40.

New Design We have retained the best of the old design to help students differentiate between what they are to *do* and what they are to *read*. The steps are clearly identified by their shaded background and numbered steps. Furthermore, this new design presents steps and screen shots in a larger, easier to read format. Some good examples of our new design are pages NC 2.27 and NC 3.24.

What features are retained in the Windows 95 and NT editions of the New Perspectives Series?

"Read This Before You Begin" Page This page is consistent with Course Technology's unequaled commitment to helping instructors introduce technology into the classroom. Technical considerations and assumptions about software are listed to help instructors save time and eliminate unnecessary aggravation. See pages NC 1.2 and NC 4.2 for the "Read This Before You Begin" pages in this book.

Tutorial Case Each tutorial begins with a problem presented in a case that is meaningful to students. The problem turns the task of learning how to use an application into a problem-solving process. The problems increase in complexity with each tutorial. These cases touch on multicultural, international, and ethical issues—so important to today's business curriculum. See page NC 1.3 for the case that begins Tutorial 1.

Step-by-Step Methodology This unique Course Technology methodology keeps students on track. They enter data, click buttons, or press keys always within the context of solving the problem posed in the tutorial case. The text constantly guides students, letting them know where they are in the course of solving the problem. In addition, the numerous screen shots include labels that direct students' attention to what they should look at on the screen. On almost every page in this book, you can find an example of how steps, screen shots, and labels work together.

TROUBLE?

TROUBLE? Paragraphs These paragraphs anticipate the mistakes or problems that students are likely to have and help them recover and continue with the tutorial. By putting these paragraphs in the book, rather than in the Instructor's Manual, we facilitate independent learning and free the instructor to focus on substantive conceptual issues rather than on common procedural errors. Some representative examples of TROUBLE? paragraphs appear on page NC 1.28.

Reference Windows Reference Windows appear throughout the text. They are succinct summaries of the most important tasks covered in the tutorials. Reference Windows are specially designed and written so students can refer to them when doing the Tutorial Assignments and Case Problems, and after completing the course. Page NC 2.19 contains the Reference Window for deleting a bookmark.

Task Reference The Task Reference contains a summary of how to perform common tasks using the most efficient method, as well as references to pages where the task is discussed in more detail. It appears as a table at the end of the book.

Tutorial Assignments, Case Problems, and Lab Assignments Each tutorial concludes with Tutorial Assignments, which provide students with additional hands-on practice of the skills they learned in the tutorial. See page NC 3.42 for examples of Tutorial Assignments. The Tutorial Assignments are followed by four Case Problems that have approximately the same scope as the tutorial case. In the Windows 95 and NT applications texts, the last Case Problem of each tutorial typically requires students to solve the problem independently, either "from scratch" or with minimum guidance. See page NC 3.43 for examples of Case Problems. Finally, if a Course Lab accompanies a tutorial, Lab Assignments are included after the Case Problems. See page NC 3.46 for examples of Lab Assignments.

Exploration Exercises The Windows environment allows students to learn by exploring and discovering what they can do. Exploration Exercises can be Tutorial Assignments or Case Problems that challenge students, encourage them to explore the capabilities of the program they are using, and extend their knowledge using the Help facility and other reference materials. Page NC 1.36 contains Exploration Exercises for Tutorial 1.

What supplements are available with this textbook?

Course Labs: Now, Concepts Come to Life Computer skills and concepts come to life with the New Perspectives Course Labs—highly-interactive tutorials that combine illustrations, animations, digital images, and simulations. The Labs guide students step-by-step, present them with Quick Check questions, let them explore on their own, test their comprehension, and provide printed feedback. Lab icons at the beginning of the tutorial and in the tutorial margins indicate when a topic has a corresponding Lab. Lab Assignments are included at the end of each relevant tutorial. The Labs available with this book and the tutorials in which they appear are:

TUTORIAL 1

The Internet
World Wide Web

TUTORIAL 3

E-Mail

Course Test Manager: Testing and Practice at the Computer or on Paper
Course Test Manager is cutting-edge, Windows-based testing software that helps instructors design and administer practice tests and actual examinations. This full-featured program allows students to randomly generate practice tests that provide immediate on-screen feedback and detailed study guides. Instructors can also use Course Test Manager to produce printed tests. Course Test Manager can automatically grade the tests students take at the computer and can generate statistical information on individual as well as group performance.

Course Presenter: This lecture presentation tool allows instructors to create electronic slide shows or traditional overhead transparencies using the figure files from the book. Instructors can customize, edit, save, and display figures from the text in order to illustrate key topics or concepts in class.

Online Companions: Dedicated to Keeping You and Your Students Up-To-Date
When you use a New Perspectives product, you can access Course Technology's faculty sites and student sites on the World Wide Web. You can browse the password-protected Faculty Online Companions to obtain online Instructor's Manuals, Solution Files, Student Files, and more. Please see your Instructor's Resource Kit or call your Course Technology customer service representative for more information. Student and Faculty Online Companions are accessible by clicking the appropriate links on the Course Technology home page at **http://www.course.com.**

Student Files Student Files contain all of the data that students will use to complete the tutorials, Tutorial Assignments, and Case Problems. A Readme file includes technical tips for lab management. See the inside covers of this book and the "Read This Before You Begin" pages for more information on Student Files.

Solution Files Solution Files contain every file students are asked to create or modify in the tutorials, Tutorial Assignments, and Case Problems.

The following supplements are included in the Instructor's Resource Kit that accompanies this textbook:

- HTML files of the Faculty Online Companion
- Solution Files
- Student Files
- Internet: World Wide Web and E-mail Course Labs
- Course Test Manager Test Bank
- Course Test Manager Engine
- Course Presenter

Some of the supplements listed above are also available over the World Wide Web through Course Technology's password-protected Faculty Online Companions. Please see your Instructor's Resource Kit or call your Course Technology customer service representative for more information.

Acknowledgments

We wish to thank John Chenoweth, East Tennessee State University, and Karleen Nordquist, Black Hills State University, for their suggestions for improving the tutorials. Many thanks to the New Perspectives team at Course Technology, particularly Mark Reimold, Acquisitions Editor; Donna Gridley, Product Manager; Rachel Crapser, Associate Product Manager; Chris Greacen, Webmaster; Brian McCooey, Quality Assurance Project Leader; and Seth Andrews, Production Editor.

Joan Carey, Patrick Carey, and Sandra Poindexter

Without the assistance of Martin Eskelinen, Helen Hack, Jane Phillips, Mike Bradley, and Steve and Anna Poindexter this book could not have been written. Finally, my thanks to Peter Heck who gave me the drive not just to finish, but to succeed.

Sandra Poindexter

Thanks also to our four little sons, Michael, Peter, Thomas, and John Paul, whose many little sacrifices made it possible for us to work on this book.

Joan & Patrick Carey

Table of Contents

TUTORIAL 3

Corresponding with Messenger and Collabra

Communicating over the Internet at Carey Outerwear

The Internet Using
Netscape Communicator™
Software

LEVEL I

TUTORIALS

Read This **Before You Begin**

STUDENT DISK

To complete Netscape Communicator Tutorials 1–3 and the end-of-tutorial assignments in this book, you need one Student Disk. You will also need a blank disk for Case Problem 4 in Tutorial 3. Your instructor will either provide you with a Student Disk or ask you to make your own.

If you are supposed to make your own Student Disk, you will need one blank, formatted high-density disk. You will need to copy a set of folders from a file server or standalone computer onto your disk. Your instructor will tell you which computer, drive letter, and folders contain the files you need. The following table shows you which folders go on your disk, so that you will have enough disk space to complete all the tutorials, Tutorial Assignments, and Case Problems:

Student Disk	Write this on the disk label	Put these folders on the disk
1	Student Disk 1: Tutorials 1–3	Tutorial.01, Tutorial.03

See the inside front or inside back cover of this book for more information on Student Disk files, or ask your instructor or technical support person for assistance.

COURSE LABS

Tutorials 1 and 3 feature interactive Course Labs that help you understand the Internet and e-mail concepts. There are Lab Assignments at the end of the tutorial that relate to these Labs. To start the Lab, click the Start button on the Windows Taskbar, point to Programs, point to Course Labs, point to New Perspectives Applications, and click the name of the Lab you want to use.

USING YOUR OWN COMPUTER

If you are going to work through this book using your own computer, you need:

■ **Computer System** Netscape Communicator must be installed on your computer. This book assumes a Complete installation of the Standard Edition of Netscape Communicator.

■ **Student Disks** Ask your instructor or lab manager for details on how to get the Student Disk. You will not be able to complete the tutorials or end-of-tutorial assignments in this book using your own computer until you have a Student Disk. The Student Files may also be obtained electronically over the Internet. See the inside front or inside back cover of this book for more details.

■ **Course Labs** See your instructor or technical support person to obtain the Course Lab software for use on your own computer.

To complete Netscape Communicator Tutorials 1–3 and the end-of-tutorial assignments in this book, your students must use a set of files on a Student Disk. These files are included in the Instructor's Resource Kit, and they may also be obtained electronically over the Internet. See the inside front or inside back cover of this book for more details. Follow the instructions in the Readme file to copy the files to your server or standalone computer. You can view the Readme file using WordPad.

Once the files are copied, you can make the Student Disk for the students yourself, or you can tell students where to find the files so they can make their own Student Disk. Make sure the files get correctly copied onto the Student Disk by following the instructions in the Student Disk section above, which will ensure that students have enough disk space to complete all the tutorials and end-of-tutorial assignments.

COURSE LAB SOFTWARE

The Course Lab software is distributed on a CD-ROM included in the Instructor's Resource Kit. To install the Course Lab software, follow the setup instructions in the Readme file on the CD-ROM. Refer also to the Readme file for essential technical notes related to running the Labs in a multi-user environment. Once you have installed the Course Lab software, your students can start the Labs from the Windows desktop by following the instructions in the Course Labs section above.

COURSE TECHNOLOGY STUDENT FILES AND LAB SOFTWARE

You are granted a license to copy the Student Files and Course Lab software to any computer or computer network used by students who have purchased this book.

Navigating the Web with Navigator

Conducting Teacher Workshops at Northern University

LABS

The Internet
World Wide Web

CASE

Northern University

Michelle Pine, an education student at Northern University, is researching the use of the Internet as a teaching tool in the classroom and as an aid for preparing class lessons. She uses the Northern University Internet connection regularly to keep in contact with friends and her professors. She also uses an online service at home to communicate with her family living in New Mexico.

Michelle has been amazed at the wealth and variety of information she has found freely available on the Internet, especially the amount geared toward educators. At forums, educators can share ideas, advice, and encouragement. Teachers can find current information about every subject that can be incorporated into the curriculum. Geography and history, for example, come alive with multimedia travel through various time periods and lands. Science is no longer limited by physical equipment, and students can conduct experiments in virtual labs that would be impossible in many classrooms. Humanities become more vibrant through tours of world-famous museums, music, and video clips from particular artists, styles, or times. The more Michelle looks, the more resources she finds. What's more, she has discovered that information is updated and added daily.

As a special project for one of her education courses, Michelle is planning a two-hour workshop for teachers on Internet basics and Netscape Navigator. The 25 educators enrolled in the workshop have little working knowledge of the Internet and Netscape Navigator but are interested in its possibilities.

Michelle asks you to help her facilitate the workshop. She'd like to give the talk while you help out at the computer keyboard. Michelle wants to begin by giving the educators an overview of the Internet and the World Wide Web. Then she'll teach them Netscape Navigator basics using a presentation she created especially for the workshop. Finally, she'll demonstrate how to connect to and navigate through pages on the Web.

Using the Tutorials Effectively

These tutorials are designed to be used at a computer. Each tutorial is divided into sessions designed to be completed in about 45 minutes, but take as much time as you need. Watch for the session headings, such as Session 1.1 and Session 1.2. It's also a good idea to take a break between sessions.

Before you begin, read the following questions and answers, which are designed to help you use the tutorials effectively.

Where do I start?

Each tutorial begins with a case, which sets the scene and gives you background information to help you understand what you will be doing in the tutorial. Ideally, you should read the case before you go to the lab. In the lab, begin with the first session.

How do I know what to do on the computer?

Each session contains steps that you will perform on a computer to learn how to use Netscape Communicator. Read the text that introduces each series of steps. The steps you need to do at a computer are numbered and are set against a color background. Read each step carefully and completely before you try it.

How do I know if I did the step correctly?

As you work, compare your computer screen with the corresponding figure in the tutorial. Don't worry if your screen display is somewhat different from the figure. The important parts of the screen display are labeled in each figure. Check to make sure these parts are on your screen.

What if I make a mistake?

Don't worry about making mistakes—they are part of the learning process. Paragraphs labeled "**TROUBLE?**" identify common problems and explain how to get back on track. Follow the steps in a **TROUBLE?**, paragraph *only* if you are having the problem described. If you run into other problems; carefully consider the current state of your system, the position of the pointer, and any messages on the screen.

How do I use the Reference Windows?

Reference Windows summarize the procedures you learn in the tutorial steps. Do not complete the actions in the Reference Windows when you are working through the tutorial. Instead, refer to the Reference Windows while you are working on the assignments at the end of the tutorial.

How can I test my understanding of the material I learned in the tutorial?

At the end of each session, answer the Quick Check questions. If necessary, refer to the Answers to Quick Check Questions to check your work.

After you have completed the entire tutorial, complete the Tutorial Assignments and Case Problems. They are carefully structured so you will review what you have learned and then apply your knowledge to new situations.

What if I can't remember how to do something?

Refer to the Task Reference at the end of the tutorials; it summarizes how to accomplish commonly performed tasks.

What are the Interactive Labs, and how should I use them?

Interactive Labs help you review concepts and practice skills that you learn in the tutorial. The Lab Assignments section includes instructions for using each Lab.

Now that you've seen how to use the tutorials effectively, you are ready to begin.

SESSION

1.1

In this session, you will learn about the Internet, the World Wide Web, and the Netscape Communicator suite. You will also learn how to start and exit Netscape Navigator, identify components of the Netscape window, work with Navigator toolbars, view Web pages, activate and abort a link, and work with frames.

The Internet

The Internet
World Wide Web

Michelle wants to begin her talk by giving an overview of the technology that makes it possible for people to communicate with each other using their computers. She also wants to familiarize her audience with common network terms that will make it possible for them to understand how the Internet operates.

When two or more computers are linked together so that they can exchange information and resources, they create a structure known as a **network**. Networks facilitate the sharing of data and resources among multiple users. Some computers, called **servers**, provide specific resources to the network, such as print capabilities or stored files. Figure 1-1 shows a small network consisting of a single server, a shared printer, and a handful of computers.

Figure 1-1 ◀
Small network

cable connects
network computers
together

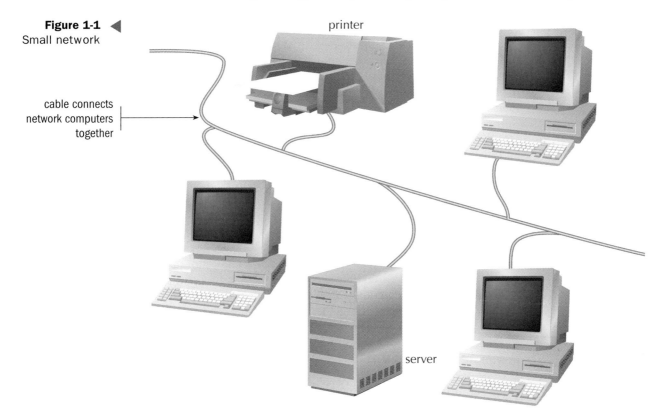

printer

server

Networks can also be connected to each other to allow information to be shared between computers on different networks. The **Internet**, the largest and most famous example of a "network of networks," is made up of millions of computers linked to networks all over the world. Computers and networks on the Internet are connected by fiber optic cables, satellites, phone lines, and other communication systems, as shown in Figure 1-2.

Figure 1-2 ◀
Structure of
the Internet

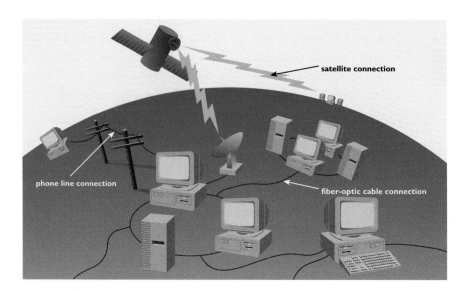

Computers on a network are often called **hosts**, and thus a computer with Internet access is sometimes called an Internet host.

The Internet, by design, is a decentralized structure. There is no Internet "company." Instead, the Internet is a collection of different organizations, such as universities and companies, that organize their own information however they want. There are no rules about where information is stored, and no one regulates the quality of information available on the Internet. Even though the lack of central control can make it hard for beginners to find their way through the resources on the Internet, there are some advantages. The Internet is open to innovation and rapid growth as different organizations and individuals have the freedom to test new products and services and make them quickly available to a global audience. One such service developed in recent years is the **World Wide Web**, an Internet service that makes finding information and moving around the Internet easy.

The World Wide Web

The foundation of the World Wide Web was laid in 1989 by Timothy Berners-Lee and other researchers at the CERN research facility near Geneva, Switzerland. They wanted to make it easy for researchers to share data with a minimum of training and support. They created a system of **hypertext documents**—electronic files that contain elements known as **links** that you can select, usually by clicking a mouse, to move to another part of the document or another document altogether. A link can be a word or phrase or a graphic image.

The system of hypertext documents developed at CERN proved to be easily adaptable to other information sources on the Internet. Within the space of a few years, hypertext documents were being created by numerous organizations for a large variety of topics. Because it was easy to link these different hypertext documents together, a single user could jump from one set of hypertext documents to another without much effort. This interconnected structure of hypertext documents became known as the World Wide Web or simply the Web.

Each hypertext document on the Web is called a **Web page** and is stored on a computer on the Internet called a **Web server**. A Web page can contain links to other Web pages located anywhere on the Internet—on the same computer as the original Web page or on an entirely different computer halfway across the world. The ability to cross-reference other Web pages with links is one of the most important features of the Web.

Figure 1-3 shows how you can click a link on one Web page that moves you to another Web page.

Web page on rock climbing

Figure 1-3
Link in one hypertext document opens another

click this link to jump to a different document

this Web page appears when you click the Tour link

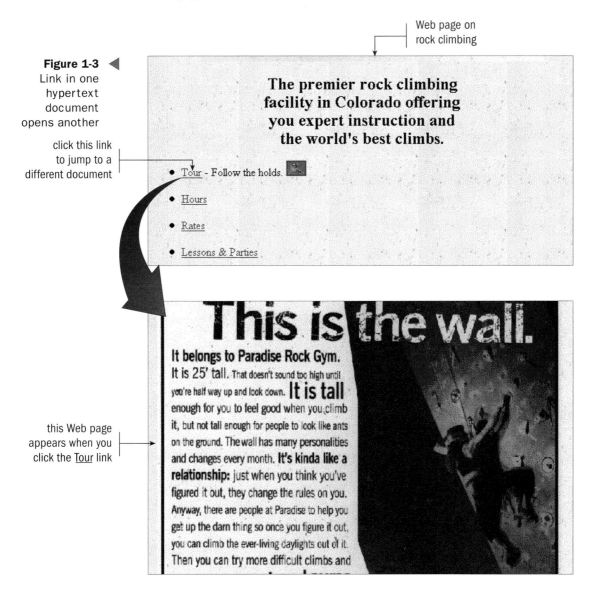

Clicking a link can also connect you to other file types, including scanned photographs, graphic images, film clips, sounds, and computer programs. A link could lead you into a discussion group called a **forum** or **newsgroup** where users share information on topics of common interest. Another link might point to the e-mail address of an individual so you can send a message.

Navigating Web pages using hypertext is an efficient way of accessing information. Michelle points out that when you read a book you follow a linear progression, reading one page after another. With hypertext, you progress through the pages in whatever way you want. Hypertext allows you to skip from one topic to another, following the information path that interests you. Figure 1-4 shows how topics might be organized in both a linear and hypertext model.

Figure 1-4 ◀
Linear vs.
hypertext
documents

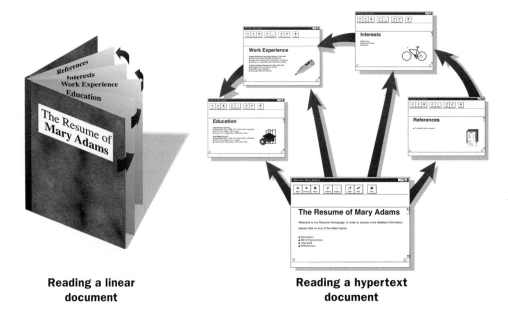

**Reading a linear
document**

**Reading a hypertext
document**

Hypertext has great appeal because a single Internet user can jump from one set of hypertext documents to another without much effort. However, perhaps the greatest source of the Web's popularity lies in the ease with which users can create their own Web pages. All you need is an account on a computer connected to the Internet that allows you to store your Web page and make it available for others to read. Many companies that sell access to the Internet, called **Internet service providers** or **ISPs**, include Web pages as part of their service.

Netscape Communicator

To access the documents available on the Web, to communicate with others, and to publish your own Web page, you need special software. Until recently, you needed to purchase one program, called a **browser**, to view and work with Web pages, another to communicate with e-mail or participate in group discussions, and yet another to create and publish a Web page. Software developers are now producing **suites**, or groups of products, that allow you to be active on the Web with a single, seamlessly integrated package. **Netscape Communicator** is Netscape Communications Corporation's Web software suite. It provides all the tools you need to communicate, share, and access information on the World Wide Web, and for this reason is Northern University's product of choice. Michelle plans to use Communicator at the workshop because it is easy to use and understand.

Michelle provides the following overview of the tools available in various installations and versions of Communicator. She emphasizes that you shouldn't worry if you don't understand the functions of each component right now. You'll learn more about the individual Communicator tools later.

You can obtain either the Standard or Professional Edition of Communicator. The Standard Edition features e-mail, browsing, discussion groups, and information sharing capabilities. The Professional Edition adds administrative and calendaring functions to the Standard Edition. Within the Standard version, you can choose a Base or a Complete installation. This book assumes a Complete installation of the Standard version, although you can perform most of the Steps with a Base installation. See Appendix A for information on downloading the Communicator software over the Web. Figure 1-5 lists the services Communicator provides for each installation.

Figure 1-5
Netscape
Communicator
components

Service	Description
Base Installation of the Standard Edition	
Navigator	Browser that retrieves, displays, and organizes documents located on Web servers on your computer.
Messenger	E-mail manager that allows you to send, receive, compose, edit, search, and sort e-mail. **E-mail**, or electronic mail, is a note you write and send across the Internet. Messenger can handle e-mail containing practically any file type—graphics, sounds, videos, and so on.
Collabra	Newsgroup manager that helps you create, manage, and participate in a discussion group.
Composer	Web page editor that you use to create and edit Web pages.
Complete Installation of the Standard Edition	
Conference	Collaboration software that allows remote users to work together in real time.
Media Player and other plug-ins	Media Player plays audio and video clips for computers with adequate hardware.
Professional Edition	
Calendar	Manages appointments, tasks, and schedules.
AutoAdmin	Helps network managers administer the computers on their networks.
Additional features	The Professional Edition includes many other features beyond the scope of this book.

Both the Complete installation of the Standard Edition and the Professional Edition include useful **plug-ins,** or software programs that extend the capabilities of the Communicator suite. You install plug-ins using instructions that come with the plug-in; once a plug-in is installed Communicator uses the plug-in's capabilities just like other built-in Communicator features. Appendix A contains more information about plug-ins. Your installation might also include **Netcaster,** a "direct delivery" service not included with the first release of Communicator. See Appendix B for information on using Netcaster.

Michelle wants to keep the workshop simple, focusing only on navigating the Web rather than on e-mail, forums, and Web page publishing. Thus she will use only the browser component of Communicator, Navigator, in her presentation.

What is Navigator?

With Navigator, you can visit sites around the world, view multimedia documents, transfer files, images, and sounds to your computer, conduct searches for specific topics, and run software on other computers. Underneath the surface, Navigator is running a variety of Internet services, but because Navigator handles the commands for you, you can be blissfully unaware of the complexity of what really happens when you navigate the Web.

When a user tries to view a Web page, the user's browser, in this case Navigator, locates and retrieves the document from the Web server and displays its contents on the user's computer. As shown in Figure 1-6, the server stores the Web page in one location, and browsers anywhere in the world can view it.

Figure 1-6 ◀
Using a
browser to
view a Web
document on a
server

Netscape
Navigator browser

browser in California
locates and displays
document stored on
server in Florida

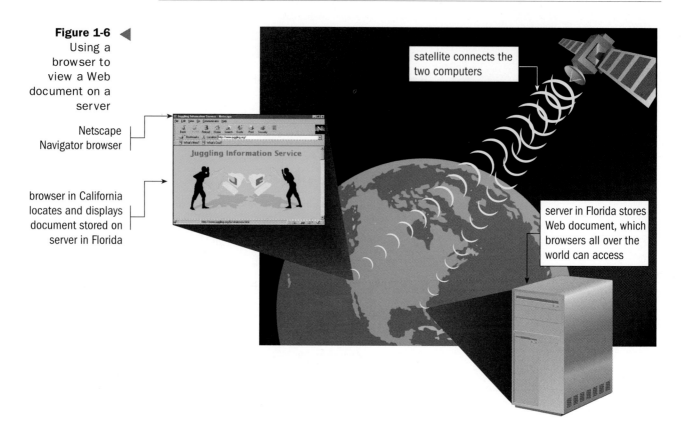

Here, a browser in California is accessing a document stored on a Web server in Florida. You might retrieve such a page without knowing or caring on which Web server it is stored. The wonder of the World Wide Web is that you can view a document stored on a Web server across the room or across the world using the same technique. Information stored on a server in Cairo is just as accessible as on one in Cleveland. Is there any doubt why the Web has been called the "information superhighway?"

Starting Navigator

Before you can start using Navigator to explore the Web, you must have an Internet connection. In a university setting your connection might come from the campus network on which you have an account. If you are working on a home computer, your connection might come over the phone line from an account with an Internet service provider. How you connect to the Internet depends on what service you have, but at a university you will most likely be already connected to the Internet and can start Navigator and immediately begin to browse the Web.

Michelle explains that, unlike many other software applications, Navigator does not open with a standard start-up screen. Instead, you see a document called the **home page**— the Web page that appears when you start Navigator. Communicator allows each computer installation to specify what home page users will see when they start Navigator. When you launch Navigator, you might see:

- the Netscape Communications Corporation home page
- your school's or institution's home page
- a page your technical support person sets as the default
- a blank page

A home page can also refer to the Web page that a person, organization, or business has created to give information about itself. A home page might include information about the host, links to other sites, or relevant graphics and sounds. When Michelle starts Navigator from home, she connects to the Netscape Communications Corporation home page, stored on servers in Mountain View, California, which provides fundamental information about Netscape and its software. When she starts it in the university's lab, she sees Northern University's home page, stored on a Web server at Northern University.

When Communicator is installed on your system, the Start menu is modified so that you can start any Communicator component from the Programs menu. Additionally, a Netscape Communicator icon is placed on your desktop that you can double-click, although it's possible that your technical support person has removed that icon. When you double-click the Netscape Communicator icon, Communicator automatically starts Navigator. These instructions show you how to start Navigator from the Start menu.

To start Navigator:

1. If necessary, connect to your Internet account.

   TROUBLE? If you are in a university setting you are probably already connected and can skip Step 1. If you don't know how to connect to your Internet account, ask your technical support person for help or call your Internet service provider's technical support line.

2. Click the **Start** button [Start] on the Windows taskbar.

3. Point at **Programs** with the mouse pointer. After a short pause, the Programs menu opens with a list of programs available on your computer.

   TROUBLE? If the Programs menu doesn't open and another menu does, repeat Step 2.

4. Point at **Netscape Communicator** in the Programs menu, and then point at **Netscape Navigator** in the Netscape Communicator menu. See Figure 1-7.

   TROUBLE? If the words "Professional Edition" appear after Netscape Communicator, don't worry. Your computer has the Professional Edition installed instead of the Standard Edition.

Figure 1-7 ◀
Starting
Netscape
Navigator

point here to open
Programs menu

Start button

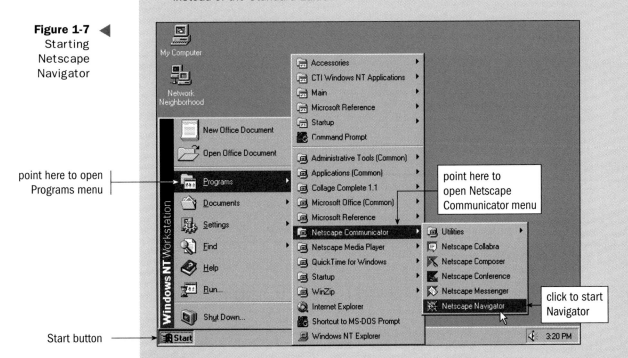

TROUBLE? If you don't see Netscape Communicator in the Programs menu, ask your instructor or technical support person for assistance. If you are using your own computer, make sure Communicator is installed.

TROUBLE? If your Netscape Communicator menu shows different entries, don't worry. You just have a different version of Communicator.

5. Click **Netscape Navigator** to start Navigator. The home page specified by your site's installation opens.

TROUBLE? If the Profile Setup Wizard window appears, this is the first time Communicator has been used on your computer. If you are using a computer that is not your own, ask your technical support person for assistance. If you are using your own computer, read the instructions, click the Next button, and then proceed through the wizard dialog boxes that appear, providing information where requested (such as your e-mail address), and clicking Next when you finish each one. If you reach a dialog box that you don't understand, you might need to call your Internet service provider's technical support line for assistance.

TROUBLE? If a message informs you that a DNS entry could not be found, you are not connected to the Internet. Click the OK button. Navigator opens, but the Navigator window will be empty. To see your home page, you must first connect to the Internet. Then click the Location box and press Enter.

6. Click the **Maximize** button 🔲 in the upper-right corner of the Welcome to Netscape window if the window is not already maximized. See Figure 1-8, which shows the Netscape Communications Corporation home page, entitled Welcome to Netscape.

TROUBLE? If your screen shows a different home page, don't worry.

TROUBLE? If your toolbar looks different (perhaps only the icons or only the names appear), click Edit, click Preferences, and then click Appearance in the Category list. In the Show toolbar as area, click the Pictures and Text option button. Click the OK button.

TROUBLE? If the right side of the Netscape Window is covered with Channel finder, click the Exit button in the Channel finder window. Channel finder is a Netcaster feature covered in Appendix B.

Figure 1-8 ◀
Netscape
window

title bar

menu bar

Navigation toolbar

Location toolbar

Personal toolbar

document window;
yours will be different

status bar

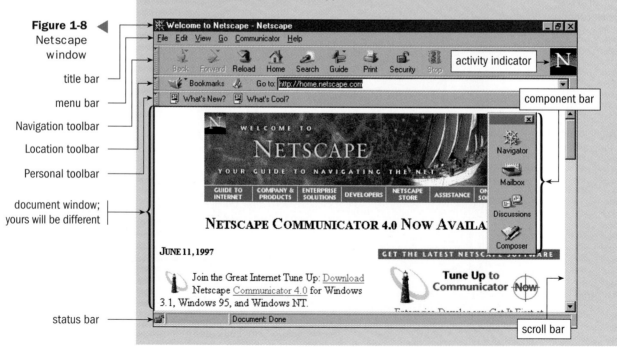

Regardless of which page appears when you first start Navigator—the Netscape home page, your university's home page, or a different home page—your window should share some common components with the one in Figure 1-8. Michelle points out the most important parts of the Netscape window, shown in Figure 1-9. Don't worry if you don't see all these components. You'll learn how to make them appear shortly.

Figure 1-9 ◀
Netscape
window
components

Window component	Description
Title bar	Identifies the active Web page.
Menu bar	Groups Communicator commands by menu name. You click a menu name to open a menu, and then click the command you want.
Navigation toolbar	Offers single-click access to the more common navigation menu commands.
Location toolbar	Provides access to favorite Web pages via the Bookmarks button and identifies the address of the active Web page—the one currently displayed in the Netscape document window.
Personal toolbar	Displays buttons that you can click to jump immediately to individual Web pages. You can add buttons for your personal favorites.
Component bar	Offers single-click access to different components of the Communicator package.
Document window	Displays the active Web page.
Scroll bars	Allow you to move through the active page content. Click the up and down arrows on the vertical scroll bar to move the page up and down, or less frequently, the left and right arrows on the horizontal scroll bar to move the page left and right. You can also drag the scroll box or click above and below it to move through a page.
Activity indicator	Displays the Netscape logo. Appears as [N] when you have successfully connected to a site. Appears as [N], with celestial bodies streaking across the sky when you are connecting. If the activity indicator is idle but the page doesn't seem to have been successfully retrieved, you know there is a problem with the connection.
Status bar	Indicates the status of the document you are retrieving from the Web server, as well as security information about the site.

Viewing and Hiding Toolbars

Every time you start Communicator, make sure that you set up your screen to match the figures shown in the tutorials. For now, you want to display all three Navigator toolbars—Navigation, Location, and Personal. If you don't see one or more of these, you'll need to select the commands in the View menu.

To show or hide toolbars:

1. Click **View** to open the View menu. The first three commands in the View menu indicate whether the three toolbars are shown or hidden. If the command begins with "Hide," then the toolbar is already visible. If the command begins with "Show," the toolbar is hidden. See Figure 1-10.

Figure 1-10 ◀
Viewing
toolbar status

toolbars are
all visible

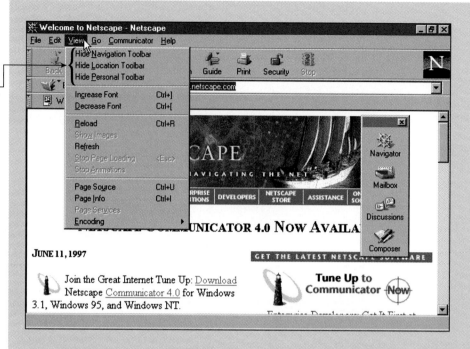

2. If one of the first three commands in the View menu begins with "Show," click that command. For example, if you see "Show Navigation Toolbar" instead of "Hide Navigation Toolbar," click **Show Navigation Toolbar**. The toolbar appears.

3. Now you'll experiment with hiding a toolbar. Click **View**, and then click one of the first three commands that begins with "Hide," such as "Hide Location Toolbar." That toolbar disappears.

4. In these tutorials, you want the toolbar visible on the screen. Click **View** once more, and click any command beginning with "Show" so that toolbar will appear.

5. Click **View**, and make sure the first three commands all begin with "Hide." If they don't, repeat step 4 until they do. All three toolbars should now appear on the screen. Each time you start Navigator, make sure all three toolbars are visible.

When you first start any of the Communicator components, the Component bar appears, offering you single-click access to other Communicator components. However, the Component bar rests on top of the active window, and when you are using the Navigator browser to view Web pages, you might find that inconvenient. You can dock the Component bar into the status bar so that it is unobtrusive.

To dock the Component bar:

1. Click the **Communicator** menu and then click **Dock Component Bar**. See Figure 1-11. The Component bar buttons now appear in the status bar.

   TROUBLE? If you can't locate the Dock Component bar command but instead see a command that says "Show Component bar," your Component bar is already docked.

Figure 1-11 ◄
Docking
Component bar

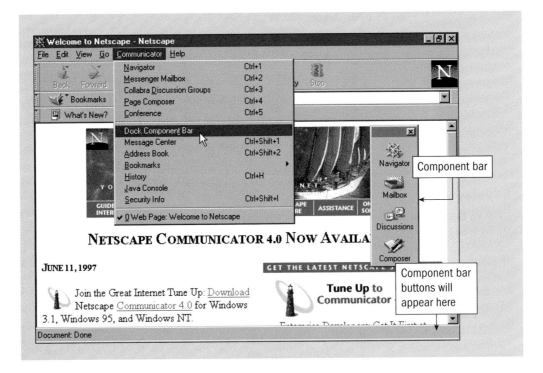

The components of your Netscape window should now match the figures. Michelle can now begin demonstrating how to navigate the Web.

Navigating the Web

Once you are connected to the Internet and you have started the Navigator browser, you can view Web pages using several different methods. If you have a Web page in the form of a file on a disk, you can simply open that page in your browser. If you are currently viewing a page with links, you can also click a link to activate it and jump to that page. You'll practice both methods now.

Opening a Web Page

Michelle has prepared a Web page that she will use at the workshop because she wants to be able to start from the same point from any computer, regardless of what home page appears in the document window. Michelle's Web page file is provided on your Student Disk. You'll open it in the Navigator browser, and then you will be viewing the same page shown in the figures and you will be able to navigate the same links.

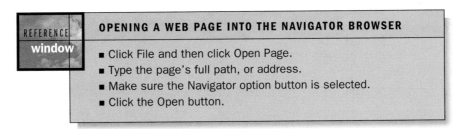

REFERENCE
window

OPENING A WEB PAGE INTO THE NAVIGATOR BROWSER

- Click File and then click Open Page.
- Type the page's full path, or address.
- Make sure the Navigator option button is selected.
- Click the Open button.

Keep in mind that you are opening Michelle's file from your Student Disk, not from the Web. You can use the Navigator browser to view Web page files on your Student Disk, on your computer's other drives, and on Web servers around the world. You'll learn how to view a file on the Web in Session 1.2.

To open a specific Web page:

1. Place your Student Disk in drive A. See the "Read This Before You Begin" page for information on the Student Disks.

   TROUBLE? If you are using drive B, place your Student Disk in that drive instead, and for the rest of these tutorials substitute drive B wherever you see drive A.

2. Click **File** and then click **Open Page**.

3. Type **a:\Tutorial.01\michelle.htm** as shown in Figure 1-12. Make sure the **Navigator** option button is selected; click it if it isn't.

   TROUBLE? If you are using drive B, type b:\Tutorial.01\Michelle.htm instead.

Figure 1-12 ◀
Opening a page

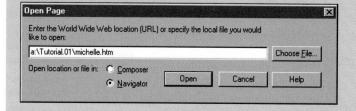

4. Click the **Open** button. The Web page Michelle has prepared for the workshop opens. See Figure 1-13.

Figure 1-13 ◀
Michelle's
workshop page

A hypertext link on the Web, like a link in a chain, is a connector between two points. Links can appear in two ways: as text that you click or as a graphic that you click. A **text link** is a word or phrase that is underlined and often boldfaced or colored differently. A graphic link is a graphic image that you click to jump to another location. When you aren't sure whether a graphic image is a link, point to it with the mouse pointer. When you move the mouse pointer over a link—text or graphic—it changes shape from ⌖ to 🖑. The 🖑 pointer indicates that when you click, you will activate that link and jump to the new location. The destination of the link appears in the status bar, and for some graphic links a small identification box appears next to your pointer.

As you'll see, Michelle's workshop page contains both text and graphic links. The text links are underlined and in color. Each link gives Navigator the information it needs to locate the page. When you activate a link, you jump to a new location, called the **target** of the link, which can be another location on the active Web page (for example, often the bottom of a Web page contains a link that jumps you up to the top), a different document or file, or a Web page stored on a remote Web server anywhere in the world.

When you activate a link, there are three possible outcomes:

1. You successfully reach the target of the link. Navigator contacts the site (host) you want, connects into the site, transfers the data from the host to your computer, and displays the data on your screen.

2. The link's target is busy, perhaps because the server storing the link's target is overwhelmed with too many requests. You'll have to try a different link, or try this link later.

3. The link points to a target that doesn't exist. Documents are often removed from Web servers as they become obsolete, or they are moved to new locations, and too often links that point to those documents are not updated.

The amount of time it takes to complete a link, called the **response time**, can vary, depending upon the number of people trying to connect to the same site, the number of people on the Internet at that time, and the site design.

Activating a Link

Activating a link starts a multi-step process. Although Navigator does the work for you, it is important to follow the sequence of events so you can recognize problems when they occur and understand how to resolve them.

Figure 1-14 illustrates the string of events that occur when you link to a site. When you point to a link, the status bar displays the address of the link's target, called its **Uniform Resource Locator** or **URL**. When you click a link, the Stop button changes to red—its active state—and the status indicator animates. The status bar displays a series of messages indicating that Navigator has contacted the host (or site) you want to visit and is waiting for a reply, is transferring data, and finally, is done.

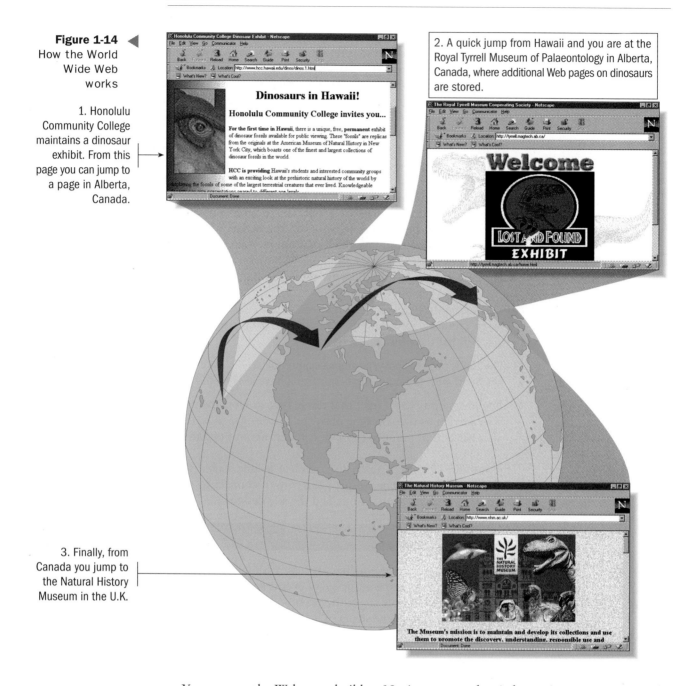

Figure 1-14 ◀
How the World
Wide Web
works

1. Honolulu
Community College
maintains a dinosaur
exhibit. From this
page you can jump to
a page in Alberta,
Canada.

2. A quick jump from Hawaii and you are at the
Royal Tyrrell Museum of Palaeontology in Alberta,
Canada, where additional Web pages on dinosaurs
are stored.

3. Finally, from
Canada you jump to
the Natural History
Museum in the U.K.

You can see the Web page build as Navigator transfers information to your screen in
multiple passes. The first wave brings a few pieces to the page and with each subsequent
pass, Navigator fills in more detail until the material is complete. The progress bar fills in
to indicate how much of the Web page has transferred. The vertical scroll box scrolls up
as Navigator adds more information and detail to the page. You don't have to wait until
the page is complete before scrolling or clicking another link, but it might be difficult to
determine links and other information until the page is mostly filled in.

Michelle's page contains links that let you experience each of the three outcomes mentioned earlier. First, you'll successfully activate a link.

To initiate a link to a Web page:

1. If necessary, scroll through Michelle's page until you find the "Click here for a Successful site link" sentence.

2. Point at the **Successful site** link. Notice that the pointer changes shape from ⌖ to 🖑, indicating that you are pointing to a hypertext link. The status bar shows the URL for that link. See Figure 1-15.

Figure 1-15 ◀
Activating
a link

link's target appears
in status bar

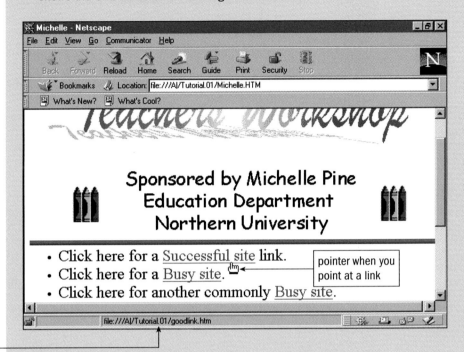

TROUBLE? If the status message area does not contain a URL, slowly move your pointer over the highlighted words. When you see the URL in the status message area, the pointer is positioned correctly.

3. Click the **Successful site** link to activate the link. The status indicator animates, and the status bar notes the progress of the link. When the status bar displays "Document: Done," the link is complete and the Web page that is the target of the link appears. See Figure 1-16.

TROUBLE? If a message dialog box opens, the link was not successful. Click the OK button to close the dialog box, and repeat Steps 1 through 3. After you click the hypertext link, make sure you do not click anywhere else on the page until the link is complete.

Figure 1-16 ◀
Completed link

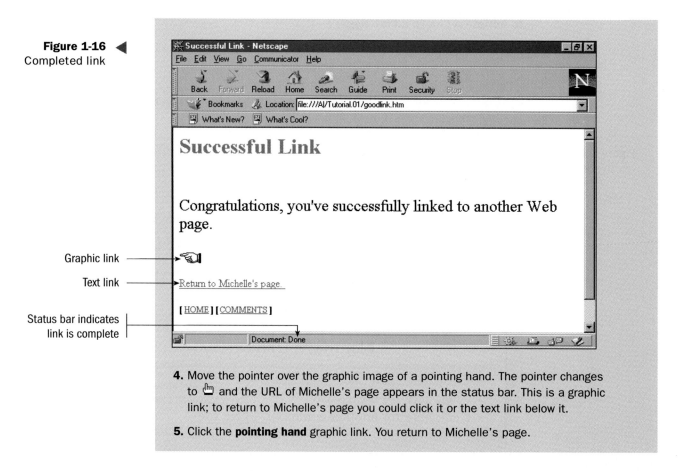

Graphic link ——————

Text link ——————

Status bar indicates
link is complete

4. Move the pointer over the graphic image of a pointing hand. The pointer changes to 🖑 and the URL of Michelle's page appears in the status bar. This is a graphic link; to return to Michelle's page you could click it or the text link below it.

5. Click the **pointing hand** graphic link. You return to Michelle's page.

You connected to a Web page with a single click, and then you used the graphic link in that page to return to Michelle's page. Using hypertext links is a simple way to move from one Web page to another. Notice that the Successful link on Michelle's page has turned color (you might need to scroll down to see this). Navigator displays text links you've already activated in a different color so you know which links you've already tried.

Aborting a Busy Link

Sometimes when you try to connect to a site, the link is not successful. Much like an expressway, the Internet can become so congested that the paths cannot support the number of users at peak times. When this happens, traffic backs up and slows to a halt, in effect closing the road. At these peak times, the load is too heavy for the Internet.

Aborting, or interrupting, a link is like taking the next exit ramp on the Internet. When the response time to a link seems too slow (longer than a few minutes) or nothing seems to be happening, you have no way of knowing how long it will take to complete a link. You can tell that a link is stalled when one of the following situations occurs:

■ The status message area does not change, but

■ the Stop button 🛑 on the toolbar is active, and

■ the activity indicator is animated ▤.

Rather than waiting for a site that has a long queue or is so busy it can't even respond to your request, you can abort the link.

Michelle wants to show the workshop how to stop an unsuccessful link. There is one site that she has tried to visit many times but has been unsuccessful. She asks you to try to link to that site.

To abort a delayed link:

1. Scroll down until you see the list of Busy site links on Michelle's page. The Busy site links target sites that are often busy — though they might not be when you perform Step 2.

2. Click the **Busy site** link to initiate the link. Watch the status message area; if the site is busy, it comes to a halt, although the status indicator remains animated and the Stop button active. The link is stalled. See Figure 1-17. The line to visit this site might be very long, or many people might be using the Internet and you just can't get to the site. Either way, you'll want to abort the link rather than wait an interminable amount of time.

Figure 1-17 ◀
Stalled link

status bar
doesn't change

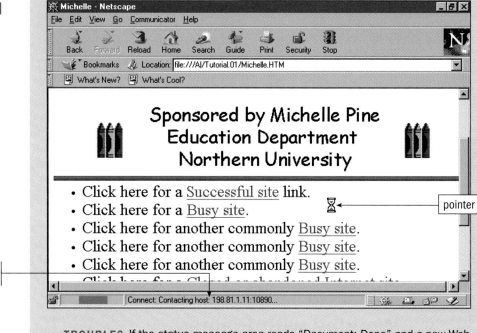

TROUBLE? If the status message area reads "Document: Done" and a new Web page opens, you were able to connect to this site. Click the Back button on the toolbar and repeat Step 2 with one of the other Busy site links. If none of the sites are busy, skip Step 3.

3. Click the **Stop** button on the toolbar to abort the link. The status indicator ceases to animate, and the Stop button dims.

Now you'll try a link that no longer exists.

Activating a Defunct Link

Michelle wants to show the workshop that a link not only might complete successfully or stall, but that it might also be aborted by Navigator. She explains that Navigator terminates a link and displays an error message indicating the site was not found because:

■ The URL specified by the hypertext link might no longer be active.

■ The URL might be typed incorrectly.

■ The server could not reach the site within the server's programmed wait time (for example, 90 seconds).

When such a message dialog box appears, you have no choice but to acknowledge the message and give up.

To end a Navigator-terminated link:

1. If necessary, scroll down the page, and then click the **Closed or abandoned Internet site** link to initiate a link to a nonexistent site. A message dialog box opens. See Figure 1-18. The dialog box indicates that Navigator is unable to locate the server containing the target of the link.

Figure 1-18 ◄
Terminated link

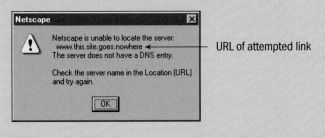

— URL of attempted link

2. Click the **OK** button to close the dialog box.

In this case, Navigator aborted the link because the server supposedly storing the target of the link does not have a proper domain name. Every host is part of a **domain,** or group, that has a unique name similar to a family surname. Just as family members can share a surname yet live in separate households both nearby and far away, a domain contains one or more hosts that might be at the same physical location or spread great distances apart. Some domains are small and contain just a few hosts. Others are very large and contain hundreds of hosts. An educational institution or a government agency might each have its own domain name.

Each host can have a domain name registered with the Domain Name Server (DNS). When you link to a site, Navigator checks to see if the domain in its URL is registered with the DNS. If the site is not registered (similar to an unlisted telephone number in the phone book), Navigator opens the message dialog box. Unless you know the correct URL for that site, you cannot link to it.

Working with Frames

Michelle wants to illustrate one more navigational concept. Web page designers often divide their pages into parts, called frames, to organize their information more effectively. A **frame** is a section of the document window. Each frame can have its own set of scroll bars and can display the contents of a different location. Many Web sites today employ frames because they allow the user to see different areas of information simultaneously. When you scroll through the contents of one frame, you do not affect the other frame or frames.

Michelle wants you to demonstrate frames using a page that she is designing for Northern University and the Education Department, listing available degree programs. She's included a link for this page on her main page.

To scroll through a frame:

1. Scroll to the bottom of Michelle's page until you see the "Click here to see how frames work" sentence.

2. Click the **frames** link. Figure 1-19 shows the page that opens. It contains three frames. The top frame identifies the page as that of the Education Department. The frame on the left identifies the two types of undergraduate programs—certification and non-certification—and the right frame displays information about the programs.

Figure 1-19 ◀
Web page
with frames

top frame
identifies page

left frame
contains links

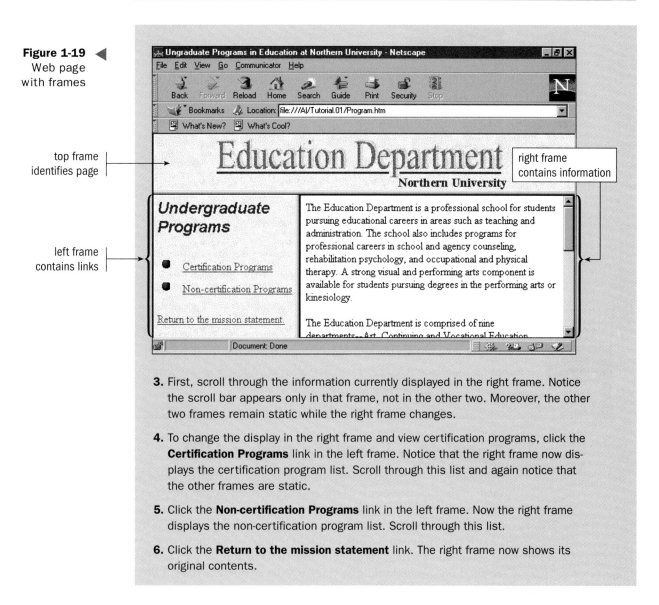

3. First, scroll through the information currently displayed in the right frame. Notice the scroll bar appears only in that frame, not in the other two. Moreover, the other two frames remain static while the right frame changes.

4. To change the display in the right frame and view certification programs, click the **Certification Programs** link in the left frame. Notice that the right frame now displays the certification program list. Scroll through this list and again notice that the other frames are static.

5. Click the **Non-certification Programs** link in the left frame. Now the right frame displays the non-certification program list. Scroll through this list.

6. Click the **Return to the mission statement** link. The right frame now shows its original contents.

By using frames, Michelle has made it possible for users to examine only the information they are interested in. Knowing how to recognize and navigate frames is increasingly important because many Web pages use them.

Exiting Navigator

Michelle decides to take a break in the workshop. Before you leave the computer, you need to close Navigator.

You can exit Navigator from any location. The next time you start Navigator, the window will show the home page designated for your installation. To return to a site you visited in this session, you will need to re-open the Web page and link to the sites you want to see.

To exit Navigator:

1. Click **File**.

2. Click **Exit**. The Netscape window closes.

You have completed Session 1.1. You have opened Navigator, opened a Web page in the Navigator browser, linked to a site successfully, aborted a stalled link, had Navigator terminate a link for you, and experimented with frames.

Quick Check

1. True or False: When you start Navigator, you will always see the same screen, no matter what computer you are using.

2. What is a home page?

3. The address of a Web page is called a(n) _____.

4. How do you hide the Component bar?

5. How does Navigator display a text link that you've already activated?

6. When you try to link to a Web site but the page you want does not immediately appear, you might need to _____ the link because of congestion on the Internet.

7. What does Navigator mean when it tells you "The server does not have a DNS entry"?

SESSION

1.2

In this session, you will learn more about URLs and how to open a Web page using its URL, how to navigate the Web with Navigator using toolbar buttons, how to speed things up by viewing images on demand, how to preview and print Web pages, and how to use the online Help feature.

Opening a Location with a URL

Michelle now wants to show the instructors how to locate specific Web pages and how to use them in their classes. Some of the educators mention that they've read journal articles about integrating the Internet into the curricula for all age groups. These articles usually supply Internet addresses for helpful online resources. Michelle explains how to access these sites.

Clicking a hypertext link is just one way of jumping to a Web page. Clicking links, often called "surfing," is an easy way to navigate the Web when you don't have a specific destination in mind and just want to follow content links. Often, however, you want to visit a particular site. In order to get to that site, you need to know its address, which must be in a certain form. Entering the uniform resource locator (URL) for a Web page is a direct route to get to a specific site.

A URL is composed of a protocol identifier, a server address, and a file pathname. For example, when Michelle saves the undergraduate program list she is creating for the Education Department, it will have the following URL:

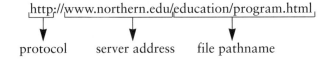

http://www.northern.edu/education/program.html

protocol   server address   file pathname

Computers use standardized procedures, called **protocols**, to transmit files. Web documents travel between sites using **HyperText Transfer Protocol** or **HTTP**, so every URL for a Web page begins with "http://" to identify its type. Another common protocol you might see is **File Transfer Protocol**, or **FTP**, a protocol that facilitates transferring files over the Web.

The server address contains the domain name and tells the exact location of the Internet server and the type of organization that owns and operates it. For example, in the domain name "www.northern.edu" the "www" indicates that the server is on the World Wide Web, "northern" indicates the name of the organization that owns the server (Northern University), and ".edu" indicates that it's an educational-type site. The entire domain name tells you that Northern is an educational site on the Web. Figure 1-20 lists common domain name types. Outside the United States, domain name types include a two-letter country code. For example, .fi indicates that the server is located in Finland.

Figure 1-20
Domain
name
types

Domain	Description	Domain	Description	Domain	Description
au	Australia	fr	France	net	Networking organizations
ca	Canada	gov	Government agencies	org	Nonprofit organizations
com	Commercial sites	int	International organizations	uk	United Kingdom
de	Germany	jp	Japan		
edu	Educational institutions	mil	Military sites		

All files stored on a network server must have a unique pathname just as files on a disk do. The pathname includes the folder or folders the file is stored in, plus the filename and its extension. The filename and extension is always the last item in the pathname. The filename extension for Web pages is .html (or just .htm), which stands for hypertext markup language. Michelle's Education Department programs file, for example, is named program.html and is located in the education folder on the Northern server.

Sometimes when you try to go to a specific site, you might see an error message such as the one shown in Figure 1-21. If you see such an error message, you should check the URL in the Location box on the Location toolbar and make sure every character is typed correctly, and then try again.

Figure 1-21
URL Not Found
error message

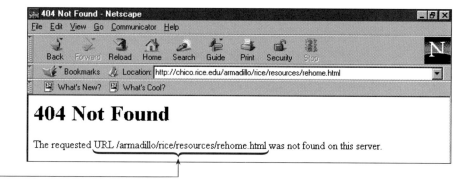

URL path you typed
will appear here

Remembering two important facts about a URL will make it significantly easier to use a URL to access an Internet site:

- Domain names in a URL are case-sensitive. A URL must be typed with the same capitalization shown. The URL http://www.Mysite.com is different from http://WWW.mysite.com. Unless the server can interpret case-sensitive addresses, you will get an error message when a URL doesn't exist with the exact name and capitalization entered. Whether you copy a URL from a magazine article or get it from a friend, make sure you copy the characters and their cases exactly.

- Internet sites continuously undergo name and address changes. A network server might have changed names, the file might be stored in a different folder, or the page you want might no longer be available. Remember, no one person or organization controls the Internet. Organizations and individuals can add files, rename them, and delete them at will. Often when a URL changes, you can find the forwarding address (URL) at the old URL. Other times, a site will simply vanish from a server, with no forwarding information.

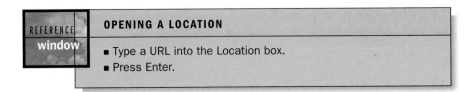

OPENING A LOCATION

- Type a URL into the Location box.
- Press Enter.

Lyle Sanchez, one of the educators, wants to find an interesting site that he can show his students as an "in-class field trip." He asks you to help him. You are going to use a set of Web pages designed by the publisher of this book for these tutorials. The URL for the Web page you need is http://www.course.com/downloads/NewPerspectives/tiuc. You can type this URL directly in the Location box on the Location toolbar.

Note that the Location box sometimes appears with the label "Netsite." This indicates that you have displayed a page coming from a Netscape server.

To open a location:

1. Launch Navigator and make sure the three toolbars are visible, the Component bar is docked, and the Channel finder window is closed.

    TROUBLE? If you need help starting Navigator or setting the options, refer to the appropriate sections earlier in this tutorial.

2. Click in the **Location** box to highlight the current entry, which should be the URL for your home page.

    TROUBLE? If the current entry is not highlighted, highlight it manually by dragging the mouse from the far left to the far right of the URL. The entire entry must be highlighted so that the new URL you type replaces the current entry.

3. Type **http://www.course.com/downloads/NewPerspectives/tiuc** into the Location box. Make sure you type the URL exactly as shown. Notice the two slashes after the protocol identifier; the protocol identifier is always followed by the two slashes. See Figure 1-22.

Figure 1-22 ◄
Opening a Web
page with
its URL

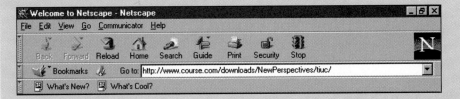

4. Press **Enter**. Netscape follows the same steps as when you clicked hypertext to link to a site and connects to the selected Web page. See Figure 1-23.

    TROUBLE? If you receive a Not Found error message, the URL might not be typed correctly. Repeat Steps 2 through 4, making sure that the URL in the Location box matches the one shown in Figure 1-22. You can correct a minor error by double-clicking in the Location box, using the arrow keys to move to the error, and then making the correction. If the URL matches Figure 1-22 exactly, or if you see a different error message, press the Enter key to try connecting to the Web page again. If you see the same error message, ask your instructor or technical support person for help.

Figure 1-23
Opened
Web page

Moving Among Web Pages

In Navigator, you can flip among Web pages you've visited in a session as though they were pages in a magazine that you have held with a finger. Rather than memorizing and retyping URLs of places you have visited, you can use toolbar buttons to move back one page at a time through the pages, move forward again one page at a time, or return to the front cover of your home page. Netscape "remembers" which pages you've been to during your current Web session, and provides navigation buttons on the Navigation toolbar so that you can easily move through those pages. See Figure 1-24.

Figure 1-24
Navigation
buttons in
Netscape
Navigator

Button	Icon	Description
Back	Back	Returns you to the Web page you were most recently viewing. If you click it twice, it returns you to the page you were viewing before that, and so on, until you reach the first page you viewed in the current session. This button is active only when you have viewed more than one Web page in the current session.
Forward	Forward	Reverses the effect of the Back button, sending you forward to the page from which you just clicked the Back button. This button is active only when you have used the Back button.
Home	Home	Retrieves your home page, the first page that Navigator displays when you begin a session.

To visit and then move among visited Web pages:

1. Click the **Tutorial 1** link in the left frame of the Web page to open the Learning to Navigate page. This Web page contains hypertext links to educational resource sites available on the Internet. Lyle wants to look at the Field Trips/Museums link.

2. Click the **Field Trips/Museums** link in the Subject Areas list to see the list of sites available from this Web page. See Figure 1-25.

Figure 1-25 ◄
Field
Trips/Museums
list

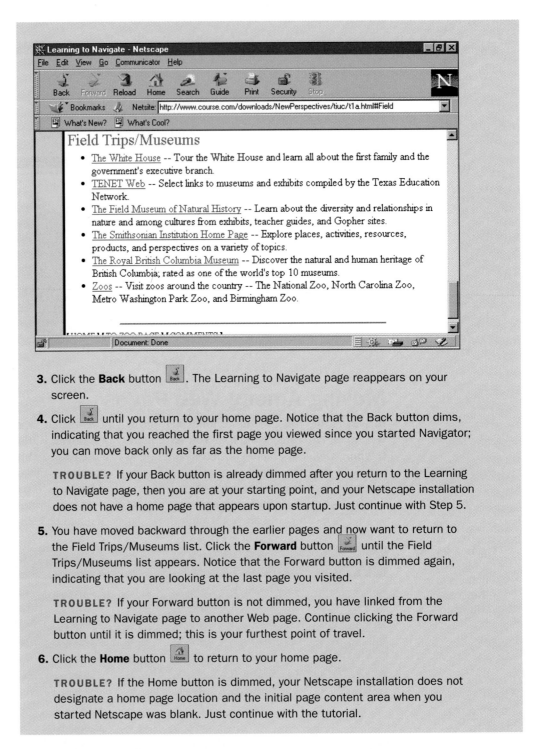

3. Click the **Back** button . The Learning to Navigate page reappears on your screen.

4. Click until you return to your home page. Notice that the Back button dims, indicating that you reached the first page you viewed since you started Navigator; you can move back only as far as the home page.

   TROUBLE? If your Back button is already dimmed after you return to the Learning to Navigate page, then you are at your starting point, and your Netscape installation does not have a home page that appears upon startup. Just continue with Step 5.

5. You have moved backward through the earlier pages and now want to return to the Field Trips/Museums list. Click the **Forward** button until the Field Trips/Museums list appears. Notice that the Forward button is dimmed again, indicating that you are looking at the last page you visited.

   TROUBLE? If your Forward button is not dimmed, you have linked from the Learning to Navigate page to another Web page. Continue clicking the Forward button until it is dimmed; this is your furthest point of travel.

6. Click the **Home** button to return to your home page.

   TROUBLE? If the Home button is dimmed, your Netscape installation does not designate a home page location and the initial page content area when you started Netscape was blank. Just continue with the tutorial.

You've seen that it's simple to navigate through Web pages, but sometimes the pages take quite a while to load. Michelle tells the workshop participants that pages load more quickly when they don't contain images.

Loading Images

Images, the graphics and pictures such as drawings or photographs that accompany a Web page, make Internet documents more attractive and informative and can enhance comprehension. For example, if you're studying modern history, you can find up-to-date information on the Internet about the geography and current events of warring countries. Because the countries' borders change so quickly, maps that accompany these articles are more current than any printed atlas.

However, the use of graphics significantly increases the time a Web page takes to load. A page that contains only text loads in seconds whereas one containing elaborate images can take minutes. Clearly, a trade-off exists between speed and quality. Deciding which factor to favor depends on the situation. When you have a lot of time or enjoy the richness of images, you might want to automatically load the images for every page. When you want to look at a large number of pages in a short amount of time, you probably want to load just text. With Netscape, you can switch between these two options as frequently as you want.

If you opt to hide images, a graphic image on a Web page is represented with an icon similar to 🖾. Although this option offers speed, the advantage of loading images automatically is that you can see and use all the links that are on the page. Remember that images also can be links to other Web pages. Unless you load the images, you won't be able to use or even see these links.

Michelle asks you to find sites that the teachers might want to use in their classes. You'll view the next pages without graphics so that they will load faster.

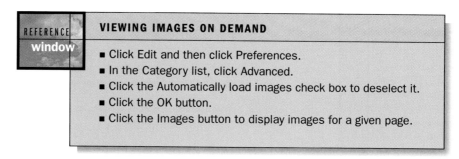

REFERENCE window

VIEWING IMAGES ON DEMAND

- Click Edit and then click Preferences.
- In the Category list, click Advanced.
- Click the Automatically load images check box to deselect it.
- Click the OK button.
- Click the Images button to display images for a given page.

To view Web pages without images:

1. Click **Edit** and then click **Preferences**.

2. In the Category list, click **Advanced**. See Figure 1-26.

Figure 1-26 ◀
Setting image preferences

click to view advanced options

deselect this check box

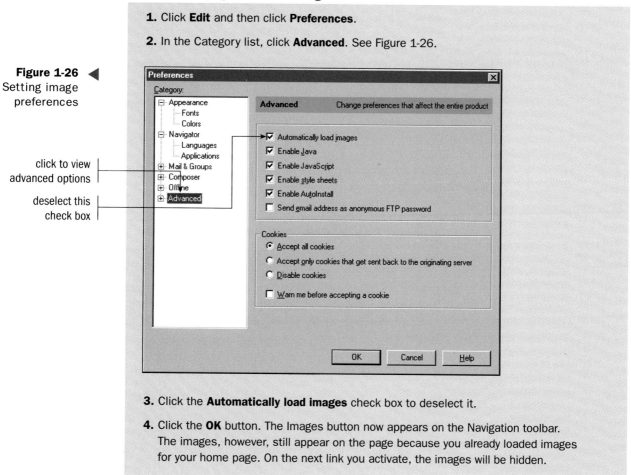

3. Click the **Automatically load images** check box to deselect it.

4. Click the **OK** button. The Images button now appears on the Navigation toolbar. The images, however, still appear on the page because you already loaded images for your home page. On the next link you activate, the images will be hidden.

5. Click the **Back** button until you see the Field Trips/Museums page.

6. Click the **Zoos** link to open the Zoos page, which contains links to several national zoos. Notice that icons replace the images. See Figure 1-27.

Figure 1-27 ◄
Zoos page with
image icons

icons replace images ────

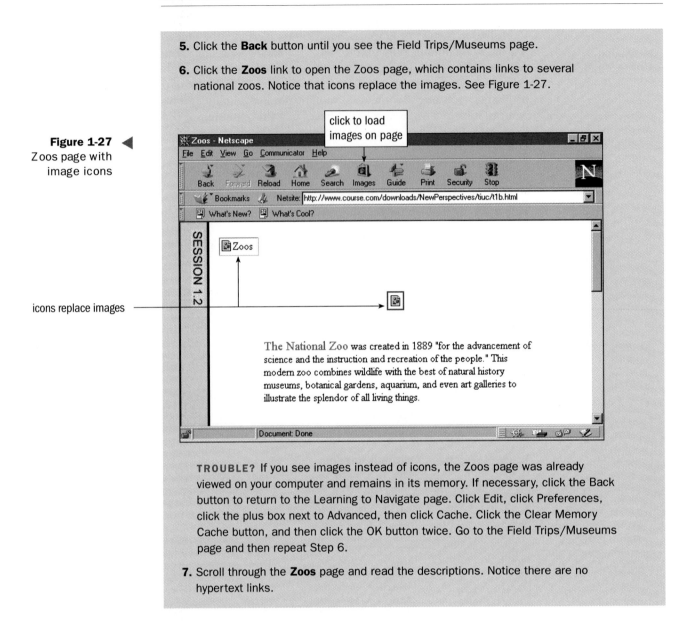

TROUBLE? If you see images instead of icons, the Zoos page was already viewed on your computer and remains in its memory. If necessary, click the Back button to return to the Learning to Navigate page. Click Edit, click Preferences, click the plus box next to Advanced, then click Cache. Click the Clear Memory Cache button, and then click the OK button twice. Go to the Field Trips/Museums page and then repeat Step 6.

7. Scroll through the **Zoos** page and read the descriptions. Notice there are no hypertext links.

You suspect that the images on this Web page might be links to other pages that the teachers might want to see because none of the text contains links. You decide to load the images to see all your link options.

To load the images for a selected Web page:

1. Click the **Images** button 📷 to replace the icons with images. The page reloads from top to bottom with the images. When it's completely loaded, your page should look like Figure 1-28. The page is much more interesting to view this way and contains other links you couldn't see with the icons. Each zoo is represented by a graphic in the large image at the top of the page. Each graphic is a link targeting each zoo.

Figure 1-28 ◀
Zoos page with
images loaded

images
replace icons

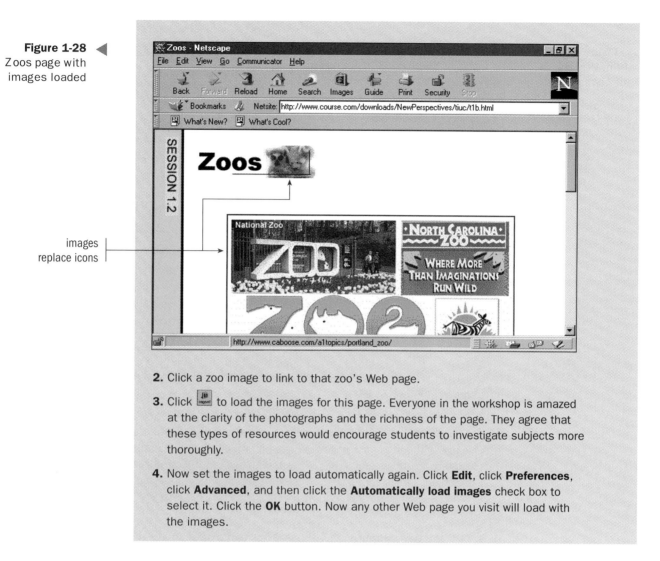

2. Click a zoo image to link to that zoo's Web page.

3. Click [icon] to load the images for this page. Everyone in the workshop is amazed at the clarity of the photographs and the richness of the page. They agree that these types of resources would encourage students to investigate subjects more thoroughly.

4. Now set the images to load automatically again. Click **Edit**, click **Preferences**, click **Advanced**, and then click the **Automatically load images** check box to select it. Click the **OK** button. Now any other Web page you visit will load with the images.

Previewing and Printing a Web Page

Although reducing paper consumption is an advantage of browsing information online, sometimes you'll find it useful to print a Web page. For example, you might want to refer to the information later when you don't have computer access, or you might want to give a copy of the Web page to someone who doesn't have access to a computer or to the Internet.

You should always preview a Web page before you print it. Although Web pages can be any size, printers tend to use 8-1/2 x 11-inch sheets of paper. When you print, Navigator automatically reformats the text of the Web page to fit the page dimension. Because lines might break at different places or text size might be altered, the printed Web page might be longer than you expect.

You decide that the directory of zoos is a good handout for the teachers in the workshop, so you decide to print out a copy. First, you'll preview it to see how many pages the Web page will print on and that it appears on the printed page as you expect.

To preview a Web page:

1. Click the **Back** button [icon] on the toolbar until you see the Zoos page.

2. Click **File**, and then click **Print Preview**. The Print Preview window opens with the first page of the Web page displayed. See Figure 1-29.

Figure 1-29
Print Preview
of Zoos page

click to send
page to printer

click to see
next page

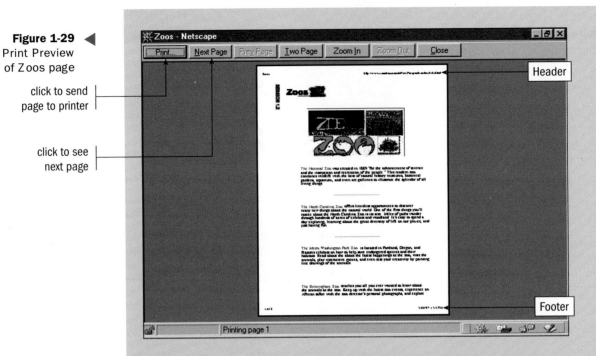

Header

Footer

TROUBLE? If you see two pages on your screen, click the One Page button on the Print Preview toolbar.

3. The pointer, when resting on the document, changes to 🔍. You can click this pointer anywhere on the document to zoom it to a larger size. Click 🔍 on the image at the top of the page to enlarge it. Notice that the name of the Web page prints in the upper-left corner of the screen and the URL for that Web page prints in the upper-right corner of the screen. Text that prints at the top of the page is called a **header**. Navigator prints a header on every page so you always know where to find that Web page on the Internet.

4. Click the **Down arrow** on the vertical scroll bar to move to the bottom of the page and look at the page number in the lower-left corner of the page and the date and time in the lower-right corner of the page. Text that prints at the bottom of the page is called a **footer**. Netscape prints a footer on every page so you can tell how many pages are in your document and when you printed it.

TROUBLE? If you do not see headers or footers, your installation of Netscape might be set up differently. Just continue with Step 5.

5. Click 🔍 twice. The page returns to its original size.

6. Click the **Next Page** button on the Print Preview toolbar to see the material that didn't fit on the first page. Notice that Netscape automatically reformats the Web page into sections that fit on letter-sized sheets of paper.

7. Click the **Prev Page** button on the Print Preview toolbar to return to page one.

8. Click the **Two Page** button on the Print Preview toolbar to view the pages side by side.

This Web page is fairly short (only two 8-1/2 x 11-inch sheets of paper). Other Web pages might convert to 30 or more 8 1/2 x 11-inch sheets of paper, which might be longer than you need or want to print. You can use the Print command to print only those pages of which you want a hard copy.

Although this Web page is only two sheets of paper, Michelle suggests that you print just the first page for the teachers. If the teachers want other information, they can return to the site and see the material online.

To print a Web page:

1. Click the **Print** button on the Print Preview toolbar to open the Print dialog box.

2. Click the **Pages** option button, type **1** in the from box, press the **Tab** key to move to the to box, and then type **1**. This indicates that you want to print only the page range 1-1 of the document, or just the first page of the document. Your completed dialog box should look similar to Figure 1-30.

Figure 1-30 ◀
Print dialog box

your printer might
be different

select page
range to print

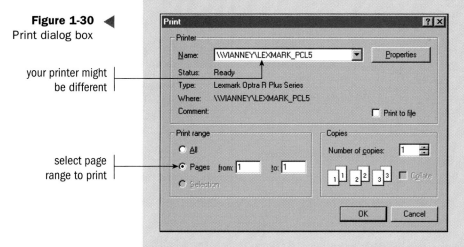

TROUBLE? If your Print dialog box looks somewhat different from Figure 1-30, don't worry. The Print dialog box changes to reflect the options available for the printer you are using. Just continue with Step 3.

3. Click the **OK** button to print the first page of the Web page.

Getting Online Help

Charlotte DuMont, another instructor at the workshop, has been taking notes about how to use Navigator, but wants to know what to do if she needs help and no one familiar with Navigator is around.

One of the best sources of information and help is always available when you're using any of the Communicator components. Netscape's NetHelp Help system is an online reference created and maintained by Netscape for use with its software; you can open the NetHelp window from the Help menu or by clicking Help buttons found in certain dialog boxes. The Help system provides a Contents window, an Index, and a Find utility that helps you locate topics by keyword.

Even though the workshop members just saw how to load images automatically, Charlotte isn't sure she remembers the precise steps. She asks you to help her find information about this option. You suggest looking up the word "image" in the Index.

To get online Help:

1. Click **Help**, and then click **Help Contents**. The NetHelp window opens. See Figure 1-31.

Figure 1-31 ◀
NetHelp
window

Index button ——

Figure 1-32 ◀
Index

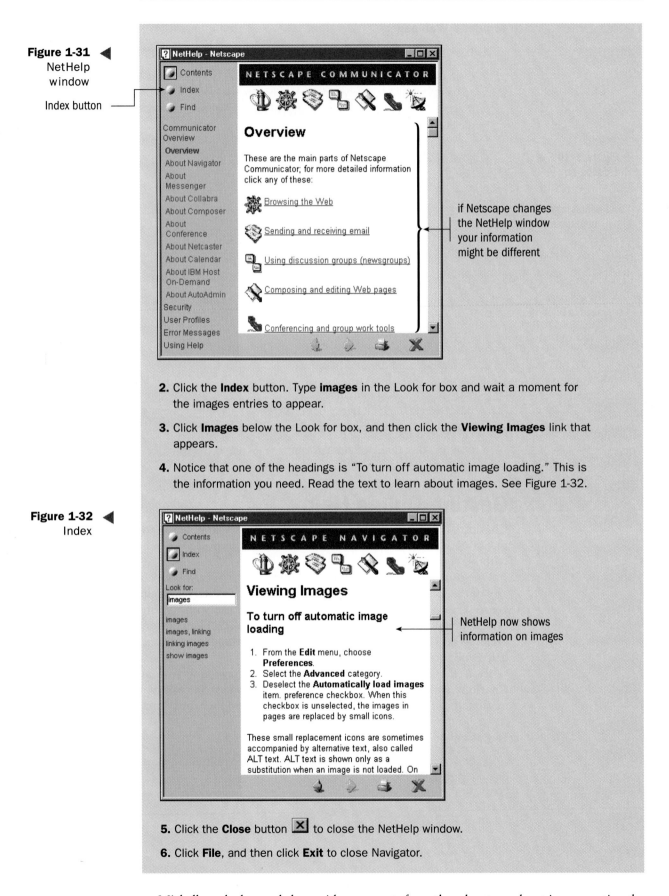

2. Click the **Index** button. Type **images** in the Look for box and wait a moment for the images entries to appear.

3. Click **Images** below the Look for box, and then click the **Viewing Images** link that appears.

4. Notice that one of the headings is "To turn off automatic image loading." This is the information you need. Read the text to learn about images. See Figure 1-32.

5. Click the **Close** button ☒ to close the NetHelp window.

6. Click **File**, and then click **Exit** to close Navigator.

Michelle ends the workshop with comments from the educators about incorporating the Internet in their classes. Lyle suggests that the information superhighway might bridge some of the gaps between metropolitan and rural schools as well as between wealthy and disadvantaged districts by providing common, equally accessible, resources to all. As technology costs decrease and states encourage network connections in their public schools, distinctions such as these will begin to fade.

Quick Check

1. Someone has given you the URL of an interesting Web page. How can you view that Web page?

2. In the URL http://www.irs.ustreas.gov/prod/cover.html, what is the protocol? What is the server address? What is the name of the Web page file? In which folder is it located?

3. Is the Web page located at the URL http://www.CTI.COM/HOME.html the same as the Web page located at URL http://www.cti.com/home.html? Why or why not?

4. What is FTP?

5. When you see a URL with ".edu" in it, what do you know about that site's Web server?

6. You can easily flip through Web pages using the _____, _____, and _____ toolbar buttons.

7. Why might you want to load text only with the Automatically load images option?

8. True or False: A printed Web page cannot contain any graphics or special formatting.

Tutorial Assignments

Michelle wants to gear her next workshop for college-level educators. She needs to find out how much the Internet is being used for educational purposes in higher education, what types of sites and information are available, and who is involved with this new approach to education.

She asks you to look at trends in the Internet and answer the following questions: How is the Internet affecting higher education? Do you think the trends overall will be positive? What are some of the possible negative side-effects?

Michelle suggested a few Web pages from which you can begin looking for answers. Do the following:

1. If necessary, launch Navigator.

2. Open the Web page at the URL "http://www.course.com/downloads/NewPerspectives/tiuc."

3. Click the Tutorial Assignments and Case Problems link.

4. Locate the Tutorial 1 Tutorial Assignments section.

5. Connect to the World Lecture Hall link in the "Universities Around the World" section.

6. Follow one of the links that interests you and see if you can find any information you can use to answer Michelle's questions.

7. Print Preview the page you connected to find out how long it is.

8. Print the first page of the World Lecture Hall page you linked to from Print Preview, and then close Print Preview.

9. Return to the Tutorial Assignments and Case Problems page.

10. Connect to the Distance Education on the WWW link in the Tutorial 1 Tutorial Assignments section.

11. Scroll through the page. Navigate links as necessary to answer these questions: What is distance education? Name three advantages or resources available on the Web to distance education.

12. Find out how many pages this Web page has. If it is more than two pages, print just the first two pages.

13. Submit to your instructor the printout and the answers to Michelle's questions based on the information you found in #6 and your answers to #11.

14. Use the online Help system to find information on two other Communicator components, such as Messenger or Collabra. Write a description of the two components you chose (between 5 and 10 sentences).

Case Problems

1. University Informational Pages Karla Marletti, director of admissions at Southern University, noticed that an increasing number of universities are placing Web pages on the Internet. She wants her university to remain current in its use of technology and decides that the school should put a Web page on the Web. She is not sure what layout or design would be most appealing for the page or what type of information should be included. She asks you to find a couple of Web pages that you think have attractive and effective designs with interesting and helpful content.

If necessary, start Navigator, and then do the following:

1. Open the Web page at the URL "http://www.course.com/downloads/NewPerspectives/tiuc."

2. Click the Tutorial Assignments and Case Problems link.

3. Scroll down until you see the Tutorial 1 Case Problems section.

4. Connect to the University Informational Pages link to find a listing of countries with universities with Web pages.

5. Visit three Web pages for universities within the United States and then visit two Web pages for universities outside the United States.

6. Choose Web pages for two universities that you think have an unusual or attractive layout and interesting and relevant content.

7. Print Preview both Web pages and find out on how many pages they will print.

8. Print the shorter university Web page. On the hard copy, explain what you liked about that Web page and submit your explanation to your instructor.

2. The Fresno Daily Helen Wu, a staff journalist for *The Fresno Daily*, a newspaper serving the Fresno, California community, just received an assignment to write a feature article on how the Internet is changing the way people spend their leisure time. As part of her article, Helen wants to discuss the current size of the Internet and its rate of growth. She asks you to find statistics on the current number of Internet domains, the current number of Internet hosts, the current number of Web sites, and the percentage these figures have grown since they were counted last.

If necessary, launch Navigator, and then do the following:

1. Open the Web page at the URL "http://www.course.com/downloads/NewPerspectives/tiuc."

2. Click the Tutorial Assignments and Case Problems link.

3. Scroll down until you see the Tutorial 1 Case Problems section.

4. Connect to one of the two Case Problems 2 links to find a listing of relevant Web pages.

5. Navigate through the Web pages to look for the statistics Helen needs.

6. When you find a Web page that contains a relevant statistic, look at that Web page in Print Preview.

7. Print only the page or pages that contain the information you need and then close Print Preview.

8. When you have all the information, write a short report about your findings on the back side of the printout.

9. Circle the URL of each page you used. *Hint*: Check the header of the printed Web page.

3. The Carpet Shoppe The Carpet Shoppe imports and sells hand-woven rugs from Thailand, Burma, and India. Four times each year, Al Sanchez, the owner, travels to these countries to replenish his inventory of new carpets.

Al has decided that it's time to convert to computerized inventory and accounting systems. Al isn't sure whether to purchase a Macintosh or an IBM-compatible system. He wants a portable computer that he could bring on his buying trips. With a laptop computer, not only will he have the most current figures at his fingertips, but he also will be able to communicate with his employees at home without worrying about the time difference or the cost of international phone calls. He wants a top-of-the-line notebook computer that won't become obsolete quickly. The more RAM, the bigger the disk storage space, and the faster the modem, the better.

He asks you to find information such as the model name, model number, and features about different brands of computers. Most of the bigger computer manufacturers place Web pages on the Internet with their latest computer models and prices, so you can begin looking there.

If necessary, launch Navigator, and then do the following:

1. Open the Web page at the URL "http://www.course.com/downloads/NewPerspectives/tiuc."

2. Click the Tutorial Assignments and Case Problems link.

3. Scroll down until you see the Tutorial 1 Case Problems section.

4. Using the Case Problems 3 links, find information about a top-of-the line notebook computer from Apple.

5. Print Preview any Web pages that contain information Al wants to see.

6. Print only those pages that contain relevant information.

7. Find information about a top-of-the line notebook computer from IBM.

8. Print Preview any Web pages that contain information Al wants to see.

9. Print only those pages that contain relevant information.

10. Write a summary report of the information you found, and make a recommendation of which notebook computer you think Al should buy.

4. Marketing 305 Consumer Behavior The students of Marketing 305 (MK305) have prepared a survey to study consumer behavior in online environments. They plan to compile a report that discusses what consumers think about two malls available on the Internet, how products' prices compare to their local malls, and what percentage of people are willing to shop online.

If necessary, launch Navigator, and then do the following:

1. Open the Web page at the URL "http://www.course.com/downloads/NewPerspectives/tiuc."

2. Click the Tutorial Assignments and Case Problems link.

3. Scroll down until you see the Case Problems 4 section.

4. Navigate through two online shopping malls looking at various products.

5. Print one sample product description from each mall. Preview each Web page to make sure it won't be longer than one page.

6. Compare a similar product available at each mall. See how information about the product is presented as well as its price.

7. Return to the Tutorial Assignments and Case Problems page and locate the MK305 survey link.

8. Connect to the MK305 survey page.

9. Answer the survey questions. When you are done, click the Submit button. Global Marketers Inc. displays a completed survey.

10. Print the completed survey and submit it to your instructor.

Lab Assignments

These Lab Assignments are designed to accompany the interactive Course Lab called Internet World Wide Web. **To start the Lab using Windows 95 or Windows NT**, click the Start button on the Windows taskbar, point to Programs, point to Course Labs, point to New Perspectives Applications, and click Internet World Wide Web. **To start the Lab using Windows 3.1**, double-click the Course Labs for the Internet group icon to open a window containing the Lab icons, then double-click the Internet Word Wide Web icon. If you do not see Course Labs on your Windows Programs menu, or if you do not see the Course Labs for the Internet group icon in your Windows 3.1 Program Manager window, see your instructor or technical support person.

   The Internet: World Wide Web One of the most popular services on the Internet is the World Wide Web. This Lab is a Web simulator that teaches you how to use Web browser software to find information. You can use this Lab whether or not your school provides you with Internet access.

1. Click the Steps button to learn how to use Web browser software. As you proceed through the Steps, answer all of the Quick Check questions that appear. After you complete the Steps, you will see a Quick Check Summary Report. Follow the instructions on the screen to print this report.

2. Click the Explore button. Use the Web browser to locate a weather map of the Caribbean Virgin Islands. What is its URL?

3. Enter the URL http://www.atour.com. A SCUBA diver named Wadson Lachouffe has been searching for the fabled treasure of Greybeard the pirate. A link from the Adventure Travel Web site leads to a Wadson's Web page called "Hidden Treasure." Locate the Hidden Treasure page and answer the following questions:
   a. What was the name of Greybeard's ship?
   b. What was Greybeard's favorite food?
   c. What does Wadson think happened to Greybeard's ship?

4. In the Steps, you found a graphic of Jupiter from the photo archives of the Jet Propulsion Laboratory. In the Explore section of the Lab, you can also find a graphic of Saturn. Suppose one of your friends wanted a picture of Saturn for an astronomy report. Make a list of the blue, underlined links your friend must click to find the Saturn graphic. Assume that your friend will begin at the Web Trainer home page.

5. Jump back to the Adventure Travel Web site. Write a one-page description of the information at the site, the number of pages the site contains, and a diagram of the links it contains.

6. Chris Thomson, a student at UVI, has his own Web pages. In Explore, look at the information Chris included on his page. Suppose you could create your own Web page. What would you include? Use word processing software to design your own Web pages. Make sure to indicate the graphics and links you would use.

Finding What's Out There

Using the Internet as a Resource at the Peter H. Martin Public Library

OBJECTIVES

In this tutorial you will:

▨ Check file associations and listen to an audio clip

▨ Use Web navigational guides

▨ Browse and return to sites with the history lists

▨ Use bookmarks to remember pages

▨ Search the Web by content and subject

▨ Save text and images to a file

▨ Download external files

▨ Consider common download concerns, including viruses, copyrights, shareware, and file compression

CASE

Peter H. Martin Public Library

The Peter H. Martin Library is a well-established public library supported by local and federal government funding as well as local civic groups. Last year, the Board of Directors authorized Anna Ferri, the library's technical assistant, to develop and implement a plan that incorporates Internet access to expand the library's existing resources. The library already had an Internet connection to a host computer within the city and a **local area network (LAN)**, a group of computers in one location that are connected so they can share data, files, and software. The library's LAN connects the microcomputers throughout the building to the server, the computer that stores the data and programs accessed by other computers in the LAN, in Anna's office. One of the programs on the LAN is a computerized cataloging system that it shares via the Internet with other regional libraries. Visitors can search for books at any participating library by title, author, or subject.

Anna wants to provide online services that supplement the library's holdings. To fulfill these goals, Anna:

- Created a home page that gives information about the library's services and layout.

- Installed Netscape Communicator on the computers throughout the building so all the library's computers have Internet access.

- Added technical support for library users who dial into the system from their home computers.

- Organized training sessions for library personnel and the general public on how to use the Internet as a research and reference tool.

The response from the community so far has been very positive. The library staff spends a lot of time showing people how to surf the Internet and find information. Anna asks you to work at the Help Desk, assisting patrons in answering questions about the Internet.

In this session, you will explore your computer's file associations, listen to an audio clip, use popular navigational guides, browse sites with the Go menu and Back and Forward buttons, and add, use, and delete bookmarks.

Viewing External Files

Anna informs you that library users often want access to files on the Internet, not just Web pages. She advises you to familiarize yourself with accessing the variety of files available on the Web. Hyperlinks on a Web page can point to many different types of files. Navigator recognizes and can display files such as HTML Web page files and certain types of graphic images. However, when Navigator encounters a file it cannot display on its own, called an **external file**, it searches your computer to see if there is other software available that it could use to display the file. Navigator uses a three-step process to determine what to do when you click a link that targets an external file:

1. First, Navigator checks the file extension of the link's target.

2. Then, Navigator matches the file extension to a list of file extensions and their corresponding programs, called **file associations**. Navigator maintains this list in conjunction with your computer's operating system.

3. Finally, Navigator checks which program is associated with that file extension, and starts that program if it can find it.

For example, if you click a link targeting a doc file, Navigator might discover that your computer associates doc files with Microsoft Word word processing software. Navigator then automatically starts Word. Figure 2-1 illustrates this process.

Figure 2-1 ◀
Linking to an
external file

You know that as you help people use the library's Internet connection, patrons will approach you for information about accessing files of many different types on the Web. You decide to explore the file association list on your computer to see which programs are associated with which files. Every computer has a different list, depending on the software it contains. You're especially curious about how audio files with the AU extension are handled.

To check your computer's file associations:

1. Launch Navigator and make sure the three toolbars are visible and the Component bar is docked. Make sure images are set to load automatically.

2. Click **Edit** and then click **Preferences**.

3. Click **Applications** in the Category list. A list of file types appears.

   TROUBLE? If Applications does not appear in the Category list and there is a plus box ⊞ next to Navigator, click ⊞. Applications now appears indented below Navigator.

4. Click any file type in the Description list. The File type details area identifies the program that handles that file type.

5. Now you're going to check how AU sound files are handled, since you know that many Web sites feature AU sound files. Click **AU** in the Description list, and notice which program handles it. See Figure 2-2. On the computer shown in the figure, AU files are handled with a plug-in. If no program is identified on your screen, you might have trouble playing AU files.

   TROUBLE? If AU does not appear in the Description list, your computer is not set up to recognize AU audio files. Ask your technical support person or instructor for assistance.

Figure 2-2 ◀
Checking file
associations

Applications category
is selected

AU file type is
selected

details about the
AU file type

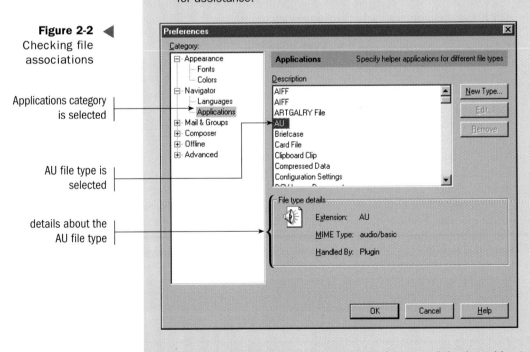

6. Click the **Cancel** button to close the Preferences dialog box without saving any changes you might have inadvertently made.

You now know that when you click a link targeting an AU file, the program indicated in the File type details section will automatically start.

What happens when you click a link targeting a file whose file extension Navigator doesn't recognize? When Navigator fails to locate a file association for the link's target, it opens the Unknown File Type dialog box, shown in Figure 2-3.

Figure 2-3 ◀
Dialog box that
appears when
you click a link
targeting an
unknown file
type

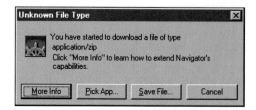

Figure 2-4 describes the four options found in the Unknown File Type dialog box.

Figure 2-4 ◀
Unknown File
Type dialog box
buttons

Option	Result
More Info	Opens a Netscape Web page that describes how Navigator handles unknown file types. Also provides information about plug-ins (extensions to Navigator that allow it to work with different types of files within the browser window) that you might want to acquire so that you will be able to view the file.
Pick App	Allows you to identify a program on your computer that you want to load whenever you click a link to this type of file. From this point on, whenever you click a link to that file type, Navigator will automatically load the file into the program you specified.
Save File	Allows you to save the file to your hard disk for later viewing, perhaps on a computer with different software.
Cancel	Cancels the connection and foregoes displaying the file.

Now that you've learned how Navigator handles external files, you're ready to assist any library patron who wants to access such a file.

Listening to an Audio Clip

Two teenagers, Sasha and Janine, stop by the Help Desk and ask you about the library's new Internet connection. You suggest that they begin by looking at the library's home page. Anna created the home page to orient visitors to the library's setup, tell them about the available services, and personally welcome them to the library with a recording by the head librarian. Sound, added to text and images, helps to make a Web page more dynamic and "alive" than a static printed page. Hearing someone greet you to a page is more welcoming than reading the same words. With sounds on a Web page, you can hear the roar of a lion, listen to the beat of a healthy heart, and play the latest song from your favorite band.

Any sound on a Web page is actually a file, called an **audio clip**, which can be stored in different formats. Some formats provide a better quality sound, but create a larger audio clip. The file extension of the audio clip indicates its file type. There is no standard audio file type, but you can expect to see audio files on the Web in the formats shown in Figure 2-5.

Figure 2-5 ◀
Audio
file types

File type	Description
AU	A basic audio file type that lacks high-fidelity quality of other audio file types; is nevertheless popular because AU files can be run on practically any computer system and are smaller than similar sounds saved in other formats.
AIFF	High-fidelity sound developed by Apple and used primarily on Macintosh computers.
WAVE	High-fidelity sound developed by Microsoft and IBM and considered a standard on Windows/PC computers.

Each type of audio file needs to be interpreted by a **playback device**, software that identifies the file and its format and then plays it through your computer's speakers. If your computer has the appropriate software and the file associations are properly set, when you click an audio clip link, a playback device starts automatically and plays the clip. (For some devices, you might need to click the Play button.) Not all software works with every type of audio file. If your computer does not have the correct playback device for an audio clip that you click, Navigator warns you and opens the Unknown File Type dialog box, which, as you have seen, gives you the opportunity to cancel, save the file to your disk so you can find a computer that can play it, or locate and acquire software that can play it. Netscape has developed a plug-in, **Media Player**, that works with the Netscape Communicator suite to play audio clips. Your computer might have this software already loaded.

If your computer doesn't have a playback device or doesn't have the necessary hardware (including a sound card and speakers) to play audio clips, you will receive an error message in the next set of steps.

To open the Peter H. Martin Library home page and listen to an audio clip:

1. Replace the current entry in the Location (or Netsite) box on the Location toolbar with **http://www.course.com/downloads/NewPerspectives/tiuc** and then press **Enter**.

2. Click the **Tutorial 2** link to open the library's home page.

3. Position your pointer over the audio clip graphic link [🔊] on the Peter H. Martin Library home page. See Figure 2-6.

Figure 2-6 ◀
Peter H. Martin
Library home
page

click to hear audio
clip

information box
appears when you
point to this link

audio clip filename

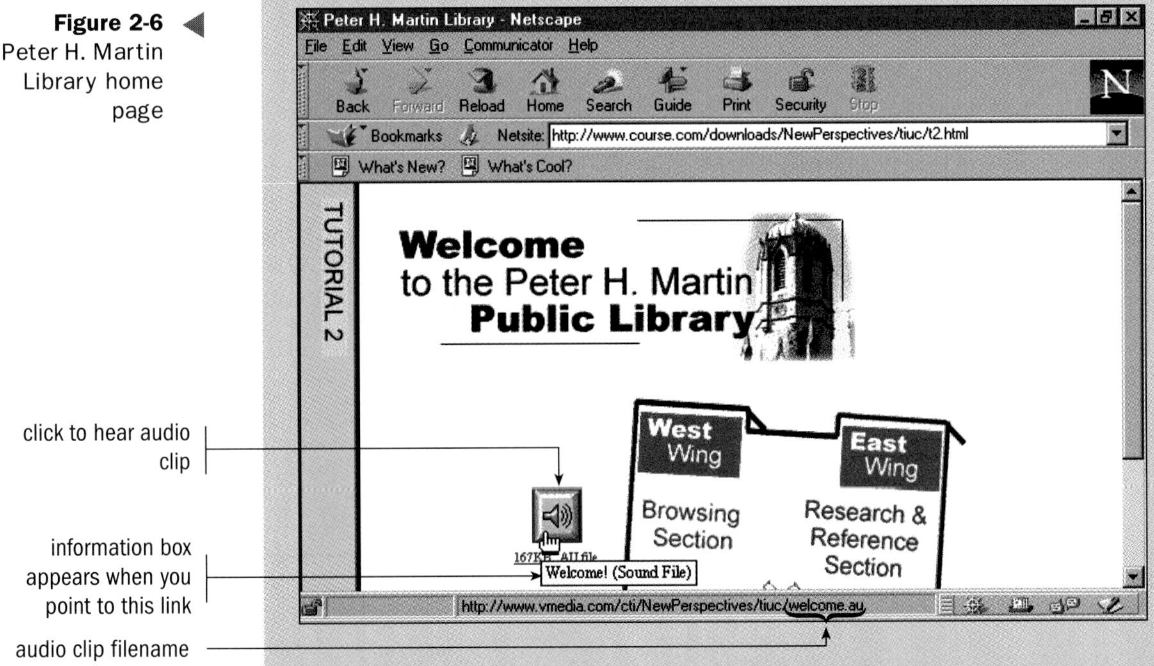

4. Click [🔊]. You might need to wait a minute or two as your playback device starts and loads the audio clip. If the playback device opens but you don't hear a sound, try clicking the **Play** button. Figure 2-7 shows the Netscape Media Player, which plays the clip automatically. Be patient; it might take a minute.

TROUBLE? If you don't hear a sound, even after clicking the Play button, your computer might not have audio capabilities or the sound might be turned down. Check with your instructor or technical support person.

TROUBLE? If an Unknown File Type dialog box opens, your computer does not recognize this type of audio file and you cannot hear the audio clip. For now, click the Cancel button to close the dialog box, and continue with the tutorial. You might need to acquire a playback device, or you might need to check your computer's file type associations. As you have seen, you can do this in the Preferences dialog box.

Figure 2-7 ◄
Playback
device

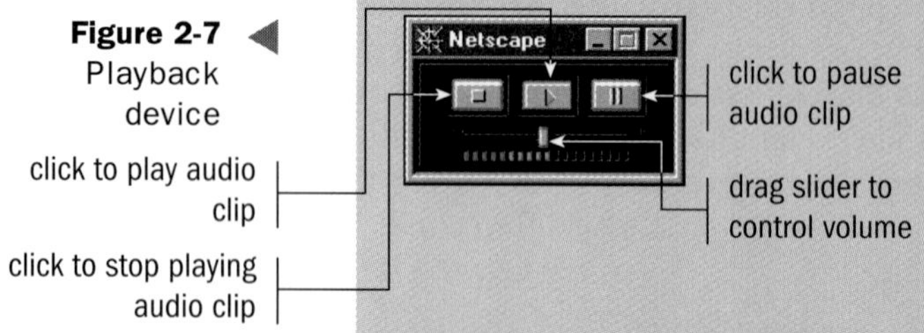

click to play audio
clip

click to stop playing
audio clip

click to pause
audio clip

drag slider to
control volume

5. Click the **Close** button ⊠ in the upper-right corner of the playback device to close it, if necessary.

Now that Sasha and Janine have seen the library's welcome page you decide to show them how navigational guides work.

Using a Navigational Guide

With so much information available on the WWW, many people spend their time searching for unique and interesting sites, with unusual layouts or interesting text, graphics, or sounds. Netscape Communications Corporation routinely scouts the Internet for unusual sites and then places links to those URLs on its What's Cool page. Netscape also maintains a What's New page, which features interesting new sites. Netscape updates both lists periodically, so they are a good starting point for surfing. You can find similar types of lists on the WWW compiled by other groups or individuals. A list or index of Web pages organized around a general theme or subject is called a **navigational guide**.

The Personal toolbar displays one or more buttons for the What's New and the What's Cool pages that link you to those pages. Sasha wants to check out the links on the What's Cool page first.

To look at the What's Cool list:

1. Click the **What's Cool** button on the Personal toolbar to link to a list of "cool" Web pages collected by Netscape Communications Corporation. See Figure 2-8. The page is updated regularly so yours will look different from the one shown here.

TROUBLE? If the Personal toolbar is not visible, click View, and then click Show Personal Toolbar.

TROUBLE? If your Personal toolbar displays a New & Cool button, click it, and then click the What's Cool button.

Figure 2-8 ◀
What's Cool
Web page

click to open
Netscape's list of
"cool" sites

description of a
"cool" Web site

advertisements such
as this appear on
many Web pages

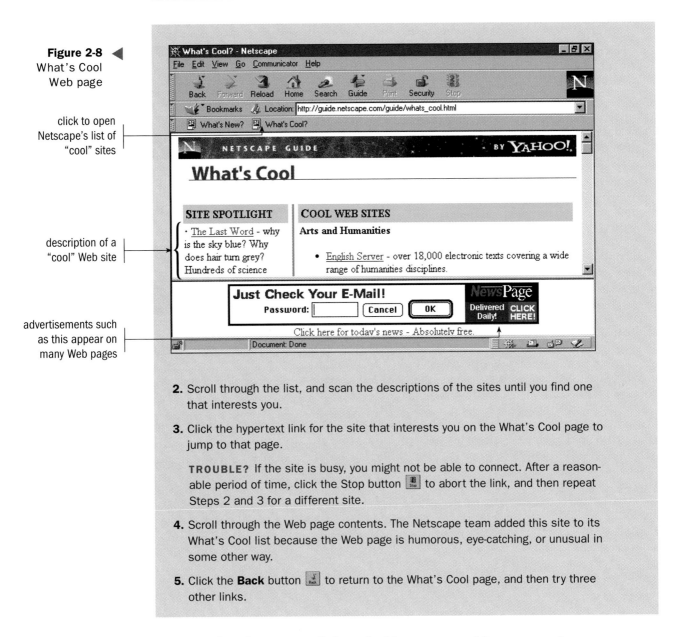

2. Scroll through the list, and scan the descriptions of the sites until you find one that interests you.

3. Click the hypertext link for the site that interests you on the What's Cool page to jump to that page.

   TROUBLE? If the site is busy, you might not be able to connect. After a reasonable period of time, click the Stop button 🛑 to abort the link, and then repeat Steps 2 and 3 for a different site.

4. Scroll through the Web page contents. The Netscape team added this site to its What's Cool list because the Web page is humorous, eye-catching, or unusual in some other way.

5. Click the **Back** button ⬅ to return to the What's Cool page, and then try three other links.

Notice the advertisement link on the Netscape page. Many corporations earn revenue by selling advertising links on their page to organizations. These advertisements change regularly.

Now that Sasha and Janine have looked at some unusual sites on the What's Cool page, Janine wants to see Netscape's What's New page. This page compiles a list of interesting new Web pages or sites that apply some new technique or technology.

To look at the What's New list:

1. Click the **What's New** button on the Personal toolbar to connect to a list of new Web sites compiled by Netscape. See Figure 2-9. Netscape frequently updates the list and images to keep the content new.

   TROUBLE? If your Personal toolbar displays a New & Cool button, click it, and then the What's New button.

Figure 2-9 ◄
What's New
Web page

click to see a list of
new Web pages

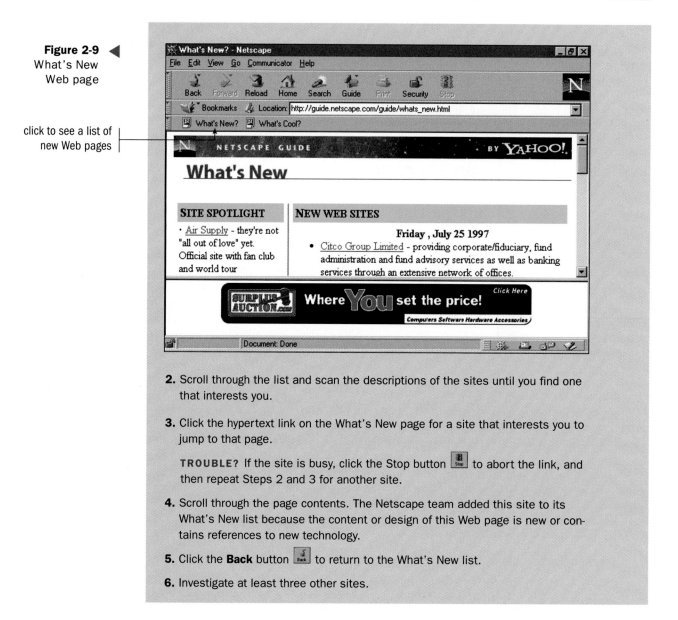

2. Scroll through the list and scan the descriptions of the sites until you find one that interests you.

3. Click the hypertext link on the What's New page for a site that interests you to jump to that page.

   TROUBLE? If the site is busy, click the Stop button to abort the link, and then repeat Steps 2 and 3 for another site.

4. Scroll through the page contents. The Netscape team added this site to its What's New list because the content or design of this Web page is new or contains references to new technology.

5. Click the **Back** button to return to the What's New list.

6. Investigate at least three other sites.

One disadvantage to sites on both the What's New and What's Cool lists is that the lists are frequented by many people and the pages suddenly can become extremely popular, overwhelming the URL's server. These pages are usually maintained by modest-sized servers, incapable of handling the large volume of requests. As a result, you'll often be unable to link to these pages or even to different pages housed on the same server.

Returning to Sites

Sasha and Janine have navigated through quite a few sites, and now they are ready to return to the library's home page. You've already seen how to use the Back button to return to a previously-visited site. Navigator also makes it easy to return to pages with the **history list**, a list of sites that you have visited since launching Navigator. You can access the history list by opening the Go menu. The history list returns you with a single click to any page you viewed earlier in the session. History list entries are numbered; 0 is your most recent connection and the bottom entry is the home page you saw when you started Navigator. The check mark indicates your current location. Although you can click the Back button repeatedly to return to a page, the history list is usually a quicker way to go where you want if you've navigated multiple Web pages.

You decide to show Sasha and Janine how to return to the library's page using the history list. Then you'll show them the navigational guide that Anna created for the Peter H. Martin library.

To return to the Peter H. Martin Library page:

1. Click **Go** to open the Go menu. See Figure 2-10. Yours will look different, depending on which sites you linked to using the What's Cool and What's New pages.

Figure 2-10 ◄
History list on
the Go menu

current Web page ──────

click to return to the
Peter H. Martin
Library home page

home page ──────

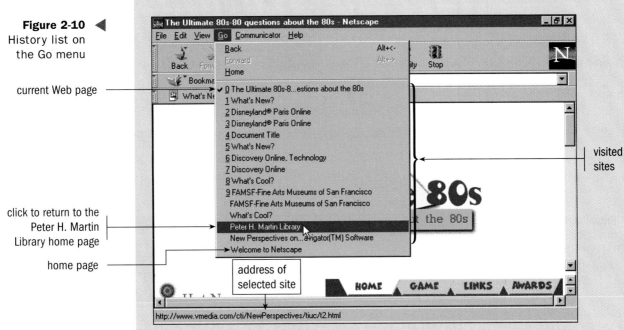

visited
sites

2. Click the **Peter H. Martin Library** entry on the history list.

   TROUBLE? If you can't find the library home page, enter http://www.course.com/downloads/NewPerspectives/tiuc in the Location box and then press Enter. Then click the Tutorial 2 link.

3. Click the **Browsing Section** area on the left side of the floor plan, shown in Figure 2-11.

   TROUBLE? If nothing happens, you might not have clicked the correct area. Make sure the pointer changes to 🖑, indicating that you are clicking a link.

   TROUBLE? If the floor plan in Figure 2-11 is not visible, Navigator might not be set to load images automatically. Click Edit, click Preferences, click Advanced, click the Automatically load images check box, click OK, click the Reload button 🔄 on the toolbar, and then repeat Step 3.

Figure 2-11 ◀
Accessing the
library's
browsing
section

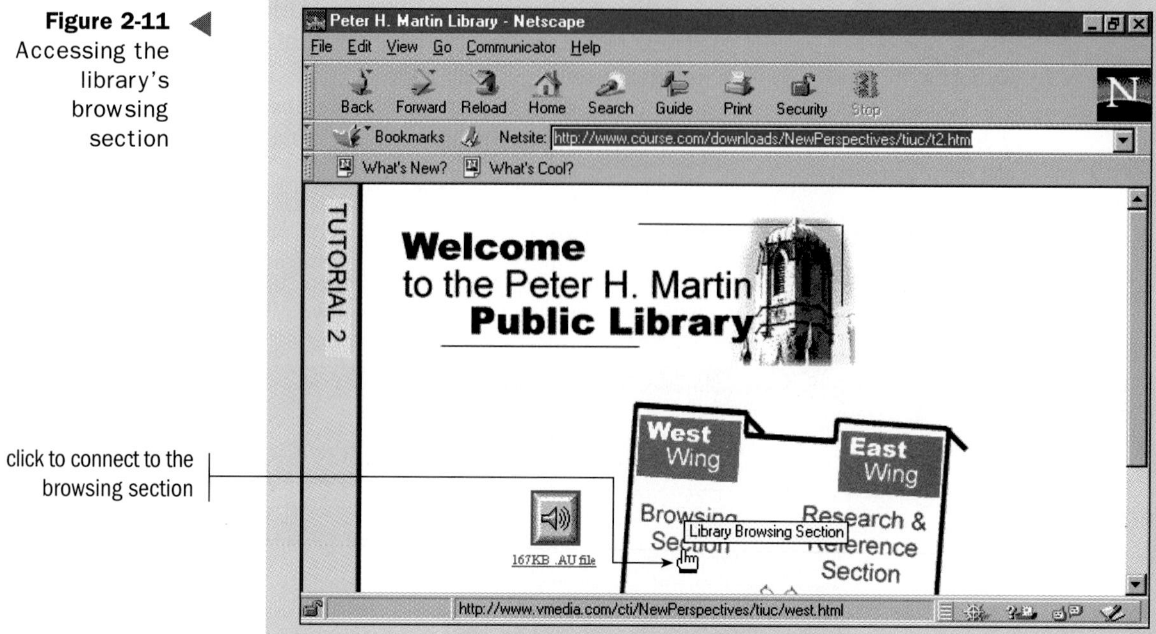

click to connect to the
browsing section

4. In the Library West Wing page that opens, shown in Figure 2-12, click the **Navigational Guides** link to see a list of popular navigational guides.

Figure 2-12 ◀
Connecting to
the library's
navigational
guides

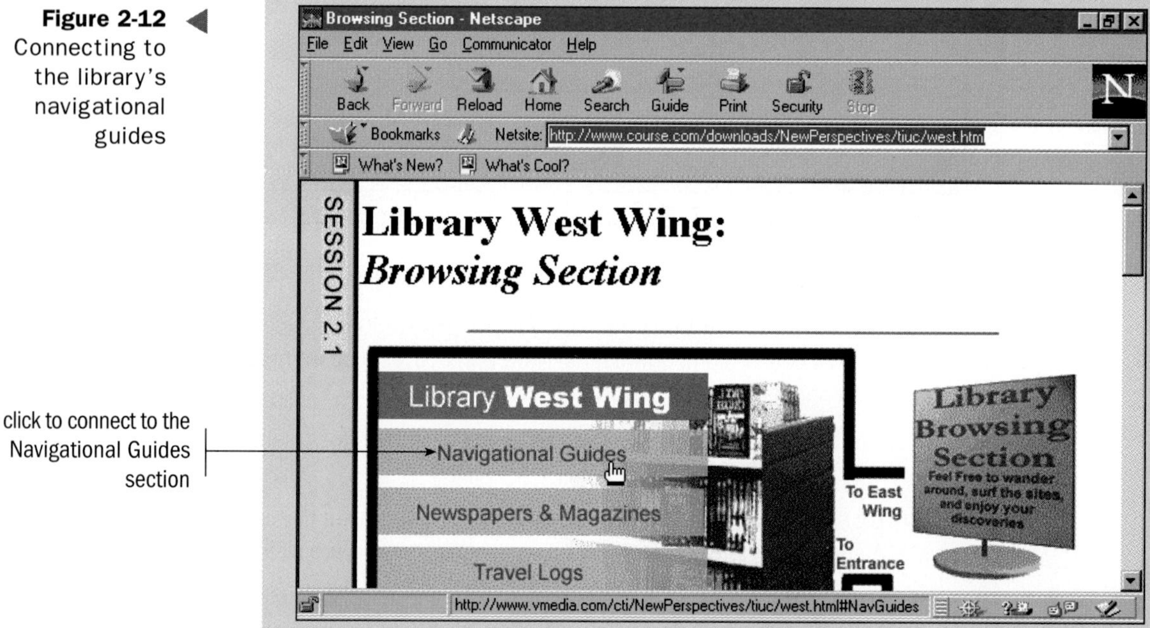

click to connect to the
Navigational Guides
section

5. Click a hypertext link from the Navigational Guides list to connect to another list of sites, and then on the navigational guide page that opens, click a hypertext link about a subject that interests you. Continue clicking links to get a sense of how you can surf the Internet.

The Go menu only recalls the last 10 or so sites you have visited in the current session (depending on your browser's settings). If you want to view information on all recently visited links, including those in previous sessions, you can open the History window. The History window provides data on each site you have visited, including the page's title, its

URL, when you first visited it, when you most recently visited it, and how often you have visited it. You can view the list of sites by title, location, or date, and you can search the History window to find a specific site.

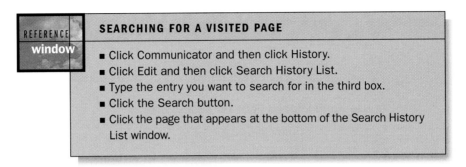

REFERENCE window

SEARCHING FOR A VISITED PAGE

■ Click Communicator and then click History.
■ Click Edit and then click Search History List.
■ Type the entry you want to search for in the third box.
■ Click the Search button.
■ Click the page that appears at the bottom of the Search History List window.

For now, you just want to show Sasha how much information this window provides, and then show him how he can use it to return to a page.

To open the History window:

1. Click **Communicator** on the menu bar, and then click **History**. The History window opens.

2. Now you'll see how to search for the Peter H. Martin Library site. Click **Edit** and then click **Search History List**.

3. Click the third box and type **peter h. martin**. Then click the **Search** button. The page you requested appears at the bottom of the Search History List window. See Figure 2-13.

Figure 2-13 ◀
Searching the History window

type what you want to search for here

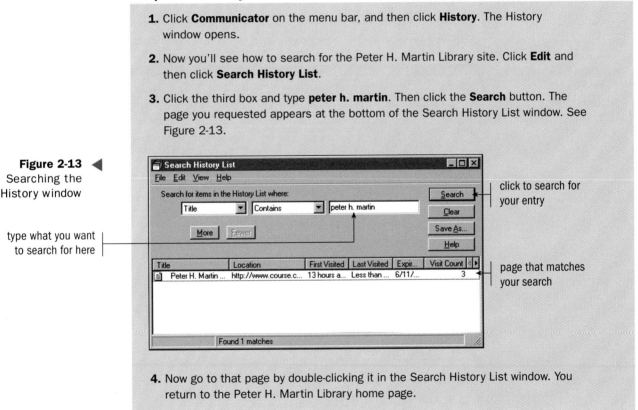

click to search for your entry

page that matches your search

4. Now go to that page by double-clicking it in the Search History List window. You return to the Peter H. Martin Library home page.

Sasha asks if the library's navigational guides might be able to help him plan his next vacation. He'd like to learn about travel in Malaysia. You assure him the information is there, and you tell him about another navigational trick he can use while locating the information and then returning to the library's home page. You can use the Back and Forward buttons to access Back and Forward history lists that show all the pages going back to a certain point and all the pages going forward to a certain point.

SEARCHING THE BACK AND FORWARD HISTORY LISTS

- Point at the Back or Forward button.
- Press and hold down the mouse button.
- Click the page you want.

You'll show Sasha this technique while you explore Malaysian travel pages.

To use the Back and Forward history lists:

1. Click the **Browsing Section** link on the Peter H. Martin Library home page to return to that site.

2. Click **Travel Logs**. The Travel Logs section of the Browsing Section page appears.

3. Click the **Virtual Tourist II** link and then scroll down to see a map of the world. See Figure 2-14. The Virtual Tourist II page is a visual presentation of links rather than text. You can click any point on the map to link to a different page and get additional information about that country or region.

   TROUBLE? If the Virtual Tourist II site is busy, try another travel link. It might not be map-oriented but will still contain links to travel destinations.

Figure 2-14 ◀
Virtual Tourist
II Web page

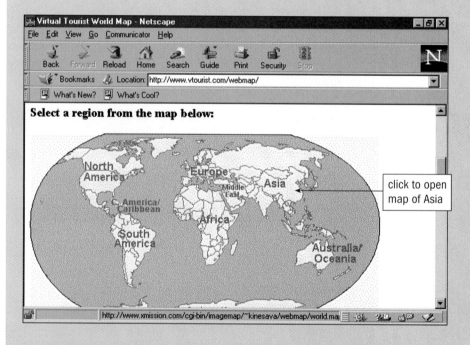

4. Click **Asia** to open a map of Asia.

5. Click **Malaysia** to link to its travel page. Scroll down until you see the Tourism link. See Figure 2-15.

Figure 2-15 ◀
Malaysia page

Tourism link ——————

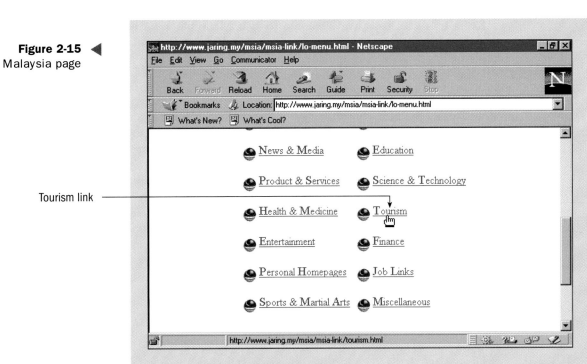

TROUBLE? If the Malaysia site is busy or you are on a travel Web page other than Virtual Tourist II, click another link until you find one that is available. Then substitute the name of the Web pages you have located for the Web pages mentioned in the steps.

6. Click **Tourism** to link to its travel page. Notice the available topics.

7. Now use the Back history list to return to the Virtual Tourist World Map. Point at the **Back** button and then press and hold down the mouse button until the Back history list appears. Then release the mouse button. See Figure 2-16.

Figure 2-16 ◀
Back
history list

history list opens
when you point at
Back button and hold
down the mouse
button

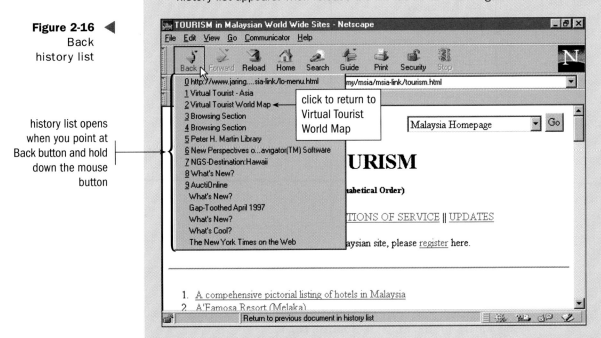

8. Click **Virtual Tourist World Map**. You return to the Virtual Tourist page. Now try returning to the Tourism page using the Forward history list. Point at the Forward button and then press and hold down the mouse button until the Forward history list appears. Then release the mouse button.

9. Click the **TOURISM in Malaysian World Wide Sites** link.

Sasha tells you he's always wanted to visit Malaysia. He'd like to explore this page some more. However, Janine wants to keep looking at other places. You'll show Sasha how to mark this Web page so he can easily find it later.

Using Bookmarks

While surfing the Net, you might find an interesting or unusual site to which you want to return. Rather than trying to remember the URL of that site, you can mark it with a **bookmark**, a shortcut back to a Web site. Just as you insert a piece of paper into a printed book to locate a specific page, you can add a bookmark to locate a specific Web page.

Navigator typically stores bookmarks in a file named bookmark.htm on your computer's hard disk. In this case, the bookmarks reside only on the computer where you add them, not on another computer. If you use a variety of computers and want to create a list of bookmarks that you can use on any machine with Navigator, you could store the bookmark file on a disk and then import that file into the machine's bookmark file. You won't do that now, however.

You decide to show Sasha how to work with the bookmark list on the library computer. Although you can access your bookmarks from the Location toolbar, to work with the bookmark file you need to open the Bookmarks window.

To open the Bookmarks window:

1. Click the **Bookmarks** button on the Location toolbar.

2. Click **Edit Bookmarks** to open the Bookmarks window, which contains a directory of all the bookmarks on that computer. See Figure 2-17. Remember that the list of bookmarks will be different for your computer.

Figure 2-17 ◄
Library's
bookmarks list

your bookmarks list
name will be different

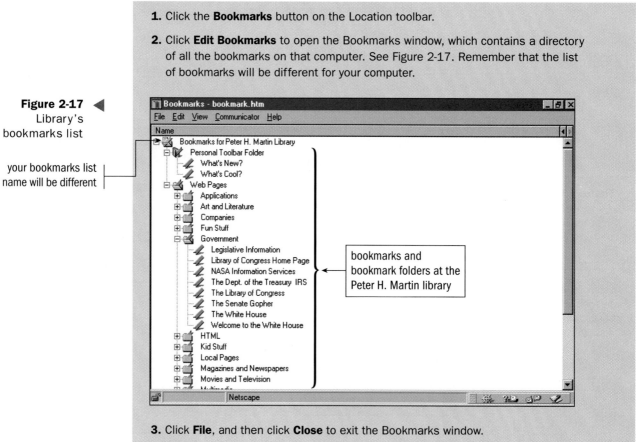

3. Click **File**, and then click **Close** to exit the Bookmarks window.

Now that Sasha has examined the library's Bookmarks window, he wants to add a bookmark for the Malaysia tourism page.

Adding a Bookmark

A bookmark is helpful when you want to return to a specific Web site, try other links from that page, or show someone else a certain site. You can add a bookmark for any Web page by using the Add Bookmarks command on the Bookmarks menu. This command adds the current page to the Bookmarks menu, at the end.

To add a bookmark:

1. Click the **Bookmarks** button to open the Bookmarks menu.

2. Click **Add Bookmark** to add a shortcut to the current Web page, the Malaysia tourism page.

3. Click the **Bookmarks** button again to open the menu and display the list of bookmarks, which now includes TOURISM in Malaysian World Wide Sites, probably at the end of the list. Notice that the page is listed by its title, which is more descriptive than its URL. See Figure 2-18.

   TROUBLE? If a different title appears, you were on a different Web page. You can either locate the Tourism in Malaysian World Wide Sites page and repeat this set of steps, or you can continue using a different page.

Figure 2-18 ◄
Bookmarks list

click to add bookmark for current Web page

your list will differ

new bookmark

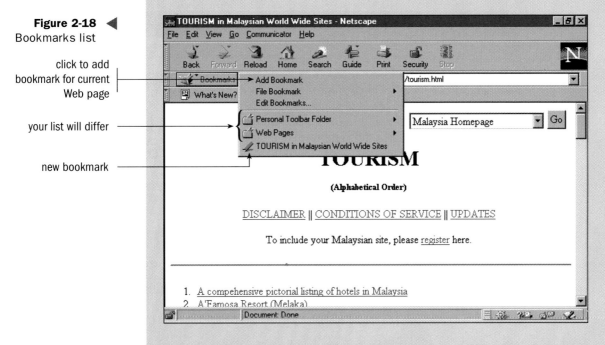

4. Click a blank area of the Netscape window to close the Bookmarks menu, then click the **Back** button twice to move to a different Web page.

Now that the Web page for which you added a bookmark is no longer the current page, you can show Sasha how to refer back to it.

Accessing a Bookmark

Because the menu bar is available no matter what Web page you are looking at or how long you have been surfing, you can click a bookmark to directly return to that Web page. A bookmark is available until you delete it from the list or the bookmark file is altered.

You'll show Sasha how to get back to the Malaysia Tourism Web page.

To access a bookmark:

1. Click the **Bookmarks** button to see the Web page bookmark you just added.

2. Click **TOURISM in Malaysian World Wide Sites** or the bookmark you added to return to that Web page.

Sasha is glad to see that bookmarks are so easy to use. He notices, however, that the Peter H. Martin Library bookmark list includes folders in addition to bookmarks. He asks you to explain.

Managing Bookmark Folders

Most bookmark users organize their bookmarks into folders grouped by category so it is easier to find a certain bookmark. The Peter H. Martin Library bookmark list, for example, organizes its bookmarks into folders with names such as Art and Literature, Government, Local Pages, and so on.

You can create folders within the Bookmarks window. The Bookmarks window lists both folders, indicated by �, and bookmarks, indicated by ✦. If a folder is preceded by ⊞, it contains additional folders or bookmarks. You can click ⊞ to open the folder and view its contents in the Bookmarks window.

You can add a bookmark to a folder from within the Bookmarks window or you can use the File Bookmark command on the Bookmarks menu.

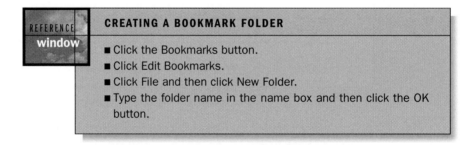

REFERENCE
window

CREATING A BOOKMARK FOLDER

■ Click the Bookmarks button.
■ Click Edit Bookmarks.
■ Click File and then click New Folder.
■ Type the folder name in the name box and then click the OK button.

You decide to show Sasha how to create a Travel folder and then add the Malaysia Tourism page to that folder from within the Bookmarks window. Then you'll show him how to add a page to a folder "on the fly" with the File Bookmark command.

To create a bookmark folder:

1. Click the **Bookmarks** button and then click **Edit Bookmarks** to open the Bookmarks window.

2. Click **File** and then click **New Folder**.

3. Type **Travel** in the Name box and then click the **OK** button.

4. Locate and click the **TOURISM in Malaysian World Wide Sites** bookmark you created earlier (it is probably at the bottom of the list).

5. Click **Edit** and then click **Cut**.

6. Click the Travel folder you just created.

7. Click **Edit** and then click **Paste**. The Tourism in Malaysian World Wide Sites bookmark now appears underneath and to the right of the Travel folder, indicating that it is now stored in that folder. See Figure 2-19.

Figure 2-19
Adding a bookmark to a folder

new folder

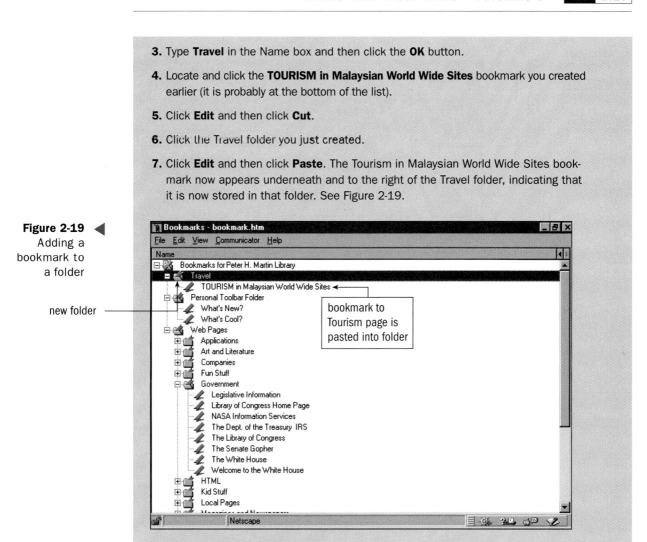

bookmark to
Tourism page is
pasted into folder

8. Close the Bookmarks window.

Once you have added a bookmark to your folder, you access it by opening the Bookmarks menu and then navigating to the folder you want. The bookmarks in that folder appear in a menu that "cascades" off to the side of the Bookmarks menu.

To access a bookmark in a folder:

1. Click the **Back** button twice to go to a different page.

2. Click the **Bookmarks** button, point to the **Travel** folder, and click the **TOURISM in Malaysian World Wide Sites** bookmark, shown in Figure 2-20.

Figure 2-20 ◀
Testing the new
bookmark
folder

new folder ──────→

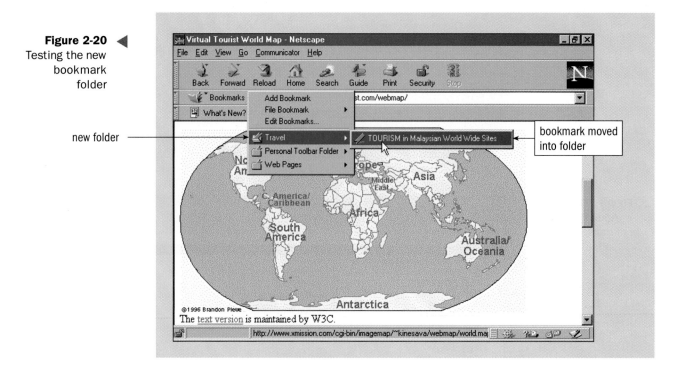

You are back to the Tourism page. Now you're going to add a bookmark to the Travel folder without using the Bookmarks window. You'll first open a different page on another place Sasha is interested in: Italy.

To add a bookmark to a folder from the Bookmarks menu:

1. Click **Go** and then click **Virtual Tourist World Map** to return to that page.

   TROUBLE? If that page title no longer appears on your Go menu, use the Navigational Guides at the Peter H. Martin Library to locate it.

2. Click **Europe**.

3. Click **Italy**. A map of Italy appears. Since Sasha isn't sure which city he wants to visit, you decide to add this page to his Travel folder.

4. Click the **Bookmarks** button, point to **File Bookmark**, and then click **Travel**. See Figure 2-21.

Figure 2-21
New folder

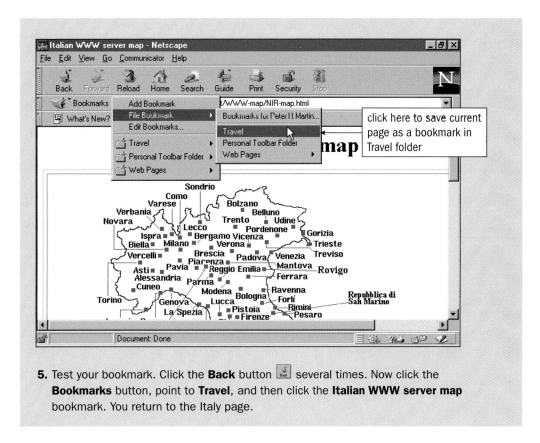

5. Test your bookmark. Click the **Back** button several times. Now click the **Bookmarks** button, point to **Travel**, and then click the **Italian WWW server map** bookmark. You return to the Italy page.

Sasha asks how you get rid of a bookmark you no longer want.

Deleting a Bookmark

Deleting, or erasing, bookmarks is almost as easy as adding them. It's always a good idea to delete the bookmark for any Web page that you no longer use or that has become outdated. This will help keep your list of bookmarks manageable and organized. In the Bookmarks window, you can work with individual bookmarks by using a **shortcut menu**, a menu that opens when you click an object on the screen with the right mouse button, called **right-clicking**. Shortcut menus display commands relevant to the object you right-clicked.

If you delete a folder, you delete not only the folder but also all the bookmarks it contains.

REFERENCE
window

DELETING A BOOKMARK

- Click the Bookmarks button, and then click Edit Bookmarks.
- Right-click the bookmark you want to delete.
- Click Delete Bookmark.

You decide to delete the bookmark to the Italy page.

To delete a bookmark:

1. Click **Bookmarks**, and then click **Edit Bookmarks** to open the Bookmarks window, which contains a list of all the bookmarks in that file.

2. Right-click the Italian WWW server map bookmark in the Travel folder in the Bookmarks window.

3. Click **Delete Bookmark** to remove the bookmark from the list.

You'll delete the Travel folder you just created.

To delete the Travel folder:

1. Right-click the Travel folder.

2. Click **Delete Bookmark**.

3. Click **File**, and then click **Close** to close the Bookmarks window.

4. Exit Navigator.

You can delete folders in the same way. When you delete a folder, the bookmarks it contains are also deleted. Sasha thanks you for your instruction and leaves for home eager to explore further the travel information available on the Internet.

Quick Check

1. True or False: Netscape uses its own software to interpret every type of file format.

2. What happens when you click a link targeting a file whose extension Navigator doesn't recognize?

3. Name three audio file types and provide a short description of each.

4. What playback device is designed to work with the Netscape Communicator suite?

5. To see a current list of unusual Web sites, you can go to Netscape's _____ page.

6. A disadvantage to using a URL link placed on the What's New page is a(n) _____ demand for the URL's server.

7. After browsing a number of Internet sites, you can trace your path by viewing the _____ from the Go menu.

8. You can use a _____ to mark a Web page you might want to visit again.

SESSION

2.2

In this session, you will conduct search queries, save text and images to a file, and explore how to download files. You will also learn about useful utilities that help you with file transfer.

Searching the Web

Surfing the Web is often a slow-paced, read-for-pleasure type of activity. Another, more focused, use of the Internet involves fact-gathering and research. You might use the Internet to find information about a term-paper topic, to learn about opening a new business, or to report statistics to a government agency. A common thread in all these research goals is that they have a specific topic, or theme.

Just as you return from lunch, Yoko Muramoto approaches the Help Desk to get assistance in finding information about opening a take-out restaurant serving Japanese food in the Marquette County, Michigan area. Some questions include: What is the population of the area? What are the current interest rates for bank loans? What government resources exist for small businesses? The answers to these questions and many others can be found on the Internet, but locating the information might be challenging.

Netscape has created a search page that makes available many popular **search services**, software that helps you find information on the Web. Search services such as Excite, Infoseek, Lycos, Yahoo, and WebCrawler are featured on the Netscape Net Search page, which you can access by clicking the Search button 🔍 on the Navigation toolbar. These services are organized on the search page so you can select the one you want. As you gain familiarity with the different search services, you'll develop preferences for which service you want to use based on the type of information you're looking for.

Search services help you find information in two ways: you can either search by query, which means you request information on a specific topic, or you can search using a subject guide, which is similar to using a subject catalog in a library. Yoko will first perform query searches and then will use a subject guide to locate information on the Japanese restaurant industry.

Searching by Query

To manage the growing number of files and documents on the Internet, commercial organizations collect information and store it in databases. A **database** is a collection of related information that can be searched by topic. The database software contains a **search engine**, which retrieves information from the database based upon a person's query. A **query** is a written request in question form that tells the search engine to find documents that contain a **keyword** (a specified word or phrase). For example, Yoko might want to search for information that matches the keywords "population statistics." The search engine generates a list of sites on the Internet that contain those words.

How is the database created? Most search services employ a **spider**, indexing software that compiles a large index of existing Web pages on a database that you can search to find references to a specific subject. Sometimes called robot, harvester, or worm, the term spider has perhaps become the most popular one for indexing software because it extends the Web analogy.

To understand how the spider creates a database, imagine a library that arranges its books randomly on the shelves and doesn't have a catalog index. The only way to locate information about any topic is to pick up a book and start reading and indexing it, jotting down keywords and references to other books. Follow these references and links until you reach a dead end, then repeat this process for all the other books in the library. The resulting list, in effect, is a database of the keywords and bibliography in each reference—a valuable way to locate all reference materials that relate to a keyword, such as Mozart. Now imagine adding to your list the books in all the libraries in your state, the country, and even the world. The resulting database, although time-consuming and tedious to compile, would yield even more information about a topic. A spider creates this type of database by circulating through millions of Web pages, one at a time, reading and storing keywords and links, until the links dead-end. The spider's helper programs organize the database by connecting some of the linked servers, removing duplicate entries, and categorizing the results.

A spider periodically (daily or weekly) connects to servers throughout the Internet in order to update its database. When you submit a query to search a spider's database, the query results include only references that were available and within the spider's range when it last updated its database. If new Web pages are added since the last update or the spider couldn't access a Web page during an update, the index doesn't contain current references to them. If a Web page is not indexed in the database, it will not turn up in a search.

The enormous task of indexing the Internet is done by relatively few organizations. Spiders on the servers of these organizations take different, but overlapping, routes as they travel the Internet. Each one independently builds and maintains a database, so each database is built on different keywords. A query performed with, for example, the Infoseek search engine usually provides a different result than asking the same query of, for example, the AltaVista search engine. To obtain a broad range of references that will more likely provide the data you need, use several search services when researching a topic.

Before you use a new search engine, you'll need to determine how you should write a query to get the results you want. When some search engines encounter two words such as population statistics, they assume you mean "population" *or* "statistics" and return pages with either word. Other search engines assume you mean "population" *and* "statistics" and return pages with both words. These types of searches take longer and return fewer pages, but the pages are likely to be more useful.

To help people learn to do research on the Net, Anna created a small database that you can use to demonstrate searching on the Web. The library's search engine assumes you mean "and," not "or," when it encounters two words. Some search engines allow you to specify what kind of search you want to perform.

To use Anna's search engine, you need to return to the Peter H. Martin Library home page. You can quickly return to a Web page whose URL you have already typed, even in a different Navigator session, by clicking the Location (or Netsite) list arrow to view a list of URLs that have been manually entered.

To conduct a query:

1. Launch Navigator. Click the **Location** list arrow and then click the **http://www.course.com/downloads/NewPerspectives/tiuc** URL, and then click the **Tutorial 2** link.

   TROUBLE? If the http://www.course.com/downloads/NewPerspectives/tiuc URL does not appear in the Location list, you'll need to enter it manually. Then click the Tutorial 2 link.

2. Click the **Research & Reference Section** link on the right side of the floor plan to connect to the Research & Reference Section page. See Figure 2-22.

Figure 2-22 ◀
Connecting to the Research & Reference Section

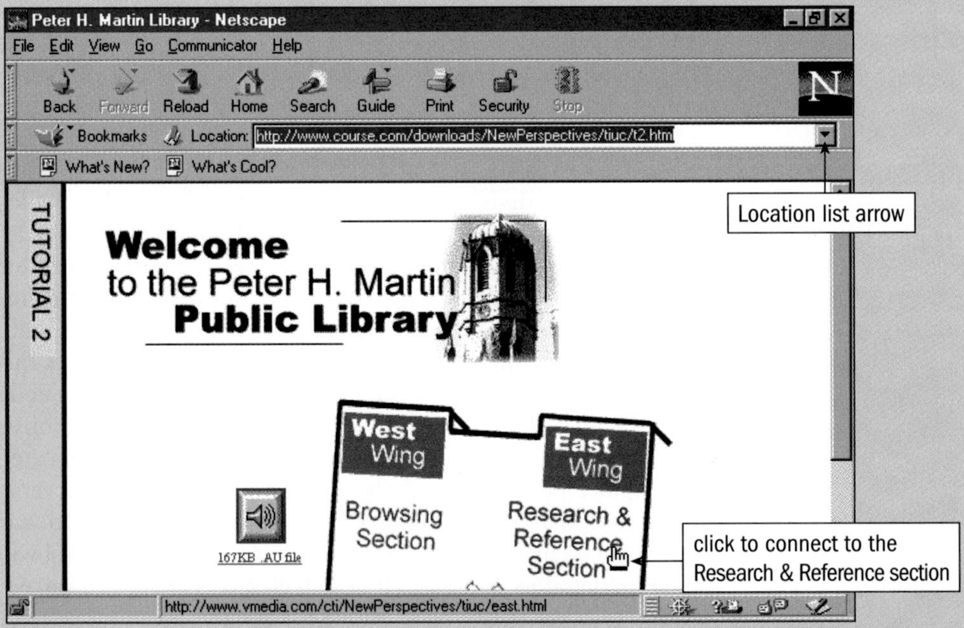

3. Click the **Query Demonstration** link (you might need to scroll down to see it) to open the Query Form used in the library's demonstration.

4. Click the query box and then type **population statistics** to indicate the keywords you want to search for. The list of references returned will include any documents that contain both the words "population" and "statistics." See Figure 2-23.

Figure 2-23 ◀
Query form

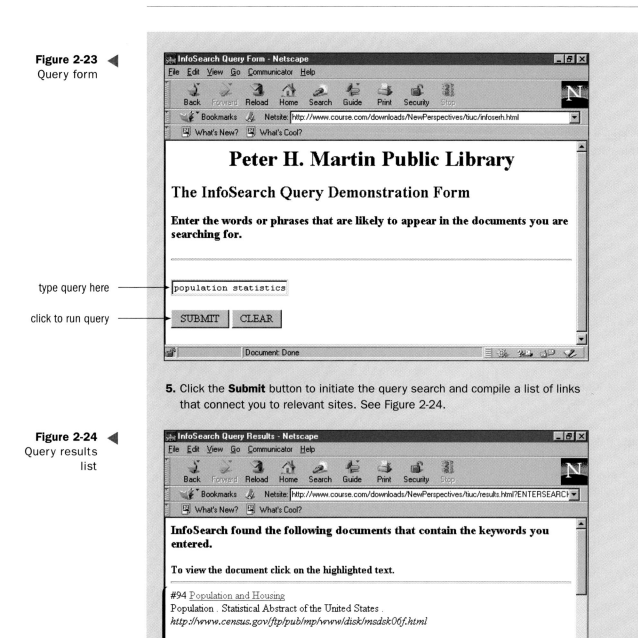

type query here ——

click to run query ——

5. Click the **Submit** button to initiate the query search and compile a list of links that connect you to relevant sites. See Figure 2-24.

Figure 2-24 ◀
Query results
list

located references ——

6. Scroll through the Query Results list and see if the data is relevant. The number on the left side of each link indicates, on a scale of 0 (least relevant) to 100 (most relevant) how relevant each link might be, based on criteria set up by the database manager. After scrolling through the links and noting those she might want to return to, Yoko decides to query the Census Bureau directly.

7. Scroll to the bottom of the page, and then click the **Click here to proceed to the next step** link to try another query.

8. Type **Census Bureau by county** in the query box and then click the **Submit** button. The first entry in the list that appears, Data Maps, has a relevance of 95. Yoko decides to explore this link.

9. Click the **Data Maps** link. The United States map appears. Click the Michigan Upper Peninsula, labelled **MI**, as shown in Figure 2-25.

   TROUBLE? If the Data Maps site is busy, read through these steps and try them again later.

Figure 2-25 ◀
State data map

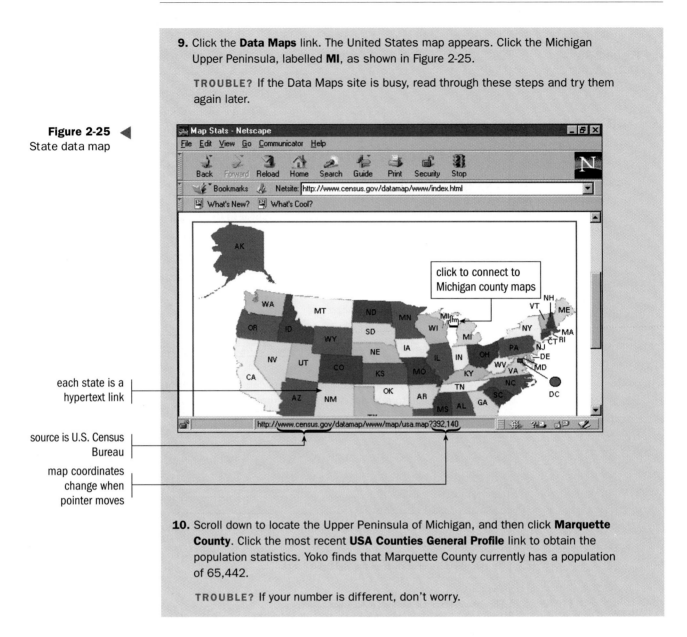

each state is a hypertext link

source is U.S. Census Bureau

map coordinates change when pointer moves

10. Scroll down to locate the Upper Peninsula of Michigan, and then click **Marquette County**. Click the most recent **USA Counties General Profile** link to obtain the population statistics. Yoko finds that Marquette County currently has a population of 65,442.

   TROUBLE? If your number is different, don't worry.

Yoko has found the population statistics she was looking for, but you add a note of caution. Sometimes a query might be too general, which results in a large list of references that includes unrelated data. Other times, the query might be too specific and returns few or no references. In either case, you'll need to revise the query so that it is more or less inclusive, as necessary. Try adding adjectives or nouns that help focus the search or choosing synonyms that are more specific to your needs. Sometimes queries are case-sensitive, so capitalize any word that might be capitalized in references.

The search engine Yoko has been using so far is the one Anna created for the Peter H. Martin library. Its database is not a large one. Now that Yoko knows how to search using a query, she wants to try one of the search services available on the Netscape Net Search page. She'll start by using Infoseek, which lets you search the Web and many other services on the Internet, such as newsgroups.

Yoko decides to use Infoseek to see what information is available on Japanese food.

To search for pages on Japanese food:

1. Click the Netscape **Search** button.

2. Click the **Infoseek** button.

3. Type **Japanese food** in the Seek box. See Figure 2-26, which shows not only Infoseek but also the other search services available from the Netscape Search page.

Figure 2-26 ◀
Searching with
Infoseek

click to access Web
search tools

click to use Infoseek

enter search query
here

click to perform
search

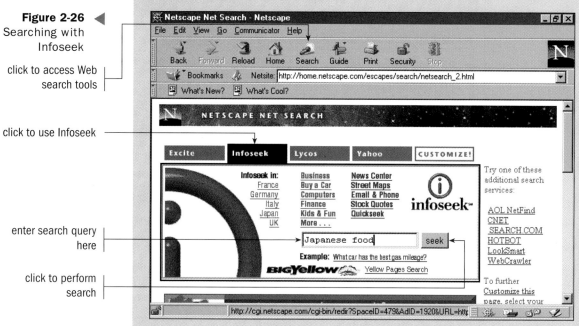

4. Click the **seek** button. Infoseek will most likely locate thousands (even hundreds of thousands) of sites, but it will display links to only the first ten.

5. Scroll through the links. Notice that Infoseek offers in addition to the Japanese food sites a list of related topics, such as Japanese restaurants and the country of Japan.

Yoko is impressed with the breadth of the Infoseek search engine. She realizes there's a lot more information here than she can ever take in, and resolves to come back later to see how other Japanese restaurants are maintaining a presence on the Web.

Now Yoko decides to use the WebCrawler search service to find additional Census information.

To use the search engine of a spider:

1. Click the **Search** button on the Navigator toolbar.

2. Click the **WebCrawler** link to connect to this popular Web search engine. See Figure 2-27.

Figure 2-27 ◀
WebCrawler
search tool

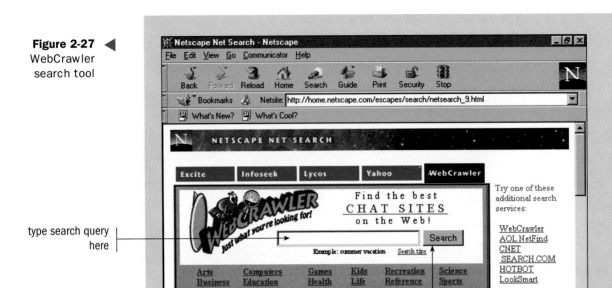

type search query here ⟶

click to perform search ⟶

3. Type **Census Bureau by county** in the Query text box, and then click the **Search** button. If a Security Information dialog box opens, warning that the information you are sending is not secure, click the **Continue** button. This simply means what you typed can be captured and read by anyone on the Internet. Notice that Navigator indicates sites that are secure sites by a solid lock icon, rather than the broken lock in the lower-left corner of your status bar.

4. Scroll through the links to see the first batch, shown in Figure 2-28. Your results will be different because the database is constantly updated.

Figure 2-28 ◀
WebCrawler
query results

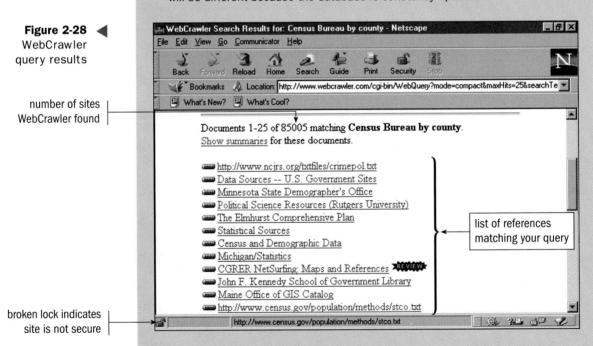

number of sites WebCrawler found ⟶

list of references matching your query ⟶

broken lock indicates site is not secure ⟶

5. Scroll through the links to see the first batch. This search resulted in 85,005 applicable pages, but only shows the first 25. To see the next 25, you scroll to the bottom and click the button that retrieves the next batch of pages.

You have now used two search services, Infoseek and WebCrawler, to locate information by performing queries. Now Yoko wants to try a different kind of search: a subject search.

Searching through a Subject Guide

Sometimes when you begin studying a topic, you don't know what keywords to use in a content search. Instead, you can search for applicable information by subject. Subject lists are organized first by general and then successively more specific subjects as you search.

Yoko knows that many new businesses fail within a short time, due in part to lack of planning and knowledge of where and how to get resources. Because her restaurant will be a small business, she thinks the government might provide funding or consulting assistance at the federal, state, or local level. She wants to know all her options but isn't sure where to begin looking. A subject search using a navigational guide is a good starting point. Yoko wants to use the Yahoo subject guide to find information on starting a small business.

To search by subject with Yahoo:

1. Click the **Search** button ⬛.

2. Click the **Yahoo** link to access an Internet subject guide. Most of these guides work similarly, so follow these steps for any of the guides. If you are using a guide other than Yahoo, the Web pages you see will differ slightly from the figures in this set of steps.

3. Scroll down, if necessary, and click a **Business** link. See Figure 2-29; the list you see might be different depending on which guide you are using.

Figure 2-29 ◀
Subject guide

main category ──→

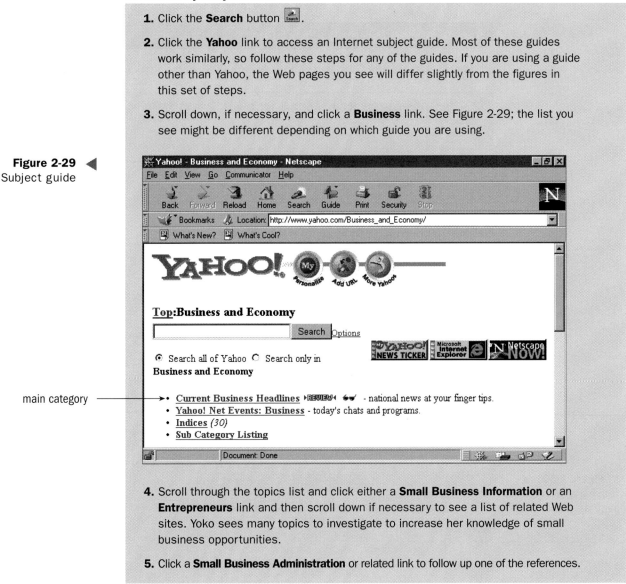

4. Scroll through the topics list and click either a **Small Business Information** or an **Entrepreneurs** link and then scroll down if necessary to see a list of related Web sites. Yoko sees many topics to investigate to increase her knowledge of small business opportunities.

5. Click a **Small Business Administration** or related link to follow up one of the references.

Yoko comments that because such a wealth of material is available about small businesses, she'll never be able to read it all before the library closes. Printing all these Web pages will require a lot of paper and time. You suggest that she save the pages she wants to look at to a disk.

Saving Text and Images to a File

Saving Web pages to a disk not only saves you paper and the time it would take to print the pages; it also reduces the amount of time you spend online. This can save you a lot of money if you pay a connection charge for using an online service provider. If the fee is charged per minute of connection time, reading Web pages online can become very costly.

You can save a Web page to disk with or without the images. When Navigator saves a file in HTML format as a text file, only the text is saved in a simple font. All the images, special fonts, links, and color are not saved. If the Web page contains a lot of graphics with important content, you will no longer be able to see or use that information. Determine if a Web page you want to save will be helpful when the graphics are not included.

Alternatively, you can save a Web page as an .html file. The saved file will look similar to the Web page, including all the special fonts and colors. However, because the file is a coded **HTML source document**, a file embedded with special characters that allow browsers to display the file, some word-processing programs will be unable to interpret the HTML codes, making the text harder to read. You can, however, open the file in Communicator or in word processors that can interpret HTML files, such as Microsoft Word.

Saving a Web Page as a Text File

Yoko wants to save the Web page about the Small Business Association that she is reading.

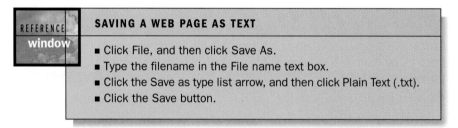

REFERENCE
window

SAVING A WEB PAGE AS TEXT

■ Click File, and then click Save As.
■ Type the filename in the File name text box.
■ Click the Save as type list arrow, and then click Plain Text (.txt).
■ Click the Save button.

To save the current Web page as a text file:

1. Insert your Student Disk (the same one you used in Tutorial 1) into drive A or the appropriate drive on your computer.

2. Click **File**, and then click **Save As** to open the Save As dialog box.

   TROUBLE? If the Save As command is dimmed, you might not have finished loading the entire Web document. Click the Reload button 🔄 on the toolbar to reload the Web page.

3. Click the **Save as type** list arrow to see the file type options.

4. Click **Plain Text (*.txt)** in the Save as type list box so the Web page is saved as readable text rather than as HTML coding.

5. Click the **File name** box, and then type **a:\business** to name the file being created. See Figure 2-30.

Figure 2-30 ◀
Saving a Web
page as a text
file

type filename here ⎯⎯⎯⎯

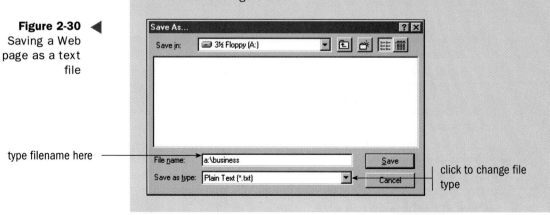

click to change file
type

6. Click the **Save** button to close the dialog box and save the file to your disk.

Before Yoko saves any more pages, she should double-check that the page saved properly.

Opening a Text File from Navigator

Because you saved the document as a text file, you could open and edit it with any word-processing program. You can also open the file from Communicator, and edit it using Netscape Composer, although for now you'll just open Yoko's file from within Navigator to verify that it saved properly.

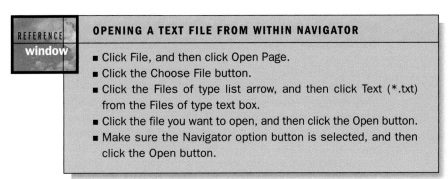

REFERENCE
window

OPENING A TEXT FILE FROM WITHIN NAVIGATOR

- Click File, and then click Open Page.
- Click the Choose File button.
- Click the Files of type list arrow, and then click Text (*.txt) from the Files of type text box.
- Click the file you want to open, and then click the Open button.
- Make sure the Navigator option button is selected, and then click the Open button.

To open a file:

1. Click **File**, and then click **Open Page**. The Open Page dialog box opens.

2. Click the **Choose File** button, click the **Files of type** list arrow, and then click **Text (*.txt)** to display the business file you just saved in the file list. Click the **business.txt** file and then click the **Open** button.

   TROUBLE? If business doesn't appear in the file list, you might be looking in the wrong drive or at the wrong file type. Make sure the Look in box lists 3½ Floppy (A:) or the appropriate drive. Make sure the Files of type text box shows Text (*.txt).

3. Make sure the **Navigator** option button is selected, and then click the **Open** button in the Open Page dialog box. Notice that you saved only the text of the Web page. See Figure 2-31.

Figure 2-31 ◀
Viewing a text
file in Navigator

images replaced by
bracketed description

content remains
though images are
not saved

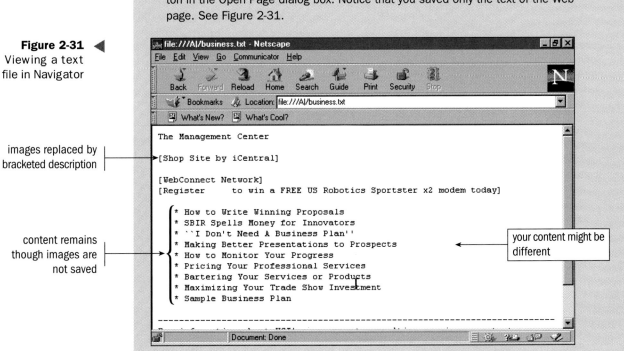

your content might be
different

> **TROUBLE?** If your text file looks exactly like your Web page, including all the special fonts, you did not save the document as a text file and you won't be able to open it in a word-processing program. Return to the Web page and save it again, this time making sure you save it as a text file.
>
> **4.** Click **Go**, and then click the lower **Research & Reference Section** to return to the library's Research & Reference Section page.

Yoko mentions that she might want to use a graphic from a Web page on her promotional material. You suggest that she save a graphic from the library's Web page so she can see how to save images.

Saving an Image from a Web Page

You can save images you see on Web pages as separate files. Image files can be saved in a variety of file formats. The two most common image file types are GIF and JPEG. As with audio files, the difference between the types of file is image quality and file size. You'll also need software that can interpret these different image file types if you want to view and use them.

You'll save an image from the library's Web page for Yoko.

SAVING AN IMAGE FROM A WEB PAGE

- Right-click the image you want to save.
- Click Save Image As on the shortcut menu.
- Type a filename in the File name text box.
- Click the Save as type list arrow, and then click GIF Files (*.gif).
- Click the Save button.

To save an image from a Web page:

1. Position your pointer over the Library East Wing image; you might need to scroll to see it.

2. Click the right mouse button to open a shortcut menu. See Figure 2-32.

Figure 2-32 ◀
Saving an
image on a
Web page

click image with right
mouse button to
open shortcut menu

click to save image
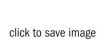

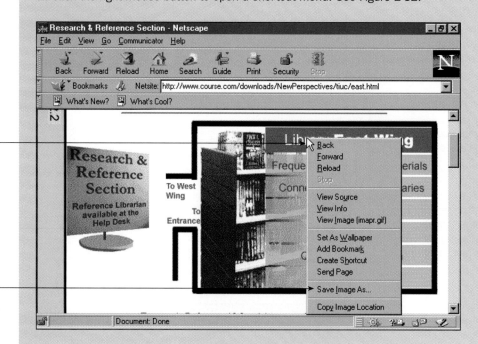

> **3.** Click **Save Image As** to open the Save As dialog box.
>
> **4.** Type **a:\image** in the File name box to name a file on your disk.
>
> **5.** Make sure that GIF File (*.gif) appears in the Save as type text box, and then click the **Save** button. The Save As dialog box closes, and the image is saved to your disk. Now you'll open the file in Navigator and view the image to verify that it saved properly.
>
> **6.** Click **File**, and then click **Open Page**. The Open Page dialog box opens.
>
> **7.** Type **a:\image.gif** in the box, make sure the **Navigator** option button is selected, and then click the **Open** button. The image appears in the Netscape window.

Yoko plans to save a number of documents and useful images that have information about starting a small business.

Downloading External Files

Yoko noticed there are many external files referenced in the Web pages she has browsed—that is, files that don't appear in the browser window but that instead can only be viewed in a separate program. She asks if there is an easy way to save those files without opening them first.

Many files on the Internet are available for transfer to your hard drive so you can use them later. For example, a financial company might place its fund prospectus on its Web site for potential investors to examine. Software developers often post trial versions of their software on the Web for potential buyers to preview.

You can transfer a file over the Internet from a Web server onto your hard drive with relative ease. File transfer over the Internet is so easy, in fact, that it has revolutionized the way people today share information.

For years, the common way to retrieve files from the Internet was with the **File Transfer Protocol** (FTP). **FTP** provides a means of logging onto, or connecting to, a computer elsewhere on the Internet, called a **remote computer**, viewing its directories, and transferring files to and from your local computer. You can quickly recognize an FTP site by its URL, which begins with "ftp://" instead of "http://." Public FTP sites are often referred to as **anonymous FTP sites** because to access the files on the site you have to log onto the remote computer, entering "anonymous" as your username and your e-mail address as the password. When you use Navigator to connect to an anonymous FTP site, the logon takes place automatically. However, in recent years, as the World Wide Web has become the primary means of accessing data from the Internet, you no longer need to store files in anonymous FTP sites to make them available to users, although it is still quite common to connect to them when you're searching for a file.

The person who owns or runs a Web server can decide whether to establish a public directory, a portion of the server that stores files that people can upload or download. **Upload** means to transfer a copy of a file from your own computer to a public directory. **Download** means to transfer a copy of a file from the public directory to your own computer.

You decide to show Yoko how to download the sound file on the library's home page. You will save it directly to your Student Disk.

To transfer a file:

> **1.** Return to the Peter H. Martin page using any of the navigation methods you learned earlier.
>
> **2.** Right-click the **audio link** 🔊.
>
> **3.** Click **Save Link As**. Click the **Save in** list arrow and click **3½ Floppy (A)**. Notice that the filename is welcome.au. Click the **Save** button. The file is saved to your Student Disk.

Now that the welcome audio file is on your Student Disk, you can run it by starting any audio utility.

You have successfully downloaded a file from the Web. Yoko asks if there is anything special she should know when downloading files from the Internet. After a moment's thought, you mention that she should check any files she downloads for viruses, she should ascertain whether or not the files are in the public domain before she does anything with them, and finally, she should learn about file compression, as she is likely to encounter compressed files if she spends much time downloading files over the Internet. You agree to go over those areas with her.

Viruses

Files stored in public directories are highly subject to viruses. You warn Yoko that she should routinely check any file that she downloads from an unknown source. A **virus** is a destructive program code embedded, or hidden, in an executable file. When you run an infected program, the virus can affect the performance of your computer, display messages or images on your screen, or even damage your data.

In order to protect your computer, you should run an anti-virus program on every file you download and every disk you get from someone else. An **anti-virus program** looks for suspicious series of commands or codes within an executable file and compares them to a list of known virus codes. If the program finds a match, it removes the virus from your disk. If you haven't opened an infected file, then it doesn't infect your computer. Anti-virus programs are frequently updated because new viruses are constantly appearing. You can download current anti-virus programs from the Internet and then run them on the files you download.

Copyrighted Material

As you've seen, saving text and images to your own disk from Internet sites around the world is easy to do, perhaps even easier than photocopying. The quality of the copied material is the same as the original; colors, shading, and graphics do not darken or distort, as they might in a photocopy. This makes it simple to copy an image or text from the Internet and reproduce it for personal, academic, or commercial use. However, similar to those for printed material, restrictions apply to the use of these files.

All printed material, such as books and magazines, and all audio material, such as music CDs or books on tape, are protected from unlimited reproduction by copyright law. A **copyright** is a federal law that allows an author (or the copyright holder) to control how his or her work is used, including how the material is reproduced, sold or distributed, adapted, and performed or displayed. Depending on how much material you want to reproduce from the Internet and your purpose in reproducing it, you might need to get permission from the Web page owner (the copyright holder) and, in some cases, pay a fee. Figure 2-33 outlines some guidelines for determining when you need to request permission before reusing material from the Internet. Remember that people, authors and artists, have made their works available over an electronic medium for increased distribution, not for increased duplication.

Figure 2-33 ◀
Copyright
notices

Copyright Notice	Academic Use	Commercial Use
Copyrighted	Can quote a certain amount without permission. Include proper citation. Request permission to reuse large amounts.	Request permission
No copyright	Assume copyrighted	Assume copyrighted
Source states "Use freely, no restrictions"	Can reuse without permission	Can reuse without permission

If Yoko found a graphic she liked on the Internet, she could use it with its citation if she were writing a research paper on starting a Japanese take-out restaurant. If she wants to use the graphic in a commercial setting for her own profit, Yoko needs to request permission from its creator to use the graphic.

Shareware

A program that you can try before buying is called **shareware**. The people who write these programs enjoy sharing their ideas and creations, hence the name shareware. The authors of shareware are not necessarily employees of software companies, but, rather, can be college students, professionals, or hobbyists, who had an idea for a program or an interest in programming. The Internet provides a convenient and inexpensive way to market a program and get feedback on its features.

The authors make their programs available for a free trial; if you decide to keep the program, you must send the author a fee, as outlined in the text file attached to the program. To help ensure that people send in the appropriate fee after a trial period, many authors usually distribute a demonstration version, which might have disabled features. When you register and purchase the program, you'll receive a full working version and information about updates, or revisions, to the program. Registering and sending payment for any shareware you plan to keep and use will encourage shareware authors to continue to write new versions or create other programs.

Compressed Files

The length of time a file takes to transfer over the Internet depends largely on the speed of the computer modem and on the size of the file. In order to conserve space on a network server and decrease the time a file takes to transfer, many files are compressed. **Compression** compacts data into a smaller size by scanning a file, eliminating duplicate words or phrases, and replacing them with reference codes, which it keeps in a small internal chart that accompanies the compressed file. For example, the word "Navigator" might be replaced by a code such as "#1" every time it appears in these tutorials, decreasing the space it takes by six characters. Apply this same coding to every repeated word in a lengthy document and its file results in a much smaller file. Often, several related files are compiled into a single compressed file. A common compression program on the Internet today creates files called **zip files**, compressed files with the file extension zip. Zip files are created with the popular PKZIP for DOS or WinZip for Windows compression programs.

Before you can use a compressed file, you must use an **uncompression program** that interprets the reference codes and restores the file to its original structure and size. Your compression program might also include an extraction feature that allows you to extract, or uncompress, one file at a time. Some compressed files are self-extracting. A **self-extracting file** is able to extract its compressed files without a separate uncompression program.

If you don't have a compression program, you can download one from a Web site that makes software utilities available. Ask your instructor or technical support person for more information. If you spend much time downloading files on the Internet you will almost certainly encounter compressed files, so learning how to handle them is time well spent.

Yoko is pleased with all the information she has gathered and what she has learned about researching on the Internet.

Quick Check

1. You submit database queries to a _____ to search the Web for keywords.

2. In a query, which kind of search—an "or" or an "and"—results in more site references? Why?

3. True or False: All sites listed in a query result are relevant to the user's needs.

4. _____ are computer software that periodically index Web page contents and URLs into topics for use in query searches.

5. When you don't know keywords to use for a search, use a _____ guide to search for general topics.

6. Web pages can be saved as _____ files, opened in a text editor, and read offline.

7. What is the difference between saving a page as plain text and saving it in HTML format?

8. What are the two most common image file types on the Web?

9. What is an external file?

10. What is the difference between uploading and downloading?

11. True or False: You can insert one GIF image, copied from the Internet, into a college term paper without requesting permission from the Web page owner.

12. True or False: Shareware is free, regardless of how long you use it.

Tutorial Assignments

Yoko Muramoto is continuing with her plans to open a take-out restaurant serving Japanese food, and she regularly checks the Web for new and useful sites that might help her. She is particularly interested in any page that deals with Michigan, small businesses, the restaurant business, or Japanese culture.

Right now Yoko wants additional information about insurance for her business. She learned from other small business owners that the Michigan Insurance Bureau provides information specially geared to small businesses. She thinks they might have a Web page. Yoko also wants to find Web pages for other businesses that deal with Japanese food. She asks you to find the Web page for the Michigan Insurance Bureau and Web pages dealing with Japanese food, recipes, or restaurants.

If necessary, launch Navigator, and then do the following:

1. Open the Web page at the URL "http://www.course.com/downloads/NewPerspectives/tiuc."

2. Click the Tutorial Assignments and Case Problems link.

3. Scroll down until you see the Tutorial 2 Tutorial Assignments.

4. Click the Search by Content link at the Peter H. Martin Library Research & Reference Section.

5. Click the WebCrawler link.

6. Enter "Michigan Insurance Bureau" in the query box and press Enter.

7. Print preview the list of sites returned by WebCrawler to make sure it's only a page or two, and then print the list.

8. Is a link to the Michigan Insurance Bureau shown? If so, click that link and then save a copy of the Michigan Insurance Bureau page to a text file. If not, connect to a link for the state or government of Michigan and look further for the Insurance site. If there is not a link to the Michigan Insurance Bureau, save the current page to a text file.

9. Use the history list on the Go menu to return to the Research & Reference Section page.

10. Link to a different spider on the Search by Content list, and type the "Michigan Insurance Bureau" query again. How do the results differ? Print this list and staple it to the first, indicating which spider you used for each query. Submit this to your instructor.

11. Return to the Research & Reference Section page using the history list, and then click the Search by Subject link.

12. Click the Yahoo link.

13. Proceed through the more detailed levels of entertainment and foods subjects to find a list of Web pages related to Japanese food by clicking appropriate links.

14. Open a Web page related to Japanese food.

15. Add this page to your computer's Bookmarks file.

16. Create a folder called Japanese Food, and move the bookmark you just created into that folder.

17. Open three additional Japanese Web pages and add a bookmark to your Japanese Food folder for each site.

18. Save an image from one of the Japanese Web pages you see. Open the image in Navigator, and then print the image.

19. Return to your favorite Japanese Web page so you can add it as a button on your Personal toolbar. Click the Bookmarks button, point to File Bookmark, and then click Personal Toolbar Folder.

20. Open the bookmarks window and delete the button you just placed on the Personal toolbar.

Case Problems

1. LaFrancois Travel Danielle LaFrancois, owner and chief agent at the LaFrancois Travel Agency, uses the Web to keep tabs on various festivals and activities taking place at tourist sites around the country. She recently learned of some inexpensive airfare to Edinburgh, the capital of Scotland. The tickets will be available at that price for only a short time so she wants to find some current information on Edinburgh and Glasgow, a nearby city, to help encourage people to purchase the tickets. She asks you to use the Web to find the following information for both cities: what activities are happening; a list of museums and galleries; and some other places of interest.

If necessary, launch Navigator, then do the following:

1. Open the Web page at the URL "http://www.course.com/downloads/NewPerspectives/tiuc" and then click the Tutorial Assignments and Case Problems link.

2. Scroll down until you see the Tutorial 2 Case Problems section.

3. Click the Travel Logs link.

4. Open the City.Net link and add a bookmark for that page to your bookmark file.

5. Navigate through the maps of Europe to locate information about Edinburgh. Save any information you find on the Edinburgh page to a text file.

6. Return to the Travel Logs in the Browsing Section page using the history list.

7. Investigate Glasgow using the Virtual Tourist II or City.Net links. *Hint:* Follow the United Kingdom links under Europe.

8. Print the Glasgow document for your instructor. Write a short note on the back stating whether you think Glasgow or Edinburgh offers the better tourist attractions at this time.

9. Locate a link to an external file, such as an audio or video clip, on one of the travel Web pages you encountered. Download the file by right-clicking the file and clicking Save Link As.

10. Once you have downloaded the file, check its file type by viewing its extension in My Computer or Windows Explorer.

11. Check which program is associated with this file type by opening up the Preferences dialog box in Navigator. Start that program if you have it, and then open the file you just downloaded. Write a short report for your instructor that identifies the file, the page from which you downloaded it, its file type, and the program associated with that file type.

12. Open the previously saved Edinburgh text file (saved in Step 5) using a word-processing program (such as WordPad or Notepad), type your name at the top, print the first page of the file, and submit it to your instructor.

2. Reading the News from Halifax Halifax, a city in Nova Scotia, Canada, northeast of Maine, is situated along the Atlantic Ocean and fishing is a major industry. In recent years, it has flourished also as a tourist town thanks to the natural beauty of the area. David Wu wants to spend his summer working at one of the fishing resorts in the area. Before he can pack his bags, he wants to learn a little more about daily living in Halifax. He asks you to use the Web to get the headlines from a Halifax newspaper, find out about the climate, and determine popular sporting events in Halifax.

If necessary, launch Navigator, then do the following:

1. Open the Web page at the URL "http://www.course.com/downloads/NewPerspectives/tiuc" and then click the Tutorial Assignments and Case Problems link.

2. Scroll down until you see the Tutorial 2 Case Problems section, then click the Newspapers and Magazines link.

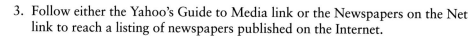

3. Follow either the Yahoo's Guide to Media link or the Newspapers on the Net link to reach a listing of newspapers published on the Internet.

4. Locate one of the Halifax newspapers using the guide's search command. (*Hint:* Search for "Halifax newspaper").

5. Connect to the newspaper and add a bookmark to your bookmark file.

6. Navigate through the pages to obtain the information about today's weather and a local sporting event that David wants.

7. When you have all the information, print the page containing the headlines of a Halifax newspaper for your instructor.

8. On the back of the page, briefly summarize the facts you gathered. Submit this page to your instructor.

9. Save one of the images on the newspaper as a gif file.

10. Open the gif file in the Navigator window and then print the gif file and submit it to your instructor.

3. Job Searching on the Web Keisha Williams, a senior at MidWest University, is actively searching for employment in marketing, her major field of study. She'd like to move to Texas. She asks you to help her use the Web to locate resources for job searches and find some tips on writing resumes. One popular site to find job listings is the CareerMosaic home page, which contains the J.O.B.S. database that you can use to search for specific jobs in different parts of the country. Unfortunately, you don't know the address of the site, so you'll have to find the Web page before you can search for job listings. The J.O.B.S. Database page contains several fields into which you can enter the information specific to the job you're seeking.

If necessary, launch Navigator, then do the following:

1. Click the Search button on the Navigation toolbar.

2. Click one search engine and type "CareerMosaic" or "Career Magazine" in the query box, and then submit the query as indicated by the search engine.

3. Scroll through the list of sites returned by the query until you see relevant page referrals.

4. Connect to the CareerMosaic or Career Magazine home page.

5. Using the search criteria given by Keisha, look for available positions. In Keisha's case, you should search for jobs related to marketing and limit the search to jobs in Texas. If you don't find any in Texas, expand your search to nearby states.

6. Connect to a link that describes a job you think is appropriate for Keisha.

7. Print the job description page for your instructor.

8. Use the history list to return to the home page of the search engine you used earlier.

9. Search for pages that contain resume writing tips.

10. Investigate the pages that seem most helpful. Select the one that looks like the best resource and save it to your disk as a text file. Then print the text file for your instructor.

4. Scavenger Hunt on the World Wide Web Now that you've had some experience using search tools on the WWW, you should be able to locate almost any type of information on the Web. Complete the following "scavenger hunt;" use any tool available at the Peter H. Martin Library. As you find an answer write it down. Submit the answers to your instructor and indicate the URL of the page you used to find the answer.

If necessary, launch Navigator, then do the following:

1. Open the Web page at the URL "http://www.course.com/downloads/NewPerspectives/tiuc" and then click the Tutorial 2 link.

2. In what Shakespearean play does a character say "There's no trust, no faith, no honesty in men; all perjured, all forsworn, all naught, all dissemblers" (specify the act and the scene)? *Hint:* Look for The Shakespeare Home Page, which contains a tool for searching the contents of all Shakespeare's plays and poems.

3. In the movie "Three Little Words," who played the part of Harry Ruby? *Hint:* Look for The Internet Movie Database page and then use a search tool to find a movie titled "Three Little Words."

4. While you are exploring movie pages, try to locate a video clip from a movie. Many movie pages include previews to upcoming movies. Save the video clip to your Student Disk, and then double-click it in My Computer to play it. What software started?

5. What is the current temperature, humidity, wind and barometric pressure at Caribou, Maine? *Hint:* Look for a page that deals with weather in the Travel Logs section of the Peter H. Martin Library home page.

6. What is the address, phone number and e-mail address of your congressional representative in the U.S. House of Representatives? *Hint:* Use the Yahoo index to search for government resources.

7. What is the current estimate of the population of the United States and of the world? *Hint:* Use the Planet Earth Home Page in the Browsing Section of the Peter H. Martin Library home page.

8. What is the ZIP code for Nome, Alaska (abbreviated AK)? *Hint:* Check the Frequently Used References at the Peter H. Martin Library.

9. What is the URL for the Smithsonian Institution's home page?

10. When you have found the answers to these questions, write them in a report and submit the report to your instructor.

Corresponding with Messenger and Collabra

Communicating Over the Internet at Carey Outerwear

In this tutorial you will:

- Configure Communicator for e-mail
- Send, receive, reply to, and forward e-mail messages
- Organize addresses in an Address Book
- Send and receive e-mail attachments
- Manage messages in mailboxes and folders
- Save messages and attachments for future reference
- Delete e-mail messages and Address Book entries
- Subscribe and unsubscribe to and from a newsgroup
- Post a message to a newsgroup
- Search a newsgroup for information

LAB E-Mail

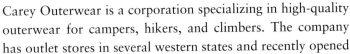

CASE

Carey Outerwear

Carey Outerwear is a corporation specializing in high-quality outerwear for campers, hikers, and climbers. The company has outlet stores in several western states and recently opened an outlet in Madison, Wisconsin and Boston, Massachusetts. The main branch in Seattle is hosting the Spring 2000 sales conference on June 12–17, 2000. Employees will spend the first part of the week in sales meetings, but for the weekend following the conference Carey Outerwear is providing its employees with a variety of opportunities to field-test Carey merchandise on organized outings throughout Washington state. You just started working as a summer intern in the Seattle sales department. Your supervisor, John Kruse, has asked you to help organize a guided climb of Mt. Rainier for the conference.

John recommends that you begin by getting in touch with Katie Herrera, one of the salespeople in the Tacoma outlet. John knows that Katie used to work as a seasonal ranger at Mt. Rainier National Park before she joined the Carey sales force, and she will be a good source of information. John gives you Katie's e-mail address and tells you that with **e-mail**, the electronic transfer of messages between hosts on the Internet, you can correspond with people around the world without having to worry about time zones, expensive long-distance charges, or answering machines.

You've also heard that newsgroups are another great Internet source of information. A **newsgroup** is a discussion group on the Internet that focuses on a single topic. There are newsgroups on just about every conceivable topic, from climbing to surfing to the Beatles to crochet. By subscribing to a newsgroup, you can see what others have to say about the topic, and can take part in the conversation. You hope that when you have some free time you can explore newsgroups and see how they work.

SESSION

3.1

In this session you will use the Messenger e-mail function to send and receive e-mail messages and attachments, organize addresses in an address book, and save attached files.

Configuring Communicator for Electronic Mail

As more people connect to the Internet and have access to e-mail programs, communicating by e-mail is becoming increasingly more common. When you need to send information to someone else, an e-mail message can save time and money because you don't need to wait for postal delivery nor do you need to make expensive long-distance phone calls. You can send e-mail to and receive e-mail from anyone in the world who has an e-mail address, regardless of the operating system and type of computer he or she is using.

You remind John that you haven't yet been assigned an e-mail account at Carey Outerwear. John replies that the company's systems administrator just finished installing Netscape Communicator on the computer you will be using, and he hands you a slip of paper with your user ID, password, and e-mail address written down. A **user ID** is the name that identifies you on the network. A **password** is a personal code that verifies you have the right to read incoming mail. An e-mail address consists of the user ID, the @ symbol, and a host name (the domain address). For example, John's e-mail address is:

jkruse@careys.com
user ID host name

Like URLs, every e-mail address is unique. Many people might use the same host, but their user IDs distinguish one e-mail address from another.

Before you can use the Communicator e-mail function, you must make sure it is **configured**, or set up, properly. Communicator needs the address of your Internet mail servers (one for outgoing mail and one for incoming mail), your name, and your e-mail address before you can use its e-mail function. Your e-mail information is included in every e-mail message you send, both as an identifier and as a return address. Your version of Communicator also might be set up to require a password before you can get your mail messages. Your technical support person might have configured these settings for you in Communicator's Preferences dialog box.

If you have any problems with your e-mail service, write down the information you find about your computer's mail settings, and ask your instructor for help.

To configure the preferences for e-mail messages:

1. If necessary, launch Communicator and make sure the toolbars are visible and the Component bar is docked.

2. Click **Edit**, and then **Preferences** to open the Preferences dialog box.

3. Click the **plus** box ☐ next to **Mail & Groups** in the Category list to view the available mail categories, and then click **Identity**. Your name and e-mail address should appear; Communicator uses this information when you send and receive e-mail. See Figure 3-1.

   TROUBLE? If the name and e-mail address boxes are blank, ask your instructor or technical support person what to enter in them.

Figure 3-1 ◀
Configuring
e-mail
preferences

plus box becomes
a minus box when
you click it

click to display
Identity settings

make sure your e-mail
address appears here

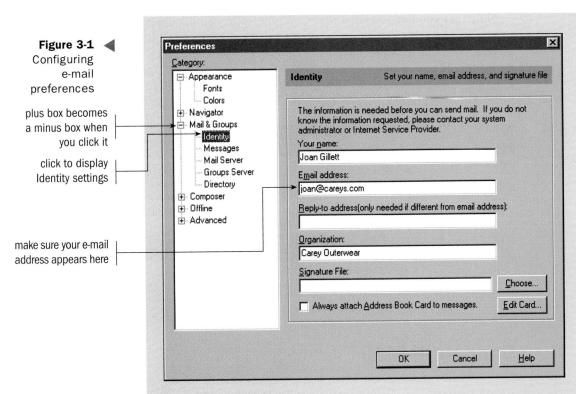

4. Click the **Mail Server** category in the Category list to check your mail server information. Your user ID should appear, along with your outgoing and incoming mail server addresses. See Figure 3-2.

   TROUBLE? If any of the three boxes are blank, ask your instructor or technical support person what to enter in them.

Figure 3-2 ◀
Checking mail
server
information

your user ID
will be different

your outgoing
mail server address
will be different

your incoming
mail server address
will be different

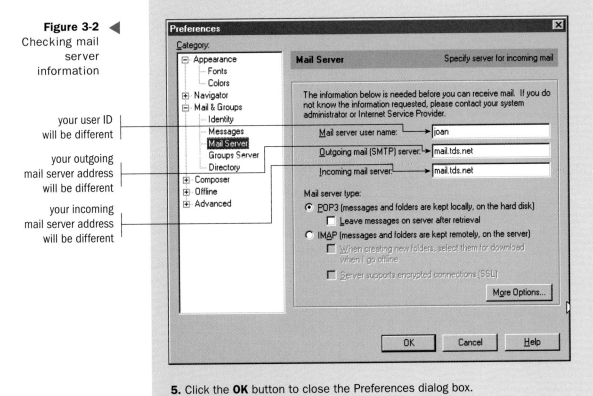

5. Click the **OK** button to close the Preferences dialog box.

Now that you have ensured that Communicator can handle your e-mail, you're ready to send e-mail messages. Communicator manages your e-mail using its Messenger component. Messenger organizes all the messages it handles, incoming and outgoing, into **mailboxes**, or compartments that allow you to sort your messages. As you'll learn later, you can also create folders within the mailboxes that allow you to file and store your messages in groups. Figure 3-3 describes the Messenger mailboxes.

Figure 3-3 ◀
Messenger
mailboxes

Mailbox	Description
Inbox	Stores all incoming messages and messages that you've read but haven't discarded or filed.
Outbox	Stores messages that you've finished composing and plan to send as soon as you connect to the Internet.
Drafts	Stores messages that you have begun but are still drafting.
Sent	Stores a copy of every message you've sent.
Trash	Stores the messages you've discarded. They remain in the Trash mailbox until you delete them, at which point they are permanently gone.

Sending E-Mail

An e-mail message uses the same format as a standard memo: Subject, Date, From, To, and the content of the message. The To line indicates who will receive the message. Messenger automatically fills in the From line with your name or e-mail address and the Date line with the date you send the message. The Subject line, although optional, tells the recipients the message's topic. Finally, the message content area contains the text of your message. You can also include additional information, such as a Cc line that indicates who will receive a copy of the message and a Followup-To line that indicates who is responsible for follow-up.

When you prepare an e-mail message, you should remember some commonsense guidelines:

- Think before you type; read before you send. Your name and your institution's name are attached to everything you send.

- Type in both uppercase and lowercase letters. Using all uppercase letters in e-mail messages is considered shouting, whereas messages in all lowercase letters are difficult to read and decipher.

- Edit your message. Keep your messages concise so the reader can understand your meaning quickly and clearly.

- Send appropriate amounts of useful information. Like junk mail, e-mail messages can pile up quickly.

- Find out if personal e-mail messages are allowed on a work account. E-mail is not free (businesses pay to subscribe to a server), nor is what you write and send from the workplace confidential.

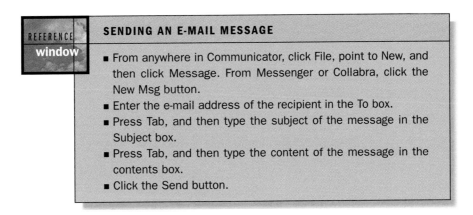

SENDING AN E-MAIL MESSAGE

- From anywhere in Communicator, click File, point to New, and then click Message. From Messenger or Collabra, click the New Msg button.
- Enter the e-mail address of the recipient in the To box.
- Press Tab, and then type the subject of the message in the Subject box.
- Press Tab, and then type the content of the message in the contents box.
- Click the Send button.

You decide to send a message to Katie in which you introduce yourself and ask for her help. Her e-mail address is kherrera@course.com. You also decide to send a copy of the message to yourself so you can make sure your mail servers are interpreting your requests correctly.

E-Mail

To send an e-mail message:

1. Click **File**, point to **New**, and then click **Message**. The Composition window opens, which allows you to compose a new message.

   TROUBLE? If you receive an error message, check your mail server settings using the procedure you learned in the previous section. Record your settings and ask your instructor or technical support person for help.

   TROUBLE? If the Password Entry dialog box opens, Messenger might be set to automatically check for incoming e-mail. Type your password in the box and then press the Enter key. If you don't know your password, ask your technical support person for help.

2. Type **kherrera@course.com** and then press **Enter**.

3. Click the **To** button that appears in the second line. Click **Cc:** in the list that opens. See Figure 3-4.

Figure 3-4 ◀
Composing a message

enter Katie's e-mail address here

click to open a menu of address options

enter message contents here

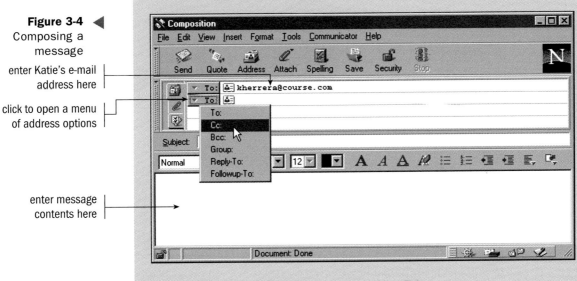

4. Type your own e-mail address and then press **Tab**.

5. Type **Spring 2000 Mt. Rainier guided climb** in the Subject box and then press **Tab**. Make sure you type this subject exactly as shown.

6. Type the following message in the content area:

I am a summer intern at Carey Outerwear in Seattle and I am helping organize the Mt. Rainier guided climb for the Spring 2000 sales conference. John Kruse suggested I contact you for information on guide services. Thanks in advance. [your name]

7. Click the **Send** button.

TROUBLE? If a message dialog box opens, indicating that Messenger was unable to connect to the server, you might need to check the configuration of your outgoing mail server. Use the procedure you learned in the previous section to do so, and ask your technical support person for help if necessary.

The time it takes to send an e-mail message depends on the size of the message, the speed of your Internet connection, and the level of Internet traffic at that time. When you send an e-mail, your local server examines the host name. Messages addressed to people at the same host site as the person sending the e-mail are processed and distributed without connecting to the Internet. Messages addressed to people at other host sites are sent out over the Internet. Because the Internet is so vast, your local mail server is not connected to every other host, so e-mail is rarely sent along a direct path to the recipient. Instead, the message is handed from one host to another until the e-mail reaches its destination. Figure 3-5 shows how the Internet routes an e-mail message from a student at the University of Alaska to a student at the University of the Virgin Islands.

Figure 3-5 ◀
Internet e-mail
routes

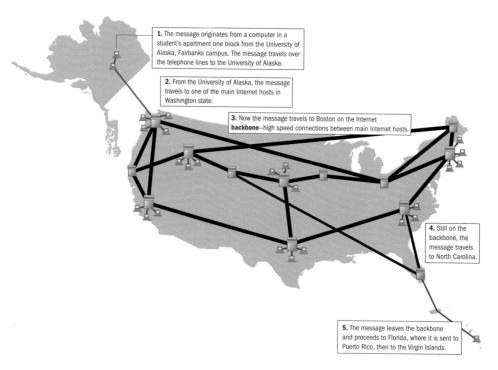

1. The message originates from a computer in a student's apartment one block from the University of Alaska, Fairbanks campus. The message travels over the telephone lines to the University of Alaska.

2. From the University of Alaska, the message travels to one of the main Internet hosts in Washington state.

3. Now the message travels to Boston on the Internet **backbone**—high speed connections between main Internet hosts.

4. Still on the backbone, the message travels to North Carolina.

5. The message leaves the backbone and proceeds to Florida, where it is sent to Puerto Rico, then to the Virgin Islands.

The message you just sent to kherrera@course.com was actually sent to a server maintained by the publisher of this book. That server is set up to send an e-mail message back to you instantly. In real life, of course, you don't usually get replies to your messages that quickly.

Receiving E-mail

Recall that e-mail messages people send you are handled by an incoming mail server. That server is similar to a post office in that it collects all mail associated with a given region (host) and holds it for pickup and delivery by a mail carrier (e-mail program). Acting as your mail carrier, Messenger contacts the incoming mail server, requests any mail addressed to your user ID, and delivers it to your computer mailbox.

Rather than being limited to a fixed delivery schedule, you can check your e-mail at any time. When you ask Messenger to check for incoming mail, the incoming mail server returns only e-mail messages that arrived since you last checked. Some people check for new e-mail messages sporadically during the day, while others check at regular intervals, such as every hour or every morning and night.

The e-mail messages can be stored on the incoming mail server or in your own computer's memory. When e-mail is left on the server, you can access it from any computer with an e-mail program, whether at school, home, or work. However, once you move the e-mail to a specific computer, you can access it only from that computer. Storing many e-mail messages on a computer can consume a lot of disk space. To conserve space, some network administrators don't allow people to store e-mail messages on the server after they have been read.

You decide to see whether or not Katie got your message and responded.

To check for incoming mail:

1. Click the **Mailbox** button ⊞ on the Component toolbar, which should be docked on the status bar. If a dialog box opens requesting your password, enter your password and then click the **OK** button.

   TROUBLE? If you don't know your password, ask your instructor or technical support person for help.

2. If the Getting New Messages dialog box opens, wait until all your messages have been received and then skip to Step 4.

3. If the Inbox window opens but there is no indication that messages have been received, click the **Get Msg** button ⊞ on the Navigation toolbar, and enter your password when requested if necessary. New messages should then be delivered. When all incoming messages are received, the status message area tells you how many messages you have received. See Figure 3-6.

Figure 3-6 ◄
Receiving
messages

new messages
are stored in the
Inbox mailbox

unread messages
appear in boldface;
you might have
additional messages

you might receive
a different number
of messages

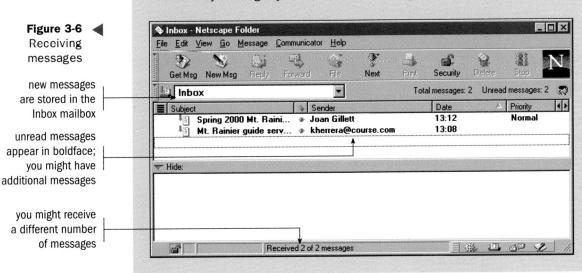

TROUBLE? If a message dialog box opens, indicating a problem with the incoming mail server, it's possible that your computer is set to remove messages from the server after they have been read. Click the OK button, then continue with the tutorial, but recognize that you might not be able to perform all the steps.

TROUBLE? If you have received no messages, it's possible that your mail server has not received or sent the messages yet. Some mail servers occasionally cause mail to be delayed. Come back later to see if your mail has arrived, or consult your technical support person.

You should have received at least two new messages since you last checked your e-mail messages, including the copy of the message you sent to Katie (Sender should be yourself) and the reply from Katie (actually sent from the publisher of this book).

Viewing a Message

Incoming messages are automatically saved to the Inbox mailbox. The mailbox windows are divided into two panes, or parts. The top pane lists the messages in that mailbox, including the subject (truncated if it's too long), an indication of whether or not you've read the message, the sender, the date, and the message's priority. You can change the width of the columns in the message list by dragging the vertical separation line between columns in the pane borders in the appropriate direction.

When you select an e-mail message in the message list, the contents of that message appear in the message contents pane below it. You can hide the lower pane if you want to view only the message list, or you can resize the two panes by dragging the pane border in the appropriate direction. For example, to enlarge the Message pane so you can see more of a message at once, drag the top border of the pane toward the top of the window until the pane is the size you want.

Messages in boldface have not yet been read.

You decide to start by reading the copy of the message you sent to Katie.

To read an e-mail message:

1. Click the message you sent yourself, which has the subject "Spring 2000 Mt. Rainier guided climb," in the message list. The contents of that message appear in the lower pane, and the message in the list is no longer in boldface. See Figure 3-7. Your Inbox folder might contain additional e-mail messages.

Figure 3-7 ◄
Viewing a
message

drag this border to the
right to enlarge
Subject column

subject is partially
hidden because
column is too narrow

list of messages

contents of
selected message

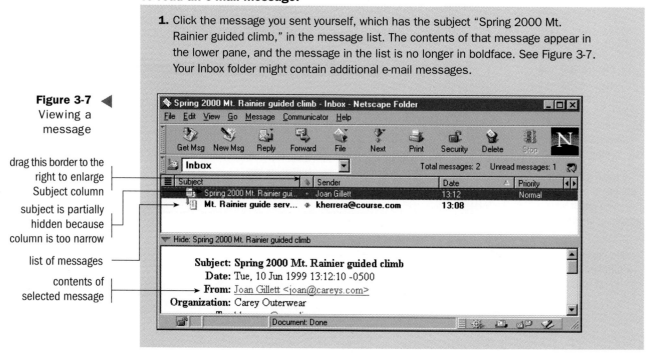

2. If the Subject column is too narrow to see the entire subject, point at the subject for a moment. A yellow box appears giving you the entire subject.

3. Now try widening the Subject column. Point at the vertical line in the pane border, shown in Figure 3-7, until your pointer turns to ◄╟►. Now drag the pointer slightly to the right to see more of the Subject column.

4. Now hide the message contents pane so you can see the entire message list. Click the ▼ arrow at the left of the border separating the two panes. The message contents pane disappears.

By successfully viewing the copy of the message you sent to yourself, you've verified that Communicator is configured properly on your computer.

Replying to a Message

Often, you'll want to respond to an e-mail message. Although you could create and send a new message, it's easier to use the Reply feature, which automatically inserts the e-mail address of the sender and the subject into the proper lines in the Composition window. The reply feature also "quotes" the sender's text to remind the sender of the message to which you are responding. When you reply to an e-mail message, you can respond to the original sender of the message, or to any other people who received the message.

You're first going to view the message Katie sent you, this time in its own window, and then you're going to reply to it. To open a message in its own window, you double-click the message in the message list. This allows you to display more of the message at once.

To open a message in its own window and then reply to it:

1. Double-click the message from Katie in the message list. The message opens in its own window. Maximize this window if necessary, and then read the message. See Figure 3-8.

Figure 3-8 ◄
Viewing a message in its own window

click to reply to Katie's address

Message window displays subject and sender information

contents of Katie's reply

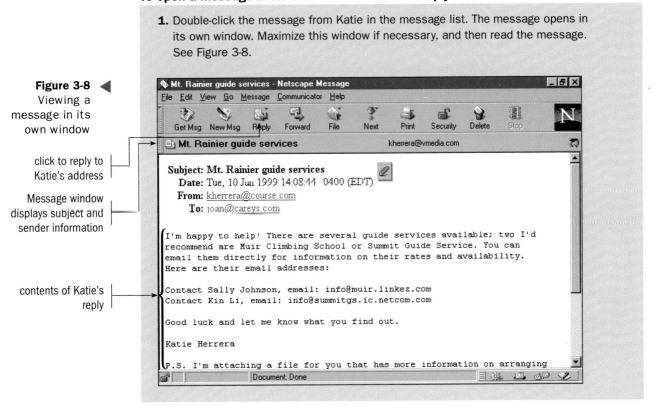

2. Click the **Reply** button and then click **Reply to Sender** in the menu that opens. The Composition window opens, this time with Katie's e-mail address and the subject already inserted, preceded with "Re:" which is short for "regarding." The message also quotes Katie's original message.

3. Press **Enter** to add a new line before the quote of Katie's message, and then press the **up arrow**. Type the following reply in the message contents area:
Thanks for your help.
[your name]

4. Scroll down to see that the original text of Katie's message is quoted after the reply you just typed.

　TROUBLE? If the original message doesn't appear, click the Quote button, and then repeat Step 4.

5. Click the **Send** button .

6. Leave Katie's message open.

Deciding whether or not to quote the sender's original message when you reply to a message depends on several factors. If the recipient might need to be reminded of the message content, it's appropriate to quote. However, long messages take longer to download, so when possible you should delete quoted material from your messages.

Printing a Message

You print an e-mail message using the File menu's Print command. You decide to print Katie's e-mail message.

To print Katie's e-mail message:

1. With Katie's message open, click **File**.

2. Click **Print**.

3. Check the print settings in the Print dialog box and then click the **OK** button. The Printing Status dialog box indicates when the print job is finished.

When you retrieve your message from the printer you might notice that some of the lines are uneven because the font your printer used caused the message word wrapping to change. If you need a high-quality printout of a message, you can save the message as a text file, open it in a word processor, and edit it there so that it looks professional.

Organizing Addresses in an Address Book

Every message sent across the Internet requires an e-mail address, but like the wrong ZIP code on a letter, any misspelled words or incorrect punctuation in an e-mail address will result in an undeliverable message. Because memorizing many e-mail addresses is a cumbersome task, prone to errors, Communicator provides the **Address Book** feature in which you can record individual e-mail addresses or groups of e-mail addresses. For each address, Communicator stores a full name, an organization, a title, an an e-mail address, a nickname, and notes on a "card," like a business card. Including a nickname can be helpful because it substitutes for the e-mail address and is much easier for you to type.

Once you have Address Book cards prepared, if you want to send an e-mail message to someone, you can just type that person's nickname or click the name from the Address Book list, and Messenger will fill in the rest of the address information. The Address Book also allows you to store other contact information, such as street addresses and telephone numbers, as well as configuration information about the individual. Only the first name and e-mail address are actually required; all other information is optional.

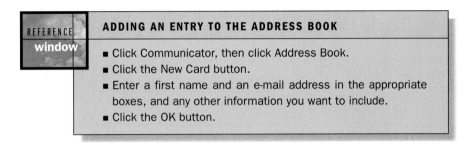

REFERENCE window	**ADDING AN ENTRY TO THE ADDRESS BOOK**
	■ Click Communicator, then click Address Book. ■ Click the New Card button. ■ Enter a first name and an e-mail address in the appropriate boxes, and any other information you want to include. ■ Click the OK button.

Katie gave you e-mail addresses for two guide services in her message. You also want to add her address to the Address Book. The Reference Window describes how to add an entry from scratch, but if the address you want to add is in a message, there is a simpler way to add it to the Address Book.

To add an address to the Address Book:

1. Right-click Katie's e-mail address, **kherrera@course.com**, in the From line of the message window and then point to **Add to Address Book**. See Figure 3-9.

Figure 3-9 ◀
Adding an
address to the
Address Book

right-click Katie's
address

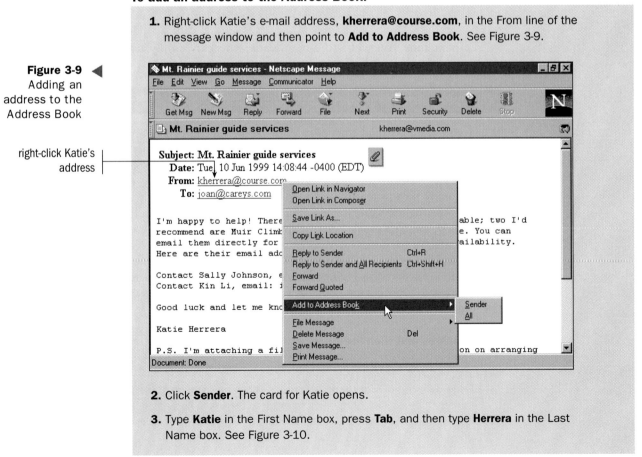

2. Click **Sender**. The card for Katie opens.

3. Type **Katie** in the First Name box, press **Tab**, and then type **Herrera** in the Last Name box. See Figure 3-10.

Figure 3-10
Katie's card

Katie's e-mail address automaticaly appears

entering a nickname makes it easier to use the address

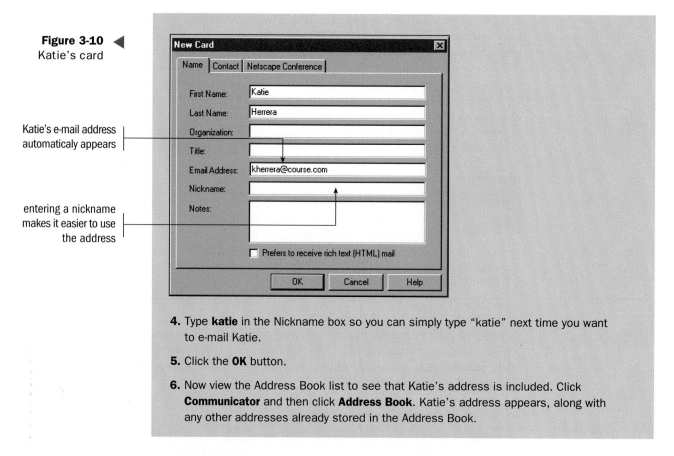

4. Type **katie** in the Nickname box so you can simply type "katie" next time you want to e-mail Katie.

5. Click the **OK** button.

6. Now view the Address Book list to see that Katie's address is included. Click **Communicator** and then click **Address Book**. Katie's address appears, along with any other addresses already stored in the Address Book.

The next time you want to e-mail Katie, you can simply use her address from the Address Book, without having to retype it.

Grouping Address Book Entries

When you want to send an e-mail message to a group of people, you could manually select each name or type multiple nicknames every time, but this can be time-consuming and it's easy to miss someone. Instead, you can create a **list**, a specified group of Address Book entries, within the main Address Book. You can copy each entry in the main Address Book into as many lists as you need. When you want to e-mail everyone on the list, you type the list name (or nickname, if you specified one) in the To box, and the message will be sent to every e-mail address on the list. When you change an individual address card, Communicator automatically updates the address in the list.

You decide to create a list called Guides that will contain the e-mail addresses of the two guide services Katie recommended. A list can be created only from addresses that already exist in the Address Book, so you'll first need to add the guide e-mail addresses to the Address Book.

To add names and then create a list:

1. Click the **New Card** button.

2. Type **Sally** in the First Name box, press **Tab**, type **Johnson** in the Last Name box, and then press **Tab** three times to move to the Email Address box.

3. Type **info@muir.linkez.com**, press **Tab**, and type **muir** in the Nickname box.

4. Click the **OK** button.

5. Click 🔲 again and enter the following information:
   First Name: **Kin**
   Last Name: **Li**
   Email Address: **info@summitgs.ic.netcom.com**
   Nickname: **summit**

6. Click the **OK** button. Now you're ready to create the list.

7. In the Address Book window, click the **New List** button 🔲. The Mailing List dialog box opens.

8. Type **guides** in the List Name box, and then click the first row of the list area. Type **muir**, and then press **Enter**. See Figure 3-11. You might only have to type the first letter or two of the word "muir," depending on what other names are in your Address Book. Messenger fills in the rest of the word for you using a technique called "pattern-matching" so you don't have to type the entire entry.

Figure 3-11 ◀
Creating a
mailing list

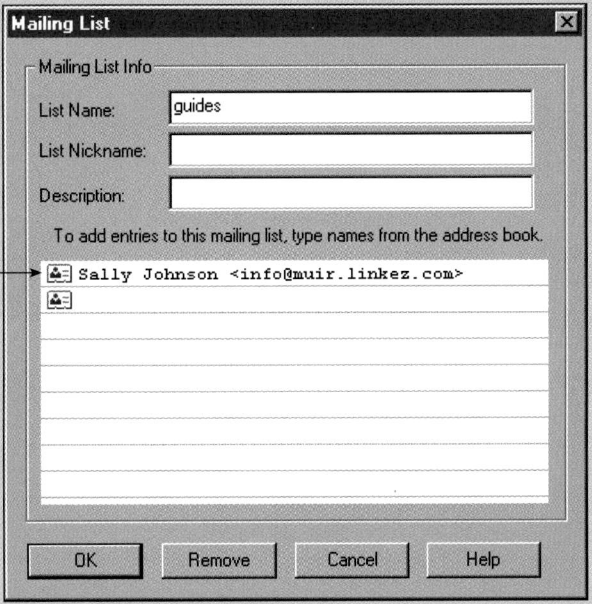

when you press Enter,
the Address Book
replaces the
nickname "muir"
with Sally's entire
e-mail address

```
Mailing List                                          [X]
┌─ Mailing List Info ──────────────────────────────────┐
│                                                        │
│  List Name:       [guides                    ]         │
│                                                        │
│  List Nickname:   [                          ]         │
│                                                        │
│  Description:     [                          ]         │
│                                                        │
│  To add entries to this mailing list, type names from the address book. │
│  ┌─────────────────────────────────────────────────┐  │
│  │ 📇 Sally Johnson <info@muir.linkez.com>          │  │
│  │ 📇                                                │  │
│  │                                                   │  │
│  │                                                   │  │
│  │                                                   │  │
│  │                                                   │  │
│  └─────────────────────────────────────────────────┘  │
│                                                        │
│  [  OK  ]   [ Remove ]   [ Cancel ]   [  Help  ]       │
└────────────────────────────────────────────────────────┘
```

9. Type **summit**, press **Enter**, and then click the **OK** button. The e-mail addresses are added to the list.

10. Click the **Close** button ☒ to close the Address Book.

   TROUBLE? If the Address Book window is not active, you might need to click it first before clicking ☒.

Now that you've finished entering names in the Address Book, you are ready to e-mail the guide services to find information about availability and rates.

Sending a Message to Multiple Recipients Using the Address Book

Using the Address Book is even easier than creating it. Whenever you want to send an e-mail message to a person or a group of people, you can select any combination or number of personal entries and list entries from the Address Book.

You want to send a message to the Guides group, and you want to copy it to Katie.

To use the Address Book to address an e-mail message:

1. Click the **New Msg** button .

2. Click the **Address** button .

3. Click **guides** in the list that appears (you might have to scroll to see it), and then click the **To:** button.

4. Click Katie's entry in the Address Book (again, you might have to scroll to see it), and then click the **Cc:** button. The names appear in the lower list of recipients. See Figure 3-12.

Figure 3-12 ◄
Selecting recipients from the Address Book

list of names in the Address Book

list of recipients of current message

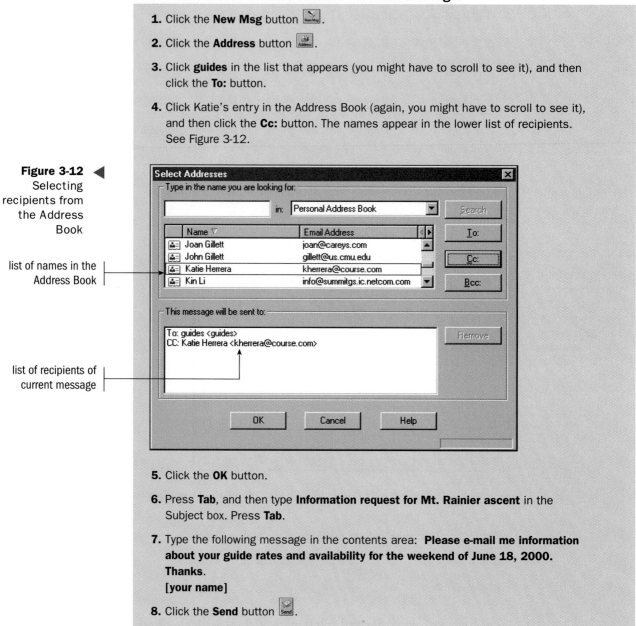

5. Click the **OK** button.

6. Press **Tab**, and then type **Information request for Mt. Rainier ascent** in the Subject box. Press **Tab**.

7. Type the following message in the contents area: **Please e-mail me information about your guide rates and availability for the weekend of June 18, 2000. Thanks.**
[your name]

8. Click the **Send** button .

You've sent your request for information, and suddenly you remember that Katie had attached a file to her e-mail message. You decide to look at the file now.

Receiving and Saving Attached Files

When you receive an e-mail message with an attached file, a paper clip icon 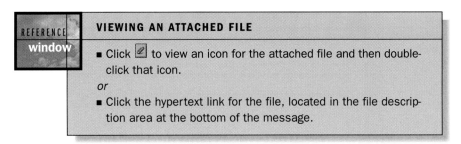 appears next to the message header and a description of the file appears below the message. With the description is a hypertext link that you can click to access the file. If Messenger recognizes the file extension of the attachment as belonging to a program on its list, it gives you the option to open the file in the appropriate program. If the file is in a format Messenger does not recognize, the Unknown File Type dialog box opens, just as it does when you click other external files, and you can choose a program to use or you can simply save the file on your disk.

REFERENCE window

VIEWING AN ATTACHED FILE

- Click ✎ to view an icon for the attached file and then double-click that icon.

or

- Click the hypertext link for the file, located in the file description area at the bottom of the message.

You decide to view Katie's attachment and then save it to your disk.

To view an attached file:

1. Click the paper clip icon ✎ in Katie's message. An icon for a Word document named ascent.doc appears at the bottom of the message window. See Figure 3-13.

   TROUBLE? If your ascent.doc icon looks different, you have a different word processor associated with doc files.

Figure 3-13 ◀
File attachment

paper clip indicates an attachment is present

icon for attached file appears when you click paper clip icon

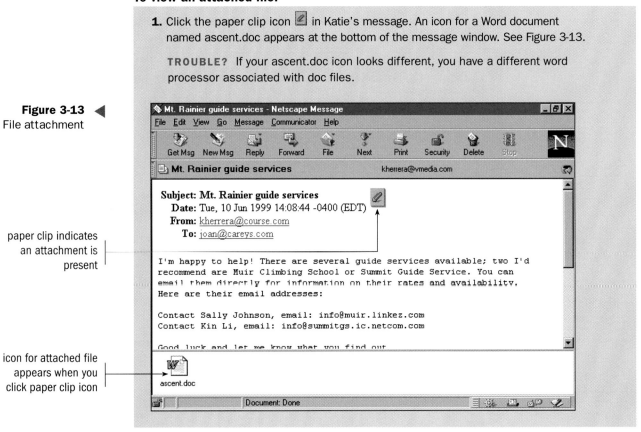

2. Double-click the **ascent.doc** icon. If your computer recognizes doc files it will start an appropriate word processing program, such as Microsoft Word, and the file will appear as shown in Figure 3-14.

   TROUBLE? If a warning dialog box opens telling you of a potential security hazard, click the Open it option button and then click the OK button.

Figure 3-14 ◄
Opening an
attached file

a different word
processor might open
on your computer

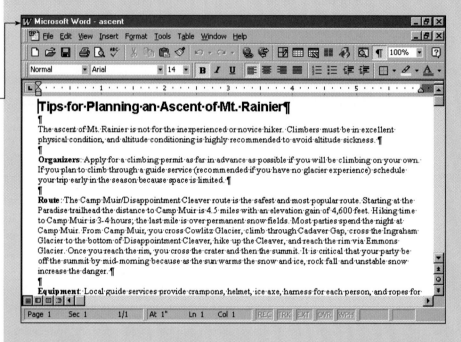

TROUBLE? If the Unknown File Type dialog box opens, click the **Cancel** button, and skip to Step 4.

3. Read the document and then click the **Close** button ⊠ to close the word processor that opened. Now save the document to your Student Disk.

4. Right-click the **ascent.doc** link in Katie's message, and then click **Save Attachment As**.

   TROUBLE? If your screen does not show Katie's message, click the Mt. Rainier button on the taskbar.

5. Type **a:\katie** in the File name box and then click the **Save** button. You can now open the file at any time from your Student Disk.

6. Click **File**, click **Exit**, and then click **Yes** to close all windows and exit Communicator.

The ability to send and receive files with e-mail messages greatly simplifies the process of sharing information over the Internet.

Quick Check

1 Identify the user ID portion and the host name portion of the following e-mail address: pcsmith@icom.net.

2 How can you check the configuration of your e-mail address and name?

3 You just e-mailed a friend with some information but you want to check what you wrote because you're having second thoughts about what you said. Where can you find a copy of the message you sent?

4 Why shouldn't you type your messages in all uppercase letters?

5 A high-speed connection between main Internet hosts is called a _____.

6 Name two advantages the Reply feature has over the New Msg feature when you are responding to an e-mail.

7 What's the quickest way to add the address of a person from whom you have received a message to your Address Book?

8 True or False: if you change someone's e-mail address in the Address Book, you must also update that address in any lists to which it belongs.

9 How do you know when you've received an e-mail message with an attached file?

SESSION

3.2

In this session you will learn how to organize your messages in folders, to attach a file to a message, to save a message to a file, to forward a message, and to delete unwanted e-mail and Address Book entries.

Managing Messages

You've already seen that Messenger uses mailboxes to organize messages passing through your computer. You can further organize your mail by creating folders. For example, a student might use a folder to file all correspondence with her Latin professor, or an architect might create one folder for each project.

Creating a Folder

Messenger includes a window called the **Netscape Message Center** that allows you to view your mailboxes and folders (and, as you'll see later, your discussion groups) in a hierarchy. When you create a new folder, you need to decide where it will be located in this hierarchy. The top level of the e-mail hierarchy is Local Mail, and the five Messenger mailboxes are on the next level of the hierarchy. Also on this level is a folder called Samples that contains sample e-mail.

You can create folders within Local Mail or within any of the mailboxes. You can also create folders within folders; these are called **subfolders**. Figure 3-15 shows the folders a student named Jo Stofflet has created within the Inbox mailbox: Homework and Student

Government. Within the Homework folder are three subfolders: History, Calculus, and Physics. Within the Student Government folder are two subfolders: Homecoming and Budget.

Figure 3-15
Message folder
structure

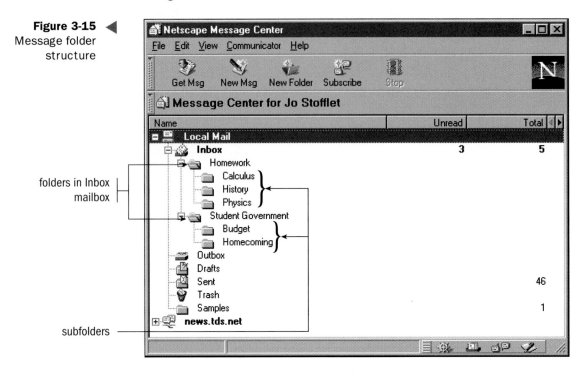

folders in Inbox
mailbox

subfolders

You can show all the folders in the hierarchy or only those at the levels you choose. The plus ⊞ and minus ⊟ boxes indicate whether the folders in that level are visible ⊟ or hidden ⊞.

REFERENCE window

CREATING A MESSAGE FOLDER

- Click Communicator and then click Message Center.
- Click the New Folder button.
- Type a folder name.
- Click the Create as subfolder of list arrow and then click the mailbox or folder in which you want to place the new folder.
- Click the OK button.

You are going to create a folder called Rainier in which you will file the correspondence you have regarding the Spring 2000 ascent of Mt. Rainier. You'll create that folder within the Inbox mailbox.

To create a folder within the Inbox mailbox:

1. Launch Communicator and make sure the three toolbars are visible and the Component bar is docked.

2. Click **Communicator** and then click **Message Center**.

3. Click the **New Folder** button [icon].

4. Type **Rainier** in the Name box.

5. Click the **Create as sub-folder of** list arrow and then click **Inbox**. See Figure 3-16.

Figure 3-16 ◀
Creating a
new folder

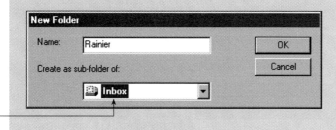

new folder will
be created in
displayed mailbox or
folder

6. Click the **OK** button.

7. Click the **Close** button [X] to close the Message Center.

Now that you have created the folder, you are ready to save messages in it.

Filing Messages

When a message comes into the Inbox, you can file it immediately or file it later.

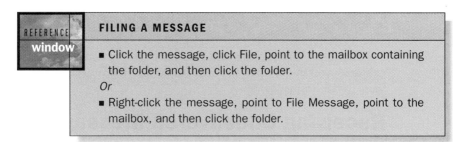

FILING A MESSAGE

- Click the message, click File, point to the mailbox containing the folder, and then click the folder.

Or

- Right-click the message, point to File Message, point to the mailbox, and then click the folder.

Once you have created a system of folders, you can view the messages in a particular folder or in one of your mailboxes by using the Location list arrow on the Location toolbar. The Location list shows all the mailboxes and folders in the Message Center. You decide to file the message Katie sent you into the Rainier folder. Then you'll use the Location list arrow to examine the contents of the Rainier folder.

To file a message:

1. Click the **Mailbox** button 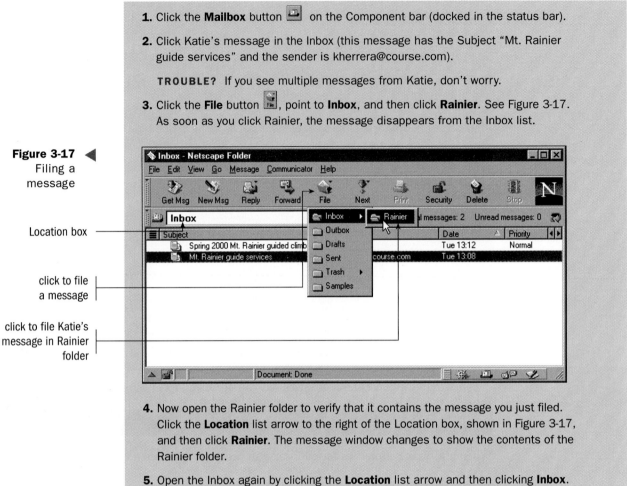 on the Component bar (docked in the status bar).

2. Click Katie's message in the Inbox (this message has the Subject "Mt. Rainier guide services" and the sender is kherrera@course.com).

   TROUBLE? If you see multiple messages from Katie, don't worry.

3. Click the **File** button, point to **Inbox**, and then click **Rainier**. See Figure 3-17. As soon as you click Rainier, the message disappears from the Inbox list.

Figure 3-17 ◄
Filing a
message

Location box ——

click to file
a message ——

click to file Katie's
message in Rainier
folder ——

4. Now open the Rainier folder to verify that it contains the message you just filed. Click the **Location** list arrow to the right of the Location box, shown in Figure 3-17, and then click **Rainier**. The message window changes to show the contents of the Rainier folder.

5. Open the Inbox again by clicking the **Location** list arrow and then clicking **Inbox**.

Some users also file relevant messages they've sent in the folders they've created. For example, you might open the Sent folder and file the message you wrote to the guide services in the Rainier folder.

Receiving Undelivered Messages

Sometimes you send an e-mail message to an Internet address that is no longer active, such as when a person changes his or her e-mail service to another server or switches to a different online service provider. When your outgoing mail server cannot locate an e-mail address that matches the recipient's address, you will receive an undeliverable mail message. This is similar to the postal service returning a letter because the street address is incorrect.

Because the guide service messages in this tutorial are actually fictional, you should have received a returned mail e-mail from the mail delivery subsystem of your outgoing mail server, telling you that the host was not found. Examine this message now.

Netscape Communicator

To read a returned mail notification:

1. Double-click the returned mail in the Inbox labeled in the Subject line as "Returned mail" or "Undeliverable message".

2. Read the message. It should inform you that the e-mail addresses of the two guide services had unknown hosts.

3. Close the returned mail message to return to the Inbox.

If e-mail messages you send are returned undelivered, you should verify the e-mail addresses that you used. Make sure that everything is typed correctly and the person is still using that e-mail address.

Attaching a File to a Message

When two people work in the same office or use the same local area network (LAN), it is relatively easy to share files because they share a common server and can open each other's files. When people not sharing the same network work in different states or even different countries, however, they need to mail disks to each other, which can be expensive and take a day or longer to receive. Attaching a file to an e-mail message is an easy and effective way to send files, as long as both people use the same or compatible e-mail programs. The recipient receives the attached file just as quickly as any other electronic message.

A file can be attached to e-mail in its original format or as a plain text file with no formatting. If the recipient will open the file with the same program you used to create it, then you should send the file in its original format. This ensures that the document retains its formatting as well as its text. For example, if you create an Excel spreadsheet and send the resulting xls file in its original format, the recipient will receive an xls file that retains the formatting and calculation codes and can open the file in Excel. If you know that the person you want to send the file to doesn't have Excel (or the program you used to create the file), you can send it as plain text, which strips a file of all its formatting and other coding, leaving only the text content.

REFERENCE window

ATTACHING A FILE TO AN E-MAIL MESSAGE

- Click the New Msg button and fill out the Composition window with the recipient and subject information and any message you want to include.
- Click the Attach button and click File.
- In the Enter file to attach window, locate and select the file, and then click the Open button.
- Click the Send button.

When you attach a file in the Composition window, you will notice that the message address area you are used to seeing has disappeared. The Composition window contains three tabs that control what information you see in that area. Figure 3-18 describes the tabs. You can view the name of each tab by resting your mouse pointer on the tab icon for a moment.

Figure 3-18 ◀
Composition
window tabs

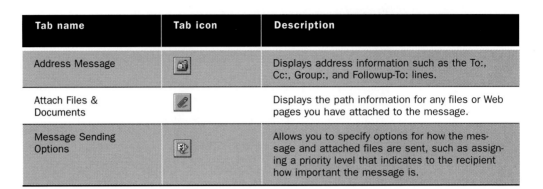

Tab name	Tab icon	Description
Address Message		Displays address information such as the To:, Cc:, Group:, and Followup-To: lines.
Attach Files & Documents		Displays the path information for any files or Web pages you have attached to the message.
Message Sending Options		Allows you to specify options for how the message and attached files are sent, such as assigning a priority level that indicates to the recipient how important the message is.

The Attach Files & Documents tab appears automatically when you attach a document. You can view the message address information again by clicking the Address Message tab.

As you worked on the Mt. Rainier ascent, you managed to locate a graphic image file of climbing Mt. Rainier that could be used as an image in the Spring 2000 packet. John Kruse asks you to e-mail it to Connie Samini, the contact person for the promotional materials. Connie's e-mail address is samini@joncag.iip.com. The file, Rainier.bmp, is located on your Student Disk. You decide to mail it to yourself too so you can test how to retrieve it.

To attach a file to an e-mail message:

1. Click the **New Msg** button .

2. Type **samini@joncag.iip.com** in the To line and press **Enter**.

3. Click the **To:** button that appears, click **Cc:**, enter your own e-mail address, and press **Tab**.

4. Type **Spring 2000 graphic file** in the Subject line and press **Tab**.

5. Type **Here's a graphic file for the Spring 2000 promotion** in the message content area.

6. Click the **Attach** button and then click **File**.

7. Type **a:\Tutorial.03\Rainier.bmp** in the File name box and then click the **Open** button. The path to that file appears on the **Attach Files & Documents** pane. See Figure 3-19.

Netscape Communicator

Figure 3-19 ◀
Attaching a file
to a message

Address Message tab

Attach Files &
Documents tab

Message Sending
Options tab

path to attached file

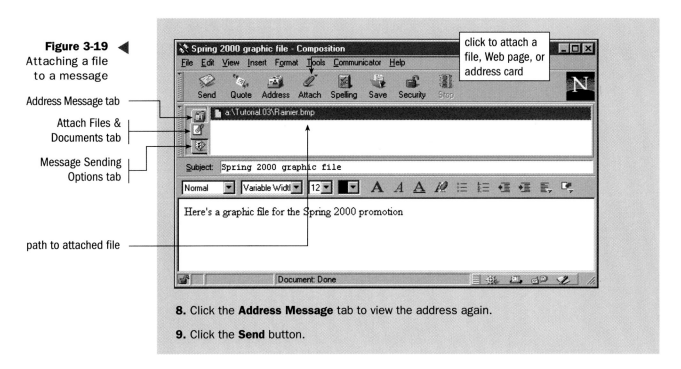

8. Click the **Address Message** tab to view the address again.

9. Click the **Send** button.

Because there is an attached file, the message is bigger than usual and takes a little longer to send. The message will arrive in Connie's incoming mail, as well as in yours. You decide to check your messages and see how the file arrived.

To receive the graphics file you just sent:

1. Click the **Get Msg** button. Because the message you sent to yourself has an attached file, it will take a little longer than usual to get messages.

   TROUBLE? If there are no messages for you, wait a few minutes and then try again.

2. If necessary, click the **Location** list arrow and then click **Inbox**.

3. Double-click the **Spring 2000 graphic file** message you just sent to yourself (your name should appear in the From column).

4. Click the attachment icon and then double-click **Rainier.bmp**. If bmp files are associated with Paint, Paint opens to display the Rainier image.

5. If asked what you want to do with the file, click the **Open it** option button and then click the **OK** button. The graphic opens in Paint. See Figure 3-20.

   TROUBLE? If the graphic doesn't open in Paint or you receive a warning that the file type is unknown, your computer might not associate bmp files with a program. Click the Cancel button and skip Step 5. If a different program starts, continue with Step 5.

Figure 3-20 ◄
Opening an
attached file
in Paint

6. Click the Paint **Close** button ☒.

Whether or not Connie can open the attached file will depend on the mail software and graphic software she has on her computer. E-mailing files only works when the mail software is compatible. You might want to check with the recipient before mailing a file to make sure the mail software can handle the message. You can also click the Message Sending Options tab to encode the message in a different format, such as Uuencode. **Encoding** saves the file attachment using coded characters that make it possible for the recipient's mail software to accept the message. The recipient can then use decoding software to interpret the message and restore the file to its original state. Ask your instructor for more information.

Saving a Message to a File

Messages exist in the Messenger mailboxes in a format that makes them inaccessible to word processing and other software. You can, however, save a message as a file so that you can store it on a disk or open it in a different program. You can also use the Copy command to copy selected parts of the message, and you can then paste the message text into a different program.

You decide to save the message Katie sent you as a text file. Because that message contains an attached file, Messenger codes the file and saves it as part of the text message. As you'll see when you open the text file in a text editor, the attached file looks like "gibberish"—a collection of stray characters. However, if you decode the text file, the attached file will be recovered. You won't do that now, but you should be aware that coding and decoding is a common solution to the problems people have sending files across the Internet.

To save e-mail messages to a disk:

1. Open the Rainier folder and then right-click Katie's message. See Figure 3-21.

   TROUBLE? After closing Paint you might no longer see your list of messages. Use the Communicator buttons on the taskbar to return to the list of messages, and then use the Location list arrow to open the Rainier folder.

Figure 3-21
Saving a
message

Rainier folder is open

Katie's message

menu of actions you
can take on Katie's
message

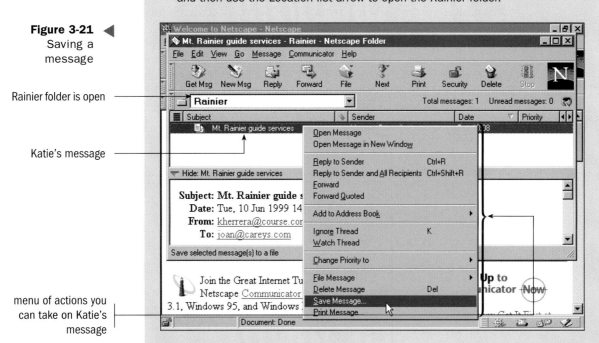

2. Click **Save Message**.

3. Type **a:\katie's message** in the File name box and then click the **Save** button.

4. Now start a text editor to open the file and view it. Click the **Start** button on the Windows taskbar, point to **Programs**, point to **Accessories**, and then click **WordPad**.

5. Click the **Open** button, type **a:\katie's message.txt**, and then click the **Open** button. Scroll down to see the message and the coded attached file. See Figure 3-22.

Figure 3-22
Viewing a
saved message
in WordPad

Katie's message

information on
coding

attached file appears
in coded characters

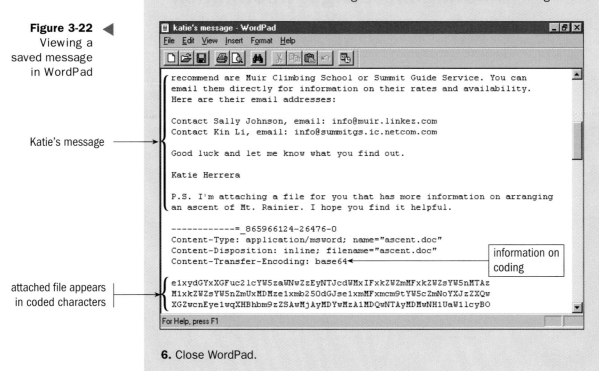

6. Close WordPad.

Katie's message is now stored as a text file on your Student Disk.

Forwarding a Message

John Kruse has decided to transfer you to a different department. Another intern, Chris Lopez, will take over the Rainier project. You realize that Chris could profit from the information you've gathered from Katie, so you decide to forward Katie's message to Chris.

Forwarding is similar to replying to an e-mail message, except that when you forward an e-mail message, you send a copy of the entire message to another person. When you click the Forward button on the Location toolbar, Messenger fills in the Subject box with Fwd: [subject] and, if applicable, includes any attached files. When forwarding a message, you can add new comments to the original text of the message in the outgoing message area.

John tells you that Chris' e-mail address is clopez@careys.com.

To forward mail:

1. If necessary, open the Rainier folder.

2. Click the message from Katie.

3. Click the **Forward** button 📷 .

4. Type **clopez@careys.com** in the To box.

5. Leave the subject as it appears (Fwd: means the message is a forwarded message).

6. Click the message contents area and then type **Here's the information you need for the Rainier project. Good luck.**

7. Click the **Send** button 📷 .

Chris now has the necessary information to handle the Rainier project, and you are almost ready to move to the new department.

Deleting Messenger Information

It's easy for your mailboxes, folders, and Address Book to get cluttered with information you no longer need. You should periodically clear out unwanted messages and remove obsolete entries from your address book. Since you're moving to a new department, you no longer need any of the Rainier messages or address information.

Deleting a Message

After you have read a message and replied to or forwarded it as necessary, you can delete it. Any message you delete from the Inbox is transferred automatically to the Trash mailbox. You can recover it from there if you need to, but once you delete the messages in the Trash folder you cannot recover them.

To delete unwanted e-mail:

1. Click the **Location** list arrow and then click **Inbox** to open the Inbox.

2. Right-click the returned mail message and then click **Delete Message**. Repeat this step for any other e-mail in the Inbox that was generated during this tutorial. If you want to delete several messages, press and hold down the Ctrl key while you click multiple messages. Then right-click the selection and click **Delete Message**.

3. Click the **Location** list arrow and then click **Sent** to open the Sent mailbox.

4. Delete any messages in the Sent mailbox that you generated during this tutorial.

You also want to delete the entire Rainier folder and all its contents. You can delete folders from the Message Center.

To delete a folder and its contents:

1. Click the **Message Center** button [icon] on the right side of the Location toolbar.

2. Right-click the **Rainier** folder.

3. Click **Delete Folder**.

4. Click the **OK** button if you are asked to confirm that you want to delete all the messages in the folder.

Deleted messages remain in the Trash folder, providing an opportunity to retrieve them, until you empty the Trash folder. To completely remove e-mail messages and free up storage space available in your computer's memory, you must empty the Trash folder.

To empty the Trash folder:

1. In the Netscape Message Center window, click **File**.

2. Click **Empty Trash Folder**. The status message area shows the process of deleting the contents of the Trash folder. Notice that the number in the Trash Total column is now zero. If asked whether you want to delete the Rainier folder and its contents, click the **OK** button.

By deleting unwanted messages regularly you save space on your hard drive.

Deleting Address Book Entries

Just as you want to keep your mailboxes and folders clean and up-to-date, you'll want to make sure that the Address Book contains only relevant entries. Periodically, you should remove outdated or no-longer-needed entries from your Address Book. You no longer need addresses you entered, so you'll delete them all from the Address Book.

To delete entries from the Address Book:

1. Click **Communicator**, and then click **Address Book** to open the Address Book window.

2. Click **Guides** to highlight it.

3. Press and hold down the **Ctrl** key and then click **Katie Herrera**, **Sally Johnson**, and **Kin Li**.

4. Click the **Delete** button .

5. Click the **Close** button ⊠ to close the Address Book window, and then exit Communicator.

You've cleaned out all unwanted information from Messenger and you're ready to move to the new department.

Quick Check

1. How can you view the subfolders of a folder in the Message Center?

2. What happens to e-mail messages that have incorrect or obsolete e-mail addresses?

3. If you attach an Excel file to an e-mail message, can you be sure the recipient will be able to open it? Explain your answer.

4. What is plain text?

5. If you receive an e-mail message containing a series of characters that looks like "gibberish" should you assume the message is ruined? What might cause it to look this way?

6. True or False: Clicking the Delete button when an Inbox message is highlighted will permanently remove the e-mail message from disk storage.

7. What window should you open to delete a folder from your mailbox?

8. What key should you press to select more than one message?

SESSION

3.3

In this session you will subscribe to a newsgroup, follow the threads in a newsgroup, sort and search newsgroup posts, and unsubscribe from a newsgroup.

Newsgroups

So far in this tutorial you've seen how you can use e-mail to communicate with others and gather information on a topic. Now you'll look at a means of bringing people with common interests together—discussion groups, most commonly called newsgroups. There are thousands of newsgroups on the Internet. Interested users subscribe to a newsgroup and then exchange messages with other subscribers on that topic using regular e-mail. The act of sending an e-mail message to a newsgroup is called **posting**; a message sent to a newsgroup is often called a **post**. Newsgroups can be open to everyone or to a private group. A private newsgroup might be created, for example, for scholars who want to limit membership to their peers.

When a newsgroup member posts a message to a newsgroup, the message is sent to a special server called a **news server**, which stores and manages the messages that are posted to various newsgroups. In order to retrieve messages posted to a newsgroup, you need special software called a **newsreader**. The newsreader that comes with Communicator is called Collabra. When you subscribe to and then open a newsgroup, Collabra retrieves the most recent message headers (the text in the Subject line) from the news server. When you see a message you want to read, Collabra can download it for you. Figure 3-23 illustrates how messages posted to a newsgroup are disseminated.

Figure 3-23 ◀
Posting to a
newsgroup

subscriber posts
a message to
newsgroup

news server
stores posts

subscribers retrieve and read
posts via newsreader software

Newsgroup Names

Newsgroup names are defined based on a hierarchy of categories. Figure 3-24 shows a small part of this hierarchy.

Figure 3-24 ◀
Examples of
newsgroup
categories in
the newsgroup
hierarchy

highest level in
newsgroup hierarchy

subcategories of
rec newsgroup

subcategories of
rec.sport.newsgroup

subcategories of
rec.sport.football
newsgroup

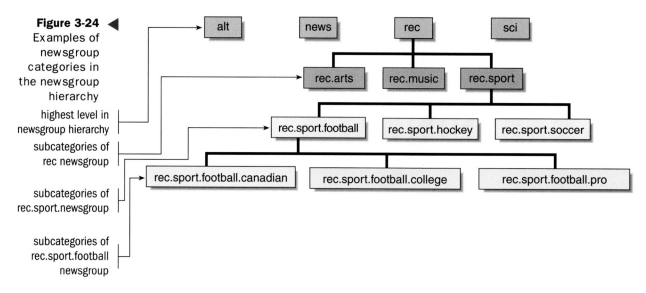

The highest level is the general category to which a topic belongs. Each category has a name (usually an abbreviation). For example, all recreational activities begin with the name "rec." Within the recreational topic category are newsgroups that deal with arts, music, sports, and so on. With the sport category you might find categories such as football, hockey, soccer, and so on. Within the football category you might find categories such as Canadian football, college football, and professional football. The newsgroup for college football has a name consisting of all the codes of the hierarchy, separated by dots: "rec.sport.football.college."

Collabra identifies newsgroups by these somewhat cryptic names. Study Figure 3-25 to become familiar with newsgroup names.

Figure 3-25 ◀
Examples of
newsgroup
names

Category	Description	Example
alt	Alternative newsgroups of many different types	**alt.guitar.bass** for discussions about bass guitars
harvard	Newsgroups about Harvard University	**harvard.course.math121** for discussions about the Math 121 course at Harvard
humanities	Newsgroups about topics in the humanities department, such as art and literature	**humanities.lit.authors.shakespeare** for discussions about the works of William Shakespeare
k12	Newsgroups about education K–12	**k12.lang.japanese** for discussions about Japanese language programs in K–12 schools
rec	Newsgroups about recreational activities	**rec.autos.sport.indy** for discussions about car racing at the Indy 500
uk	Newsgroups about the United Kingdom	**uk.politics.electoral** for discussions about electoral politics in the United Kingdom

Threads

When you subscribe to a newsgroup, you have access to all the messages posted by all the subscribers within a time frame established by the news server. Keeping your e-mail organized might seem an easy task when compared to organizing newsgroup messages, given that there can be thousands of people posting on thousands of conversations in a given newsgroup. Newsreader software such as Collabra allows you to organize the list of message headers so that subscribers can follow the many conversations without losing the flow.

Collabra by default sorts message headers into threads. A **thread** is a batch of messages that follow a single "line of conversation." One person posts a message, several people reply to it, more reply to the replies, and so on until the topic is dropped. Multiple threads can develop simultaneously, just as in a busy room there can be many conversations. Figure 3-26 illustrates how threads are developed in a newsgroup.

Figure 3-26 ◄
Threads you
mightfind in
rec.arts.
calligraphy

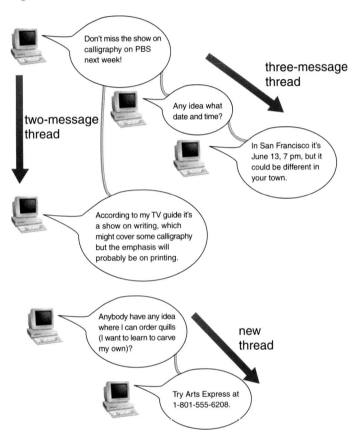

Most threads generate just a few posts, but some (especially controversial topics) can go on for days.

Starting Collabra

The first time you start Collabra, the newsreader must download a copy of the list of all newsgroups supported by your news server to your computer, which could be time-consuming. Once the initial list is downloaded, however, starting Collabra will be almost instantaneous, because Collabra will simply load the list stored on your computer. If any new newsgroups are created after the initial download, you can view them with the New Groups feature. You can also retrieve an updated version of the entire list using the Get Groups feature. You won't do either of those things in this tutorial, though, because the list of newsgroups on your news server is unlikely to change over the course of this tutorial.

A few days have passed since you joined the new department at Carey Outerwear, and you decide to spend your lunch hour exploring newsgroups. You don't have any particular goal in mind; you just want to get a feel for what's out there.

To start Collabra:

1. Launch Communicator and make sure the three toolbars are visible and the Component bar is docked.

2. Click the **Discussion Groups** button ⬚ on the Component bar. The Message Center opens, with the news service highlighted. See Figure 3-27. The domain name of your news server should appear; it will probably be different than the one shown here. If you have already subscribed to one or more newsgroups, they might appear below the news service line.

Figure 3-27 ◀
Message
Center with
news service

click to subscribe
to a newsgroup

your news service
might be different

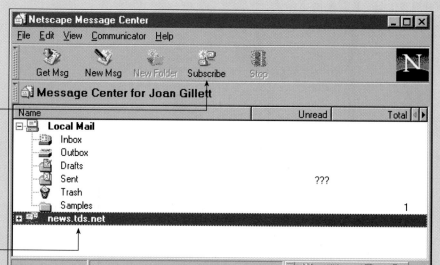

3. Click the **Subscribe** button ⬚. The Subscribe to Discussion Groups dialog box opens. See Figure 3-28. If this is the first time you have clicked this button in Communicator, the Discussion group name area will be blank. You must wait for the newsreader to download the names of all existing newsgroups on your news server. This could take a considerable amount of time, depending on the speed of your Internet connection and the number of newsgroups your news server supports. Be prepared to wait 10 minutes or more.

TROUBLE? If 15 minutes have elapsed and the Discussion group name area is still blank, your Internet connection might be slow. Ask your technical support person whether you should continue to wait or whether there might be a problem with the connection. You can check discussion group settings by clicking Edit, clicking Preferences, clicking the Mail & Groups plus box, and then clicking Groups Server. If you can determine that you are still receiving data (perhaps your computer indicates data transfer with a blinking icon in the Windows taskbar), continue to wait.

Figure 3-28 ◀
List of
discussion
groups

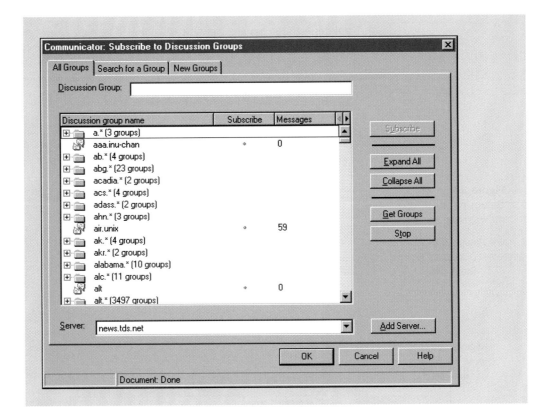

The list of newsgroups appears in alphabetical order.

Subscribing to a Newsgroup

To subscribe to a newsgroup you can either search for a particular one, as you'll see later, or you can navigate the hierarchy of newsgroups until you find the one you want. Like other lists you've seen, the newsgroup list uses plus ⊞ and minus ⊟ boxes to show and hide levels in the newsgroup hierarchy. To view the newsgroups in a given category, you click ⊞ next to the category.

You decide to look at the newsgroups contained in the alt category, and when you find one that's interesting, you'll subscribe to it.

To explore the list of newsgroups in the alt category:

1. Scroll down to the **alt** category 🗀.

2. Click the **plus** box ⊞ next to alt.

3. Scroll down the list of newsgroups in the alt category. The alt category contains many subcategories, indicated with the 🗀 icon: alt.animals, alt.autos, and alt.books are just a few examples. Click ⊞ next to one of those subcategories if you want to view additional categories or newsgroups. Categories are indicated by 🗀 and newsgroups by 📰.

4. Scroll through the hierarchy of alt categories and locate a newsgroup that interests you. Click next to that newsgroup. See Figure 3-29. Make sure the newsgroup you select has more than 100 messages, indicated in the Messages column, so that you'll be able to experience the full flavor of newsgroups.

TROUBLE? If you can't find a newsgroup that interests you, click any newsgroup with more than 100 messages.

TROUBLE? If your Discussion group name list shows different newsgroups, don't worry. Not all news servers service the same newsgroups.

Figure 3-29 ◀
Selecting a
newsgroup

newsgroup name
appears in Discussion
Group box

newsgroup you
choose will be
different

number of messages

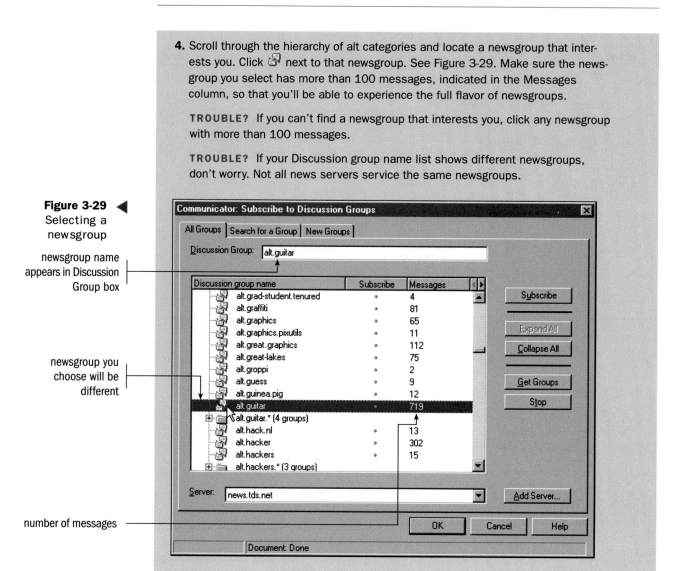

Now that you've found a newsgroup, you're ready to subscribe to it.

To subscribe to a newsgroup:

1. Make sure the newsgroup you want to subscribe to is highlighted.

2. Click the **Subscribe** button. A check mark appears in the Subscribe column. You can subscribe to another newsgroup by clicking the newsgroup and again clicking the Subscribe button, but you won't do that now.

3. Click the **OK** button. You return to the Message Center.

4. If necessary, click the **plus** box next to the news service line in the Message Center. (Remember this is the line of your news server's domain name.) A list of newsgroups to which you have subscribed appears. See Figure 3-30.

Figure 3-30
List of
subscribed
newsgroups

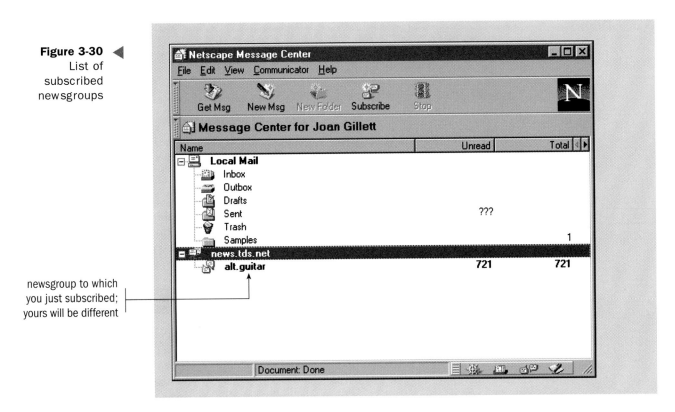

newsgroup to which
you just subscribed;
yours will be different

Now you are ready to open the newsgroup to which you just subscribed. When you open a newsgroup for the first time, Collabra gives you the opportunity to specify how many message headers you want to download: all, or just the first 100. Some news servers store thousands of messages, though most only store the most recent. To save time, you should download 100 message headers at a time until you've had more experience with newsgroups.

To download the first 100 message headers:

1. Double-click the newsgroup to which you just subscribed.

2. Click the **Download _____ Headers** option button. Make sure 100 headers are specified. If not, type **100** in the box. See Figure 3-31.

   TROUBLE? If the Download Headers dialog box doesn't appear, skip to Step 4. Your groups settings might specify that this dialog box needn't appear.

Figure 3-31
Selecting
number of
headers to
download

number of new
message headers

make sure you
download 100
message headers

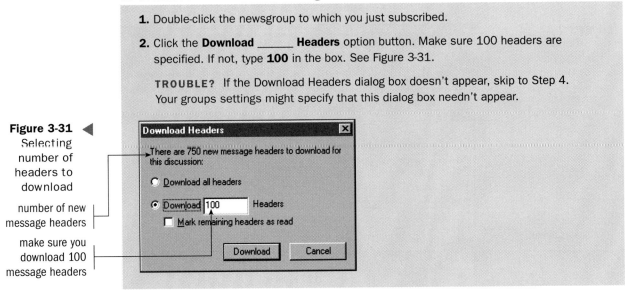

3. Click the **Download** button. It might take your computer a few minutes to download the headers; the status bar reports the download progress. Once the download is complete, the message headers appear in a list.

4. Maximize the newsgroup list window.

Now that you have subscribed, you can view the message headers you have retrieved and select the messages you want to read.

Reading Newsgroup Messages

You read a newsgroup message the same way you read an ordinary e-mail message: you either click it, and the text appears in the lower pane, or you double-click it and the message opens in its own window. Once the first message is open, you proceed through the list of messages using the Next button.

Sorting Newsgroup Posts

The order in which the message headers appear when you click Next depends on how they are sorted in the newsgroup list. By default, Collabra sorts message headers by thread, but it can be helpful to sort in a different order. For example, a newsgroup on a popular TV series might have regular posts from the series producer. If you want to read only the posts by the producer, you could sort by sender to locate all posts from that sender.

For now, you should make sure the sort order is by thread, so when you read your messages you are able to follow a thread of conversation.

To check the sort order:

1. Click **View** and then point to **Sort**.

2. Click **by Thread** to ensure the messages are sorted by thread. You can also click the column heading buttons to sort by those columns. For example, you click 🔲 to sort by thread. See Figure 3-32.

Figure 3-32
Sorting
messages
by thread

can click to sort
by thread

spool icon
indicates thread

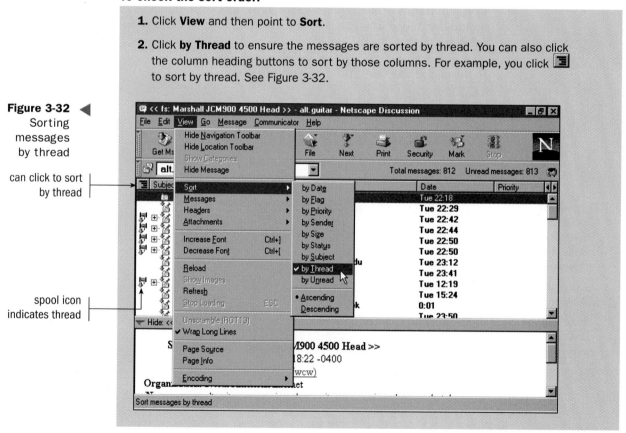

Note that you can also sort your regular e-mail (not just your newsgroup messages) by thread. When you replied to an e-mail earlier in this tutorial, you were actually taking part in a conversation—and Messenger tracks replies just as Collabra tracks newsgroup threads.

Following a Thread

Collabra provides many visual clues to help you keep track of threads of newsgroup conversation. For example:

- Any message preceded by a plus box ⊞ or minus box ⊟ is the beginning of a thread. ⊞ indicates that the responses to the initial message are hidden and ⊟ indicates they are visible.

- Messages without ⊞ or ⊟ aren't part of any other conversation in the headers you have downloaded.

- Boldfaced messages with a green bullet 🌼 have not yet been read; messages without boldface and with a gray bullet 🌼 have.

Figure 3-33 introduces some of the icons you'll see when you examine your newsgroup list; study them so you know how to interpret them.

Figure 3-33
Thread icons

Icon	Description
🖳	Spooled thread indicates messages are hidden; you click the plus box ⊞ to reveal them. Arrow indicates the thread contains messages you haven't yet read.
🖳	Spooled thread indicates messages are hidden; you click the plus box ⊞ to reveal them. Absence of arrow indicates that you have read all the messages in that thread.
🖳	Unspooled thread indicates messages are all displayed; you click the minus box ⊟ to hide them. Arrow indicates the thread contains messages you haven't yet read.
🖳	Unspooled thread indicates messages are all displayed; you click the minus box ⊟ to hide them. Absence of arrow indicates that you have read all the messages in that thread.
📑	Thumbtack on message balloon indicates the message hasn't been read.
📋	Blank message balloon indicates the message has been read.

Now you're ready to read your newsgroup's messages. Because your list of messages will be different from the list shown in the figures, you'll have to adapt the steps to the newsgroup you selected.

To read the messages in a thread:

1. Click ⊞ next to the first message in a thread to view the thread. See Figure 3-34, which shows a thread beginning with a message that asks why stage performers smash their guitars at the end of a concert. Messages indented one level are replies to the first message in the thread. These messages are joined by a vertical dotted gray line. Messages indented two levels are replies to the message in the message indented one level, and so on.

Figure 3-34 ◀
Viewing a thread

original message in thread

these messages, replies to the original message, generated additional replies

six replies to original message

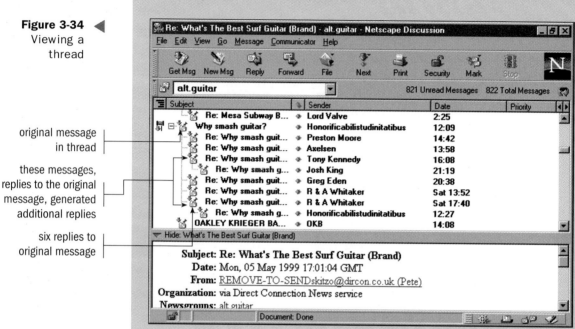

2. Double-click the first message in the thread.

3. Once you've read the message, click the **Next** button. The next message in the thread appears. Notice that the thread name is the same as the subject of the original message and is identified at the top of the message contents area. See Figure 3-35.

Figure 3-35 ◀
A newsgroup post, replying to a message

thread name appears as subject

this post quotes original post

sender of this post agrees with sender of original post

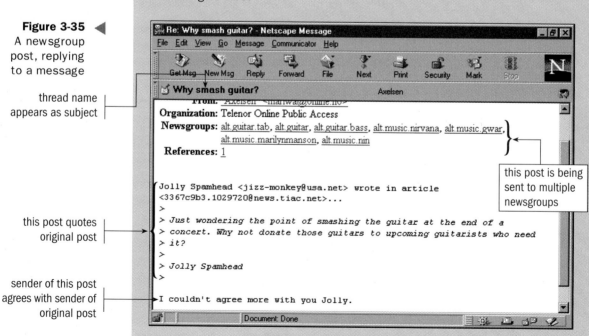

4. Continue viewing the messages in the thread until you finish the thread. If there are too many messages, just view the first several messages. Now click the message window's **Close** button ☒ to return to the newsgroup's window. Notice that all the message headers you read are no longer in boldface, and observe how the icons have changed, according to the table in Figure 3-33.

As you read through the thread, you probably noticed that new posts often quote the previous posts to which they are replying. When you respond to a post, quote as sparingly as possible to keep your message short. Some newsreaders do not let you post a message unless there is more new material than quotes.

Downloading Additional Messages

If you like what you see in a newsgroup, you will probably want to download additional messages. Or you might read messages from a thread but you don't have the first message that initiated the conversation. Try downloading more of the messages in your newsgroup.

To download additional messages:

1. Make sure the newsgroup is open.

2. Click **File** and then point to **Get Messages**.

3. Click **Next 100**. (If you clicked New instead, only new messages since your last download would be retrieved.)

Collabra places the message headers into the list according to the current sort order. Thus if you added headers belonging to a thread, those headers would be placed in the correct position in the thread. The spool icon would change from 🔳 to 🔽 to indicate that new headers have been added to the thread since you last read through it.

Posting a Message

Once you have read through some of the posts in a newsgroup, you might be ready to post a message of your own. You can post a follow-up message to a post you are currently reading, or you can post a message on a completely new topic. When you post a response, you can choose to:

■ Send a private e-mail message to the sender.

■ Send a private e-mail message to the sender and any other e-mail addresses in the sender's original To list.

■ Post a response to the entire newsgroup.

■ Post a response to the entire newsgroup and to the private e-mail address of the sender.

In a newsgroup you should usually reply to the group and not the sender, unless there's a good reason for wanting the reply to be private. The idea of a newsgroup is that it is an open forum. Moreover, people don't want their personal e-mail account cluttered up with e-mail from the newsgroup.

You should perform these next steps only if you have a valuable post to send to the newsgroup you chose. If you don't have anything valuable to say, then read through these steps without performing them.

To post a reply to an existing message:

1. Open the message.

2. Click the **Reply** button 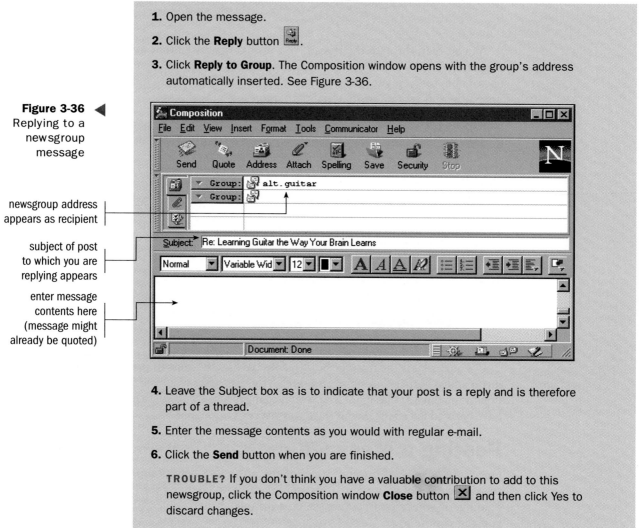.

3. Click **Reply to Group**. The Composition window opens with the group's address automatically inserted. See Figure 3-36.

Figure 3-36 ◄
Replying to a newsgroup message

newsgroup address appears as recipient

subject of post to which you are replying appears

enter message contents here (message might already be quoted)

4. Leave the Subject box as is to indicate that your post is a reply and is therefore part of a thread.

5. Enter the message contents as you would with regular e-mail.

6. Click the **Send** button when you are finished.

   TROUBLE? If you don't think you have a valuable contribution to add to this newsgroup, click the Composition window **Close** button 🗙 and then click Yes to discard changes.

Your message is added to the list of newsgroup messages as a reply within a thread.

You can also raise a new issue in a newsgroup that might start a new thread, depending on whether other newsgroup members reply. Again, make sure you post a new message only if you have something to say.

To post a new message:

1. Open the newsgroup and then click the **New Message** button. The address is again filled in for you.

2. Enter a subject and the message contents.

3. Click the **Send** button.

   TROUBLE? If you have nothing important to post, cancel this message.

If you have asked a question or if your message is provocative enough to generate discussion, when you next download messages you might find responses to your message. Depending on how active the newsgroup is, you might need to wait a few days to get an answer, or an answer might appear within the hour.

Searching a Newsgroup

Collabra offers search features that make it easy for you to find the newsgroup you want and the information you want. For example, within the Subscribe window you can search your news server's list of newsgroups for a particular newsgroup. You hope to drive down to California after your internship is over so you decide to look for newsgroups on surfing.

To search for a newsgroup on surfing:

1. Click the **Discussion Groups** button 🖳 on the Component bar (docked in the status bar) to open the Message Center.

2. Click the **Subscribe** button 🖳.

3. Click the **Search for a Group** tab.

4. Type **surfing** in the Search for box.

5. Click the **Search Now** button. A list of all newsgroups with "surfing" in their names appears. See Figure 3-37. You could click one of these newsgroups and then click the Subscribe button to subscribe to that group from the Search tab, but you won't do that now.

Figure 3-37 ◀
Searching for a
newsgroup

surfing newsgroups;
your list might
be different

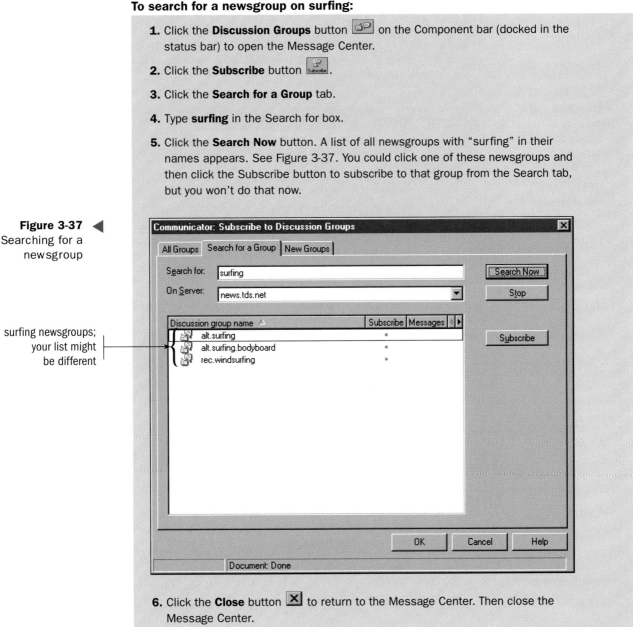

6. Click the **Close** button 🗙 to return to the Message Center. Then close the Message Center.

Within a newsgroup, you can search for posts on particular topics. For example, perhaps you subscribed to a newsgroup of people who like backcountry camping. You are curious about whether there's been any discussion lately about taking dogs into the backcountry.

To search a newsgroup for messages on a topic:

1. If necessary, open the newsgroup.

2. Click **Edit** and then click **Search Messages**.

3. Click the sender list arrow and click **subject**.

4. If necessary, click the adjacent list arrow and click **contains**.

5. Type **dog** in the third box.

6. Click the **Search** button. Any messages with "dog" in the subject field appear in the list. See Figure 3-38. You could double-click a message to open it directly from the Search Messages dialog box.

Figure 3-38 ◀
Searching a
newsgroup for
a post on a
topic

choose either
sender or subject

list of posts
matching criteria

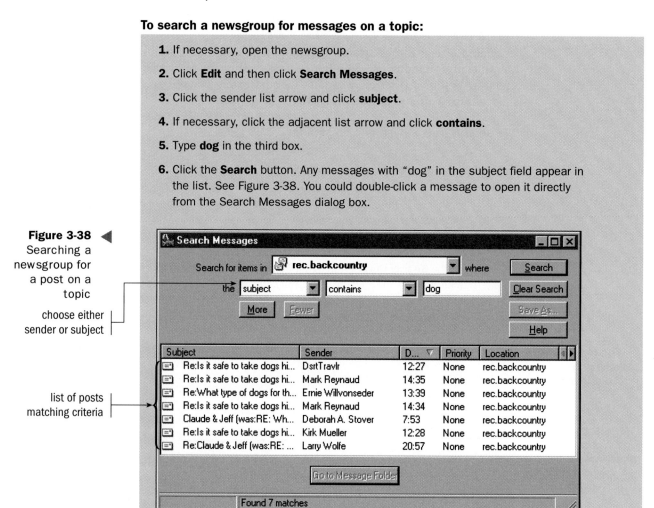

The ability to search a newsgroup makes it easier to find information, but you should be aware that since newsgroup contents change so quickly, an unsuccessful search you perform one day might be successful the next.

Unsubscribing

When you have lost interest in a newsgroup you will probably want to unsubscribe from it so it doesn't clutter up your newsgroup list.

To unsubscribe from a newsgroup:

1. Close the newsgroup window (it can't be open when you unsubscribe from it).

2. Click **Communicator** and then click **Message Center** to open the Message Center.

3. Right-click the newsgroup you joined in this tutorial.

4. Click **Remove Discussion Group**.

5. Click the **OK** button when asked if you are sure you want to unsubscribe from the newsgroup.

6. Click **File** and then click **Exit** to exit Communicator.

Newsgroups can be an excellent source of information. Some newsgroups exist just to support people going through hard times, such as coping with a serious illness. Others exist to exchange information and advice on challenges such as home repair. Still others provide an open forum to discuss a hot topic, such as current election issues. The "conversation" in some newsgroups can get rather intense, because people are less inhibited in an anonymous e-mail message than they tend to be face-to-face. Insulting e-mail in newsgroups is so common that it even has a name: **flaming**. If you avoid taking and giving offense, however, your newsgroup experience will probably be positive.

Quick Check

1 True or False: messages posted to a newsgroup are automatically forwarded to all subscribers.

2 A server that stores the messages posted to a newsgroup is called a _____.

3 When you subscribe to and open a newsgroup, does your newsreader download the text of the messages? Explain your answer.

4 A friend who knows nothing about newsgroups sees rec.arts.oil on your computer screen and asks you to explain what it means. Draw a diagram to accompany your explanation.

5 What is a thread?

6 Why does it take so long for Collabra to open the first time?

7 What might you do to read only the posts by a certain sender?

8 If a message header has no plus box ⊞ or minus box ⊟ next to it in the list of posts, what does that tell you?

9 What is flaming and why is it more prevalent in newsgroups than in public?

Tutorial Assignments

Your internship is over at Carey Outerwear and you're back at school, after an exciting weekend trip where you climbed Mt. Rainier. You want to implement some of the things you learned while in Seattle, especially about e-mail and newsgroups. You plan to e-mail the graphic image of Mt. Rainier to your instructor to show off what you climbed, and then you want to add your instructor's address plus the addresses of some of your friends to your Address Book. You also want to create folders to store your course-related e-mail. Finally, you want to explore more newsgroups to find one that you'd like to join and participate in.

1. Make sure Communicator is properly configured to send and receive e-mail.

2. Create a new e-mail message to your instructor (your instructor will provide you with the e-mail address to use) and Cc: it to yourself. Enter "From your student [name]" as the subject (insert your name between the brackets). In the message contents area, write your instructor a message about what you hope to gain from taking this course.

3. Enter your instructor's name as a new card in your Address Book. After you have entered information on the Name tab, click the Contact tab and enter any other contact information your instructor has given you.

4. Add the e-mail addresses of three friends to your Address Book (make sure you assign a nickname to each). Create a list called "friends" and add the names of your three friends.

5. Create a short message to the friends list you just created and Cc: the message to your instructor. Enter "Class assignment" as the subject and explain briefly in your message that you are testing your e-mail system.

6. In the "Class assignment" message from the previous step, attach the Rainier.bmp file in the Tutorial.03 folder on your Student Disk.

7. Send the "Class assignment message." Once you have sent it, open the Sent mailbox and then open the message you just sent.

8. Print the message you sent in step 7.

9. Create a folder in the Inbox named "Courses." Within the Courses folder, create a folder for each course you are taking.

10. Create another folder in the Inbox named "Personal" for storing personal e-mail. On the back of the printout you created in step 8, draw a picture of your mailbox hierarchy.

11. From the Message Center, click the Subscribe button.

12. Subscribe to one of the newsgroups in the rec category.

13. Download the first 100 message headers in the newsgroup you just subscribed to.

14. Open any of the messages and print it. On the back of the printout, write the full address of the newsgroup you subscribed to.

15. Search for all newsgroups on the topic "basketball." On the back of the print-out you created in step 14, write the addresses of a basketball newsgroup in the alt category and in the rec category, plus three additional addresses of any other basketball newsgroups in other categories.

Case Problems

1. E-mailing Freelancers at Custom Cartoons Custom Cartoons provides its clients with cartoon drawings for their promotions and advertisements. Often, when their own cartooning staff is busy with projects, Custom Cartoons contracts projects out to freelance cartoonists. Janey Killips has been assigned to manage a project for a jugglers guild that is hosting a conference in San Antonio next summer. Janey e-mails you and asks if you would be interested in handling the job. You will correspond with Janey via e-mail to get the job done.

If necessary, launch Communicator, and then do the following:

1. Create a new message to janey@customcartoons.netez.com.

2. Enter "Jugglers Guild" in the Subject line and use your own words in the message contents area.

3. In the message contents area, confirm your availability and willingness to do the job.

4. Check the spelling of your message. Click the Spelling button in the Composition window. If an error is found, click the correct spelling in the Suggestions box, and then click the Replace button.

5. Copy the message to your instructor. Use the Address Book entry you created in the Tutorial Assignments.

6. Add another Cc: line and copy the message to yourself.

7. Add formatting to the message. In the message contents area, bold at least one word and italicize at least one word. To bold a word, you select it and then click the Bold button **A**. To italicize it, you select it and then click the Italic button *A*.

8. Now color one word red. Select the word, press and hold down the Font Color button, and then drag the mouse up and down the color grid that opens and click the color red.

9. Attach the file juggler.bmp, located in the Cases folder of the Tutorial.03 folder on your Student Disk, to the message. Explain in the message content that this file is a draft of a juggler cartoon.

10. Send the message.

11. Now check your mail. The copied message should appear. Open the message. Print the message, and submit the printout to your instructor.

2. Joining a Newsgroup at Camp Yahara George Hendriks, the maintenance person at Camp Yahara, a summer camp for children with special needs, has hired you to help with some summer maintenance jobs. Many of the outdoor facilities such as the tennis courts, the lake dock, and the obstacle course, need work. Everyone at Camp Yahara has a computer with an Internet connection, and you ask George if he would mind if you spent a little time checking the Internet for advice on some of the repair projects. George replies that a second opinion never hurts, so you decide to subscribe to the newsgroup alt.home.repair, which you know addresses many indoor and outdoor repair and mainte-nance problems.

If necessary, launch Communicator, and then do the following:

1. Open the Message Center and click the Subscribe button.

2. Click the Search for a Group tab and type alt.home.repair in the Search for box. If nothing appears, your news server doesn't support this newsgroup. Ask your instructor which newsgroup you should select.

3. Subscribe to the alt.home.repair newsgroup.

4. Open the newsgroup and download the first 100 message headers.

5. Scroll through the message headers until you locate a thread that looks like it might apply to any outdoor or indoor repair job underway at Camp Yahara.

6. Open the first message in the thread and read it. Click the Next button to read through all messages in the thread.

7. Click the Forward button to forward the newsgroup message to your instructor; use the Address Book to enter your instructor's e-mail address in the To line.

8. Enter "Camp Yahara" in the Subject line.

9. In the message contents area, inform your instructor that you found this mes-sage in the alt.home.repair newsgroup.

10. Unsubscribe from the newsgroup.

3. Corresponding with College Students You are interested in what's going on at other col-leges and decide to subscribe to one of the many college newsgroups on the Internet. Once you have found a college newsgroup that interests you, you'll post a message to that newsgroup.

If necessary, launch Communicator, and then do the following:

1. From the Message Center, click the Subscribe button.

2. Click the Search for a Group tab.

3. Search for all groups with the word "college."

4. Scroll through the list that appears until you find one that interests you. There are many such newsgroups, ranging from alt.art.college to alt.college.fraternities to soc.college.financial-aid, and so on.

5. Subscribe to the newsgroup that interests you. Make sure there are at least 100 messages. If the college newsgroups don't have many messages, search for a newsgroup that interests you and subscribe to that one instead.

6. Download the first 100 messages.

7. Read through the messages until you find one to which you'd like to respond. Make sure you have something worthwhile to say; the newsgroup won't appreciate it if you write a worthless post. Use the "flavor" of the messages you've read as your guide to tone and length.

8. Click the Reply button, and use the Reply to Group option to reply to the entire newsgroup. Copy the message you post to your instructor. Send the message.

9. Wait at least a day. Open the newsgroup again, and if necessary, click File, point to Get Messages, and then click New. Locate your message and print it. Submit the printout to your instructor and write down the name of the newsgroup to which you subscribed.

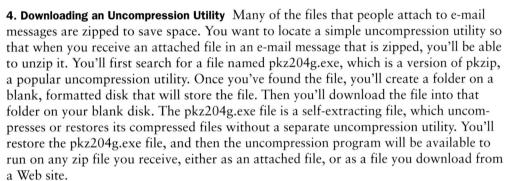

10. If there are any responses to your post, reply to that post and add another contribution to the newsgroup. Again, make sure you have something worthwhile to say.

4. Downloading an Uncompression Utility   Many of the files that people attach to e-mail messages are zipped to save space. You want to locate a simple uncompression utility so that when you receive an attached file in an e-mail message that is zipped, you'll be able to unzip it. You'll first search for a file named pkz204g.exe, which is a version of pkzip, a popular uncompression utility. Once you've found the file, you'll create a folder on a blank, formatted disk that will store the file. Then you'll download the file into that folder on your blank disk. The pkz204g.exe file is a self-extracting file, which uncompresses or restores its compressed files without a separate uncompression utility. You'll restore the pkz204g.exe file, and then the uncompression program will be available to run on any zip file you receive, either as an attached file, or as a file you download from a Web site.

If necessary, launch Communicator, and then do the following:

1. Create a folder on a blank, formatted disk named pkzip. Do not use your Student Disk. To do this, minimize the Communicator window. Open My Computer, click 3½ Floppy (A:), click File, point to New, click Folder, type pkzip, press Enter, and then close My Computer.

2. Maximize the Communicator window and click the Navigator button on the Component bar to activate the Navigator browser.

3. Click the Search button and then perform a search for the file pkz204g.exe. Navigator will likely inform you that thousands of sites match the search.

4. Read through the links and click the one that looks most promising. A site with the word "utilities" or "archive" will probably have a copy of this file. Once you locate a promising site, click the PKZ204G.EXE link. The Save As box should appear. If you have trouble, ask your instructor for a workable site.

5. In the Save As dialog box, locate and click the pkzip folder you created on drive A. Click the Save button.

6. If you have a virus checker, run it on this file. If you don't, realize that you are putting yourself at risk by running a program that has not been checked. If you are in doubt, ask your instructor.

7. Click the Start button on the Windows taskbar and then click Run.

8. Type a:\pkzip\pkz204g.exe in the Open box, and then click the OK button. A DOS window opens, because the program is a DOS utility, and shows the steps for uncompressing the file. If you receive a message saying your disk is full, you'll need to copy the file you downloaded over to a blank disk. Once the program is uncompressed, you are ready to run it. It uncompresses into several files; one is pkunzip.exe, the uncompression utility.

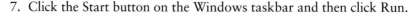

9. To run the pkunzip program, you click the Start button, click Run, and type:

   a:\pkzip\pkunzip.exe path

where path is the path to the file you want to unzip. For example, if you had a file named flowers.zip on drive C and you wanted to unzip it into a folder named c:\flowers, you would type:

   a:\pkzip\pkunzip.exe c:\flowers.zip c:\flowers

The first "phrase" in this command indicates the uncompression program you are running; the second indicates the file you are uncompressing, and the third indicates where you want to put the uncompressed files.

Lab Assignments

These Lab Assignments are designed to accompany the interactive Course Lab called E-mail. To start the Lab using Windows 95, click the Start button on the Windows 95 taskbar, point to Programs, point to Course Labs, point to New Perspectives Applications, and click E-Mail.

E-Mail E-mail that originates on a local area network with a mail gateway can travel all over the world. That's why it is so important to learn how to use it. In this Lab you will use an e-mail simulator, so even if your school's computers don't provide you with e-mail service, you will learn the basics of reading, sending, and replying to electronic mail.

1. Click the Steps button to learn how to work with E-mail. As you proceed through the Steps, answer all of the Quick Check questions that appear. After you complete the Steps, you will see a Quick Check summary report. Follow the instructions on the screen to print this report.

2. Click the Explore button. Write a message to re@films.org. The subject of the message is "Picks and Pans." In the body of your message, describe a movie you have recently seen. Include the name of the movie, briefly summarize the plot, and give it a thumbs up or a thumbs down. Print the message before you send it.

3. Look in your In Basket for a message from jb@music.org. Read the message, then compose a reply indicating that you will attend. Carbon copy mciccone@music.org. Print your reply, including the text of JB's original message before you send it.

4. Look in your In Basket for a message from leo@sports.org. Reply to the message by adding your rating to the text of the original message as follows:

Equipment:	Your rating:
Rollerblades	2
Skis	3
Bicycle	1
Scuba gear	4
Snowmobile	5

Print your reply before you send it.

5. Go into the lab with a partner. You should each log into the E-Mail Lab on different computers. Look at the Addresses list to find the user ID for your partner. You should each send a short e-mail message to your partner. Then, you should check your mail message from your partner. Read the message and compose a reply. Print your reply before you send it. *Note: Unlike a full-featured mail system, the e-mail simulator does not save mail in mailboxes after you log off.*

Answers to Quick Check Questions

SESSION 1.1

1 False

2 The Web page that appears when you start Navigator or the page that a person, organization, or business has created to give information about itself.

3 URL

4 Click Communicator and then click Hide Component Bar.

5 in a different color

6 abort

7 The domain in the URL is not registered with the Domain Name Server (DNS).

SESSION 1.2

1 Type the URL in the Location box and then press Enter.

2 protocol: http; server address: www.irs.ustreas.gov; filename: cover.html; folder: prod

3 No. URLs are case-sensitive.

4 file transfer protocol, used to transfer files

5 It is located at an educational institution.

6 Back, Forward, and Home

7 Page loads faster without images

8 False

SESSION 2.1

1 False

2 The Unknown File Type dialog box opens

3 AU (basic audio file), AIFF (high-fidelity sound used on Macintosh computers), and WAVE (high-fidelity sound used on Windows/PC computers)

4 Media Player

5 What's Cool

6 high

7 history list

8 bookmark

SESSION 2.2

1 search engine

2 or, because either word can be present

3 False

4 Spiders

5 navigational or subject

6 text

7 When you save a page as a text file, only the text is saved: not the images, links, and color.

8 GIF and JPEG

9 a file that doesn't appear in the browser window but must be viewed in a separate program

10 Uploading means to transfer a copy of a file from your computer to a public directory; downloading means to transfer a copy of a file from a public directory to your computer.

11 True

12 False

SESSION 3.1

1 user ID: pcsmith; host name: icom.net

2 Click Edit, click Preferences, click Mail & Groups plus box, and then click Identity.

3 Sent mailbox

4 The recipient might interpret the uppercase letters as shouting.

5 backbone

6 Recipient's e-mail address is automatically inserted; contents of the original are quoted

7 Right-click person's e-mail address, point to Add to Address Book, then click Sender.

8 False

9 a paper clip icon appears

SESSION 3.2

1 Click the plus box or double-click the mailbox containing the folder, then double-click the folder or subfolder.

2 They are returned undeliverable.

3 Not necessarily. The recipient needs Excel or another program that can open Excel files.

4 text without special fonts or images

5 No. It might be encoded.

6 False. It will be stored in the Trash mailbox.

7 Message Center

8 Ctrl or Shift

SESSION 3.3

1 False

2 News server

3 No. It downloads only the message headers; to download the message text you must double-click a message.

4 The newsgroup is in the rec category, which stands for recreational. It is in the arts subcategory, and its subject is oil; probably oil painting.

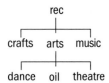

5 a batch of messages that follow a single "line of conversation"

6 Collabra must download the list of all newsgroups

7 sort by sender

8 It is not part of a thread in the message header list you downloaded.

9 Insulting e-mail; because e-mail senders are anonymous.

The Internet Using
Netscape Communicator™
Software

LEVEL II

TUTORIALS

Read This **Before You Begin**

STUDENT DISK

To complete Netscape Communicator Tutorials 4 and 5 and the end-of-tutorial assignments in this book, you need a Student Disk. Your instructor will either provide you with a Student Disk or ask you to make your own.

If you are supposed to make your own Student Disk, you will need one blank, formatted high-density disk. You will need to copy a set of folders from a file server or standalone computer onto your disk. Your instructor will tell you which computer, drive letter, and folders contain the files you need. The following table shows you which folders go on your disk, so that you will have enough disk space to complete all the tutorials, Tutorial Assignments, and Case Problems:

Student Disk	Write this on the disk label	Put these folders on the disk
1	Student Disk 1: Tutorials 4 and 5	Tutorial.04
		Tutorial.05

When you begin each tutorial, be sure you are using the correct Student Disk. See the inside front or inside back cover of this book for more information on Student Disk files, or ask your instructor or technical support person for assistance.

USING YOUR OWN COMPUTER

If you are going to work through this book using your own computer, you need:

■ **Computer System** Netscape Communicator for Windows must be installed on your computer. This book assumes a Complete installation of Netscape Communicator Standard Edition.

■ **Student Disk** Ask your instructor or lab manager for details on how to get the Student Disk. You will not be able to complete the tutorials or end-of-tutorial assignments in this book using your own computer until you have a Student Disk. The Student Files may also be obtained electronically over the Internet. See the inside front or inside back cover of this book for more details.

TO THE INSTRUCTOR

To complete the Netscape Communicator Tutorials 4 and 5 and end-of-tutorial assignments in this book, your students must use a set of files on one Student Disk. These files are included in the Instructor's Resource Kit, and they may also be obtained electronically over the Internet. See the inside front or inside back cover of this book for more details. Follow the instructions in the Readme file to copy the files to your server or standalone computer. You can view the Readme file using WordPad.

Once the files are copied, you can make Student Disks for the students yourself, or you can tell students where to find the files so they can make their own Student Disks. Make sure the files get correctly copied onto the Student Disks by following the instructions in the Student Disks section above, which will ensure that students have enough disk space to complete all the tutorials and end-of-tutorial assignments.

COURSE TECHNOLOGY STUDENT FILES SOFTWARE

You are granted a license to copy the Student Files software to any computer or computer network used by students who have purchased this book.

Developing Web Pages with Netscape Composer

Creating a Home Page at Avalon Books

Avalon Books

CASE

You work at Avalon Books, a large bookstore in the city of Lakeside. The store offers its customers more than books; it also includes reading rooms, play areas for the kids, and a small cafe. The bookstore sponsors special events such as author signings, poetry readings, and live music. The manager of Avalon Books, Mark Stewart, prepares paper flyers featuring the month's events, and the Avalon Books salespeople insert these flyers into the books customers purchase. However, Mark would like to publicize these events to a wider audience. He especially wants to reach those who have never visited the store or who haven't purchased a book recently and so are unaware of upcoming events. He has asked you to create a Web page to advertise Avalon Books on the World Wide Web. He plans to advertise his Web site in all his promotions.

Netscape provides three methods to create a Web page with the Composer component of Netscape Communicator. The Page Wizard method allows you to select page elements from a predetermined list to build your page. Your opportunity for creativity when using the Page Wizard is limited to this preselected list. A second method of creating a new page is using a **template**, a professionally designed page that you retrieve and use as a model for your own page. Although using a template relieves you from having to spend time on page design, you might find that the template designs don't appeal to you or that your page ends up looking like a lot of other pages whose creators have also used the templates. You can also use an existing page on the Web as your model by saving it to your local disk and modifying it. You can use both the Page Wizard and the templates to "jump start" your page by creating the page and then using Composer to modify it. A third method of creating a new page is starting from scratch with a blank page in Composer. You enter and format your own text and create your own design using the Composer tools.

After spending some time thinking about the project Mark has asked you to take on, you decide to use this third method to create the Avalon Books page.

In this session you will use Netscape Composer to create a Web page from scratch. You will learn how to define properties for your document and to enter and then format text in your page.

Creating a New Page with Netscape Composer

The Composer component of Netscape Communicator gives you the ability to create and edit intranet and Web documents. An **intranet document** is just like a Web page except that it is available only to an internal network, not to all users on the Web. See Figure 4-1.

Figure 4-1 ◀
Storing a Web page on the Internet or an intranet

Internet Server

intranet Server

Web page you store on Internet server is available to anyone on the Web

Web page stored on intranet server is available only to those on the intranet who have rights to your document

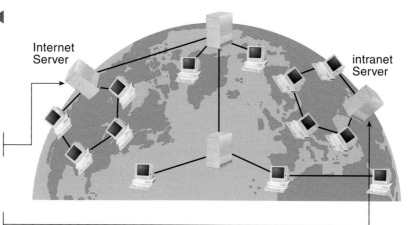

When you create a Web page, you need to decide if your audience will be only your local intranet, if you are on one, or the entire Internet community. Your content should always be dictated by your audience. Once you've created your page, Communicator can help you publish it. With Composer you can:

■ Create Web documents from scratch or using composition aids.

■ Edit and format your documents in a WYSIWYG (what you see is what you get) environment, so that you will see an immediate preview of how the final document will appear.

■ Use familiar word processing features such as spell-checking and table creation.

■ Quickly and easily insert graphic objects and hypertext links into your document.

■ Publish your document to a server.

Elements of a Web Page

Creating a Web page involves planning both the content and the appearance. You can plan the content by asking questions like: What information do I want to convey? What links do I want to include?

Once you have settled on your content, you should plan your design. You can include colors, interesting fonts, a stylized background, graphics, and other design elements like lines and tables. Keep in mind, however, that a browser takes much longer to retrieve a Web page that contains a lot of graphics. If your page takes too long to retrieve, your target audience might lose patience and skip your page.

Mark shows you a flyer he uses to advertise the bookstore's current events, shown in Figure 4-2. He suggests you use this flyer as a basis for the Web page contents.

Figure 4-2 ◀
Mark's flyer

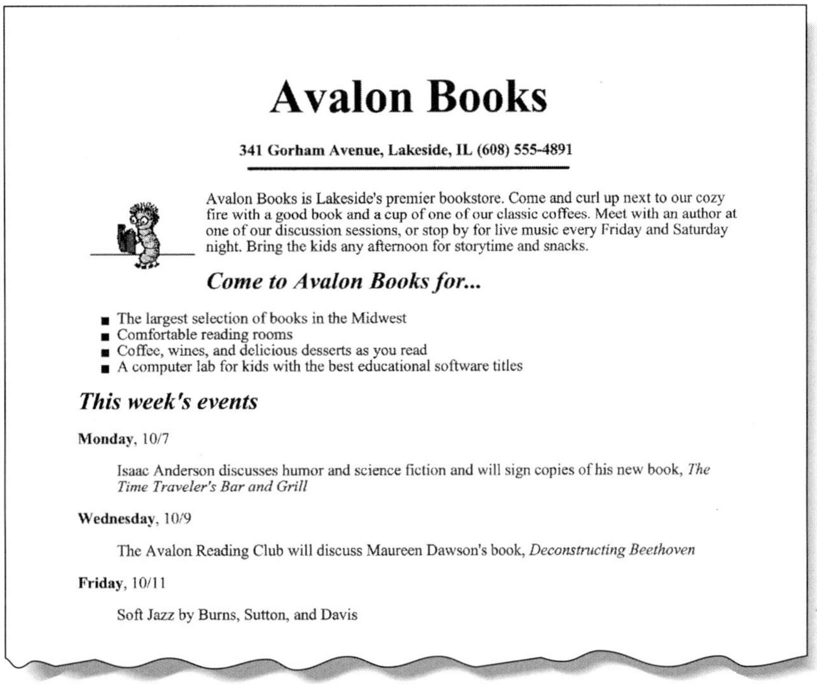

Avalon Books

341 Gorham Avenue, Lakeside, IL (608) 555-4891

 Avalon Books is Lakeside's premier bookstore. Come and curl up next to our cozy fire with a good book and a cup of one of our classic coffees. Meet with an author at one of our discussion sessions, or stop by for live music every Friday and Saturday night. Bring the kids any afternoon for storytime and snacks.

Come to Avalon Books for...

- The largest selection of books in the Midwest
- Comfortable reading rooms
- Coffee, wines, and delicious desserts as you read
- A computer lab for kids with the best educational software titles

This week's events

Monday, 10/7

Isaac Anderson discusses humor and science fiction and will sign copies of his new book, *The Time Traveler's Bar and Grill*

Wednesday, 10/9

The Avalon Reading Club will discuss Maureen Dawson's book, *Deconstructing Beethoven*

Friday, 10/11

Soft Jazz by Burns, Sutton, and Davis

The page that Mark sketched contains the following elements:

- A main heading and several subheadings at different levels.
- A description of the contents and purpose of the page.
- A bulleted list.
- A horizontal line that improves the page's appearance.
- A graphic image.
- Text in different fonts and sizes.
- Indented text.

You decide to create this page from scratch, by first entering and formatting the text and then by creating a page design.

Going Offline

You can use many Communicator features without actually being connected to the Internet—a plus if you are paying for your Internet connection. When you work without an Internet connection, you are working **offline**. When you start Communicator, your computer will probably attempt to connect to the Internet. If you will be using only Composer without requiring any Internet resources, you could click the Cancel or Stop button on your Internet connection dialog box to halt the connection. Creating a Web page with Composer can usually be done offline.

Starting Composer

How you start Composer depends on your circumstances. If you plan to use the Page Wizard or one of the templates developed by Netscape, you can start those features from anywhere in Communicator. Alternatively, you can retrieve any page on the Web in the Navigator browser and open it in Composer so that it functions as a template. Keep in mind that most Web pages contain copyrighted material that you cannot use without permission. You can also start Composer and then open a document from there.

REFERENCE
window

STARTING COMPOSER

- To create a new page from scratch, click File on the Communicator menu bar, point to New, then click Blank Page, Page From Template, or Page From Wizard.
- To open an existing page that is already open in the browser, click File and then click Edit Page.
- To open a page from Composer, click the Composer button to start Composer, click the Open File button, locate and select the file, and then click the Open button.

To create a new document in Composer:

1. Launch Communicator. If your computer attempts to connect to the Internet, you can cancel the connection.

2. Click the **Composer** button 🖉 in the docked Component Bar. The Netscape Composer window opens to a blank page. See Figure 4-3.

Figure 4-3 ◀
Composer
window

Composition toolbar —

Formatting toolbar —

document window
displays the page as
you create it

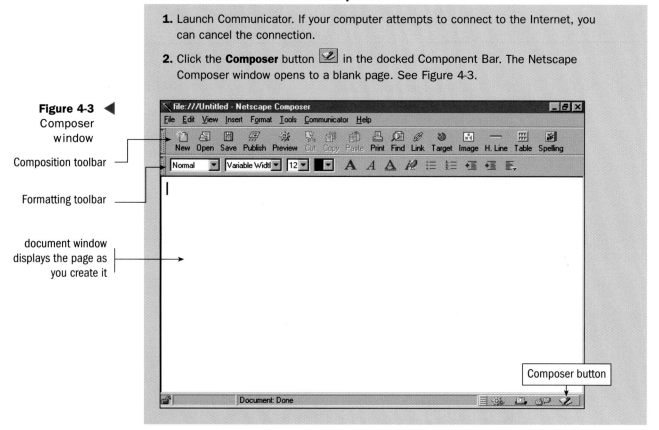

Composer button

Notice that the toolbars in Composer are no longer the Navigation, Location, and Personal toolbars you're used to seeing in the Navigator browser. Instead, Composer includes two toolbars: Composition and Formatting. The Composition toolbar includes tools that aid you in composing your page, and the Formatting toolbar includes tools that help you format your page.

Setting Document Properties

Before you actually begin entering text into your new document, you decide to fill out the Document Properties dialog box, which stores information about your page, including a title, a description, the author, and other record-keeping details. None of the information you enter in the Document Properties dialog box appears on the page itself. Instead, Composer uses this information to identify your page to other users, as well as to provide background information on the page. Although you don't have to fill out this dialog box, it does allow you to include additional information about you and your page—information that might not be appropriate to include on the page itself.

The Document Properties dialog box also allows you to specify **keywords**—descriptive words that identify the contents of your page to other Internet users—and classification labels that classify your page. For the Avalon Books Web page, you might enter the keywords "books" or "bookstore." Internet search pages such as the popular one developed by Yahoo use keywords to categorize a page in their Web page database. An Internet user who searches for information on books is more likely to locate the bookstore's page if you've included keywords. Since Mark has told you that he wants people to be able to locate this page easily, you decide to include keywords when you enter the document's properties, and you decide to enter his name as the page's author.

To enter information for your Web page:

1. Click **Format**, and then click **Page Colors and Properties**. The Page Properties dialog box opens.

2. If necessary, click the **General** tab.

3. In the Title box, type **Avalon Books**, and then press **Tab**.

4. Type **Mark Stewart** in the Author box, then press **Tab**.

5. Type **This is the home page for the Avalon Books bookstore** in the Description box, and then press **Tab**.

6. Type **Avalon, books, bookstores, novels, Lakeside** in the Keywords box, then press **Tab**.

7. Type **bookstore** in the Classification box. Figure 4-4 shows the completed dialog box.

Figure 4-4 ◀
Entering page
properties

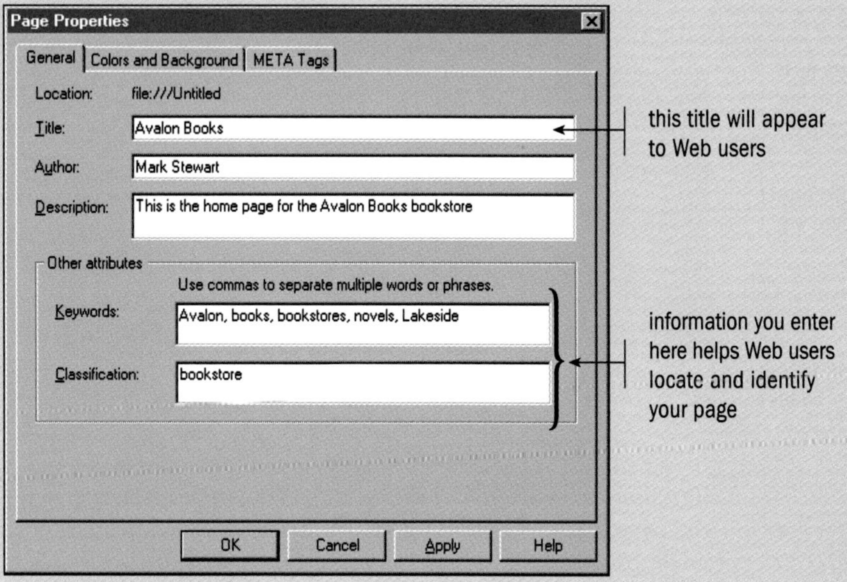

this title will appear
to Web users

information you enter
here helps Web users
locate and identify
your page

8. Click the **OK** button.

Before adding any text to your page, you should save the blank page to your Student Disk.

To save the Avalon Books page:

1. Place your Student Disk in the drive, click **File**, and then click **Save As**.

   TROUBLE? Check the Read This Before You Begin page to ensure you are using the correct Student Disk.

2. Locate then select the drive containing your Student Disk.

3. Open the **Tutorial.04** folder.

4. Type **Avalon** in the File name box.

5. Click the **Save** button to save your new Web page document in the Tutorial.04 folder on your Student Disk.

Note that Composer's title bar now displays the filename you entered.

Markup Tags

Composer works much like a word processor. However, there are some important differences between a document created with a software program such as Microsoft Word and one created by Composer for use on the Web. When you create a document using Composer, you are actually creating a file that consists of HTML codes. **HTML**, which stands for Hypertext Markup Language, is the language in which a Web page is written. HTML uses special codes to describe how the page should appear on the screen. Figure 4-5 shows a Web page as it appears on your computer screen, and behind it, the underlying HTML code. It is this code that is actually transferred over the Web when someone accesses your page.

Figure 4-5
Web page and
the HTML code
it employs

Web page as it
appears in the
browser

An example of a
markup tag

Underlying HTML
code

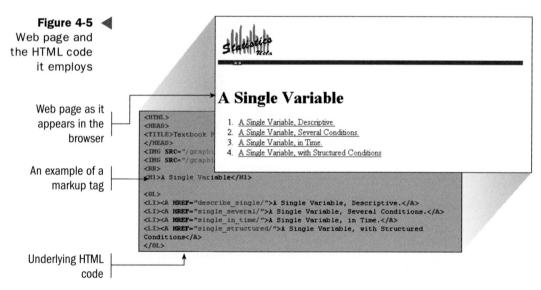

When the HTML code is transferred over the Web, the browser accessing the page interprets the code to determine the page's appearance. The appearance of each element in the page, such as a heading or a bulleted list, is indicated by a **markup tag**—a label within angle brackets that identifies the element to a browser. A tag with the label <H1>, for example, stands for "Heading 1" and indicates that the text that follows is a top-level heading in the document. Markup tags are necessarily very general so that many different kinds of browsers can read the document and determine how to display it. Not all browsers display text the same way. Some browsers, called **text-based browsers**, often can't display formatting such as bold or italics and might be able to display only one type of font. These browsers will display Heading 1 text very differently from a browser like Netscape that can display a variety of fonts and formatting. Figure 4-6 shows how two different browsers might interpret text formatted with a Heading 1 tag.

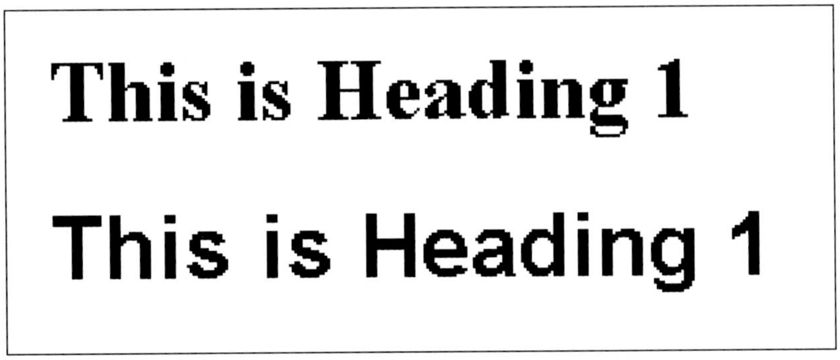

Figure 4-6
Same heading
as it appears in
different
browsers

This is Heading 1

This is Heading 1

You can assign fonts and font sizes to text, just as you do in a word processor, but you should be aware that not all browsers will be able to display the font you choose. Suppose you format text with a Heading 1 tag with a 14-point bold Century Gothic font. If a browser on an operating system without Century Gothic installed retrieves your page, it will use the default font for the style you've assigned rather than Century Gothic. If you designed your page around interesting fonts, you could sell yourself short if the majority of browsers don't have your font.

As a Web page author, you don't have the same kind of control over your page's appearance as you would in creating a word-processed document. Although you can use different fonts and font sizes, the appearance of text is determined by the browser, not by you. Even with these limitations, you can still create interesting and visually attractive documents. And as the Web increases in popularity, new tags will be developed that give Web authors more flexibility and control in creating pages.

In creating your Avalon Books Web page, you'll be using tags with the following document elements:

- paragraphs

- individual characters

- graphic images

- tables

Some tags simply contain information about the document. When you were entering document information earlier you were actually inserting tags of this kind into your document. While these tags do not show up on the page, they do appear in the HTML code. You can see this by viewing the source code, or the actual HTML tags, that define the document.

To view a page's source code:

1. Click **View** and then click **Page Source**. The View Document Source window opens. See Figure 4-7. Notice that each property you entered is actually part of a tag. When you enter your page's contents, it will appear between the Body tags.

   TROUBLE? If your source code is slightly different, don't worry. Even typing an extra space can make the HTML code look different.

Figure 4-7 ◀
HTML source
code

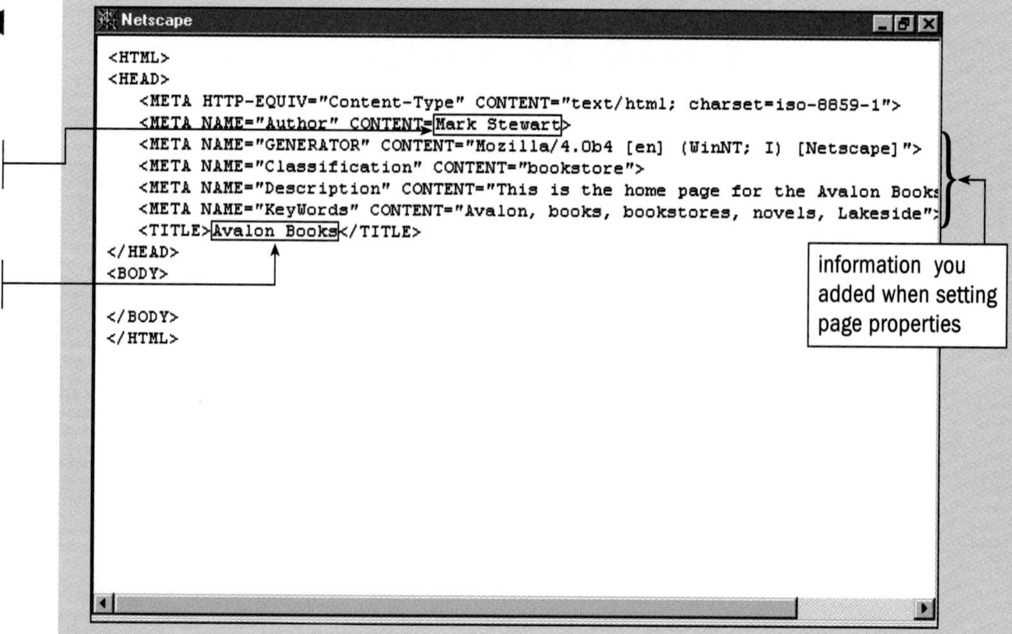

page author appears
here

page title within
TITLE tag

```
Netscape                                                          _ ☐ ☒
<HTML>
<HEAD>
    <META HTTP-EQUIV="Content-Type" CONTENT="text/html; charset=iso-8859-1">
    <META NAME="Author" CONTENT=Mark Stewart>
    <META NAME="GENERATOR" CONTENT="Mozilla/4.0b4 [en] (WinNT; I) [Netscape]">
    <META NAME="Classification" CONTENT="bookstore">
    <META NAME="Description" CONTENT="This is the home page for the Avalon Book
    <META NAME="KeyWords" CONTENT="Avalon, books, bookstores, novels, Lakeside"
    <TITLE>Avalon Books</TITLE>
</HEAD>
<BODY>

</BODY>
</HTML>
```

information you
added when setting
page properties

2. Click the **Close** button ☒ to return to the Composer window.

Entering and Formatting Text

You are now ready to start formatting the Avalon Books Web page to mirror the appearance of Mark's flyer. As you look over Mark's flyer from Figure 4-2, you identify the following elements:

- main heading for the title

- smaller heading listing store's address and phone number

- heading for each of the two sections of the document

- bulleted list of bookstore features

- bolded weekdays on which Avalon Books has scheduled events

- indented descriptions of events

- horizontal line separating headings

- graphic that makes the page visually attractive

In trying to recreate this flyer on the Web, you will need to apply a tag to each of these elements: headings, bulleted lists, formatted text, indented text, and graphics. Composer makes it easy for you to choose the appropriate tags for each element. When you want to apply the style to an entire paragraph you choose a paragraph tag. When you want to apply a style to just a phrase, word, or character, you choose a character tag.

To start, you decide to apply the paragraph tags for the headings. HTML offers six different heading tags, labeled H1, H2, H3, and so on through H6. Composer has assigned a style name to each HTML tag and placed all available style names on a list that is available through the Formatting toolbar. The HTML tag H1, for example, appears as the Heading 1 style in this list. Figure 4-8 shows how a typical browser might display paragraphs with each of these heading tags applied.

Netscape
Communicator

Figure 4-8
Heading styles
as they appear
in browser

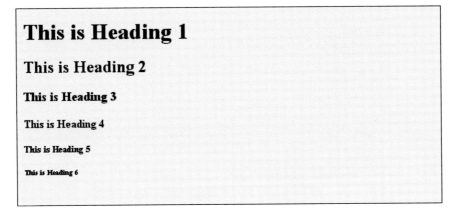

This is Heading 1

This is Heading 2

This is Heading 3

This is Heading 4

This is Heading 5

This is Heading 6

To apply a style to a paragraph, you click anywhere in the paragraph and then choose the style you want from the Paragraph style list. You can apply a style before or after you type the paragraph, and you can apply a different style at any time.

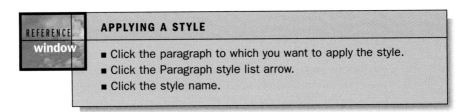

REFERENCE window

APPLYING A STYLE

- Click the paragraph to which you want to apply the style.
- Click the Paragraph style list arrow.
- Click the style name.

Applying Heading Styles

You decide to use the Heading 1 style (corresponding to the H1 HTML tag) for the page's main heading, "Avalon Books," and the Heading 4 style (corresponding to the H4 HTML tag) for the store's address and phone number.

To enter text and styles for the first two paragraphs:

1. Click the upper-left corner of the document window. The blinking insertion point indicates you are ready to type.

2. Click the **Paragraph style** list arrow on the Formatting toolbar. The list of available styles opens. Each style corresponds to an HTML tag. See Figure 4-9.

Figure 4-9
Paragraph style
list

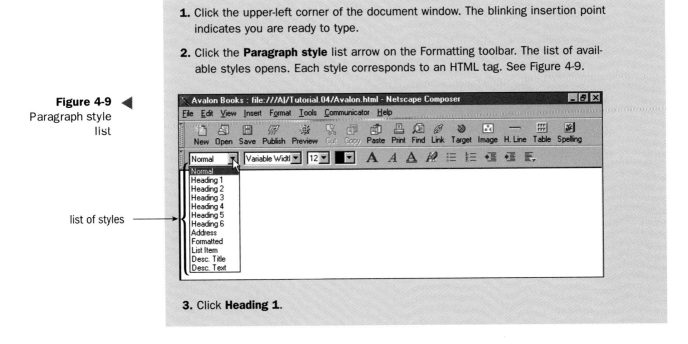

list of styles

3. Click **Heading 1**.

4. Type **Avalon Books** then press **Enter**. Now tag and enter the second line.

5. Click the **Paragraph style** list arrow on the Formatting toolbar, then click **Heading 4**.

6. Type **341 Gorham Avenue, Lakeside, IL (608) 555-4891** then press **Enter**. Notice that because you applied a different style to this paragraph, Composer displays it differently. See Figure 4-10.

Figure 4-10 ◀
Entering
headings

paragraph formatted
with Heading 1 style

paragraph formatted
with Heading 4 style

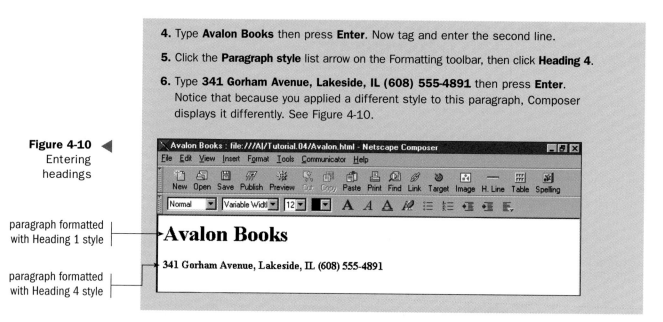

Within each tag, you can make some additional choices regarding the appearance of text formatted with that tag. These choices are called **properties**. While tag properties are not as extensive as what you may be accustomed to with word processors, you can still use them to add variety and interest to your text. One such property for a paragraph tag is alignment. Paragraphs can be left-aligned, centered, or right-aligned.

You decide to center the two headings you just created to follow the format of the flyer.

To center the headings on the page:

1. Use the mouse to select the two headings.

   TROUBLE? To select the two headings, drag the mouse with the left mouse button held down from the left side of the first heading to the right side of the second.

2. Click the **Alignment** button and in the list that opens click the **Center** button . Your headings are now centered.

You now add the next two headings to the page. Unlike the first two, they will be aligned with the left edge of the page.

To add additional headings:

1. Click the end of the second line and press **Enter**. The new line is also centered, so you need to set it to left alignment.

2. Click the **Alignment** button and then click the **Align Left** button on the Formatting toolbar.

3. Type **Come to Avalon Books for...** then press **Enter**.

4. Type **This week's events**, then press **Enter**.

5. Select the two headings you just entered, then click **Heading 2** from the Paragraph style list. See Figure 4-11.

Figure 4-11
Applying
Heading 2 style

paragraphs formatted
with Heading 2 style

You've entered your headings, and now you want to enter the introductory paragraph on Mark's flyer.

Inserting Text with the Normal Style

Most Web pages include a descriptive paragraph that serves as an introduction to the page, usually in the Normal style. This text can describe the page, its goals, and its resources, or it can give brief instructions about how the page operates.

Unformatted sections of text such as descriptive or informational paragraphs are called **normal text**. You tag normal text with the Normal style. Inserting additional text into a Web page with Composer works much as it would with a word processor. You move the mouse pointer to the spot on the page where you want the new text to appear, click the left mouse button, press Enter if you want a new line, and start typing the new text.

Mark's flyer includes a paragraph describing Avalon Books attractions. You are ready to enter this information into your Web page.

To add normal text to a page:

1. Click the end of the line containing Avalon's address and press **Enter**. When you press Enter, Composer automatically formats the next paragraph with the Normal style, as you can see from the Paragraph style list box.

2. Click the **Alignment** button and then click the **Align Left** button on the Formatting toolbar.

3. Type the following text into the document window:

   Avalon Books is Lakeside's premier bookstore. Come and curl up next to our cozy fire with a good book and a oup of one of our classic coffees. Meet with an author at one of our discussion sessions, or stop by for live music every Friday and Saturday night. Bring the kids any afternoon for storytime and snacks.

   Your page should now look like Figure 4-12.

Figure 4-12 ◀
Entering normal
text

normal text ⟶

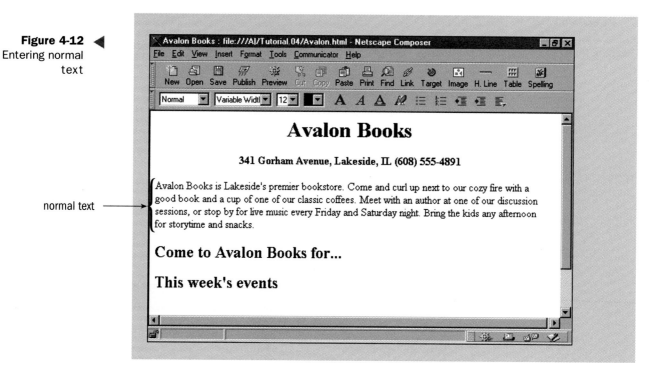

You are satisfied with your page so far. You decide to save your work and then take a break.

To save your changes to the Avalon Books Web page:

1. Click the **Save** button 🖫.

2. Click **File**, click **Exit**, and then click the **Yes** button when Communicator asks whether you want to close all windows and exit Netscape.

Your Web page is well on its way. You've entered document properties and the page's headings and normal text.

Quick Check

1. What is a WYSIWYG document?

2. Under what circumstances would you want to work offline?

3. Why should you enter keywords for your Web page?

4. The language in which a Web page is written is called _____.

5. What is the difference between a markup tag and a style?

6. Why might you choose not to use a special font in your page?

7. How does Composer differ from a word processor like Microsoft Word?

8. What style do you use for unformatted sections of text such as descriptive paragraphs?

SESSION	*In this session you will learn how to enhance the appearance of your documents with numbered and bulleted lists, how to indent text, and how to format text using character formats.*
4.2	

Creating Lists

As you look over Mark's flyer, you notice the next thing you want to add is a list of attractions. You can use Composer to create two kinds of lists: a numbered list or a bulleted list. You use a numbered list, also called an **ordered list**, when you want to display, for example, chronological information such as a list of the steps needed to complete a task. You use a bulleted list, known as an **unordered list** because the order doesn't matter, to distinguish between items in the list with bullet symbols.

You decide to try both the numbered and bulleted list formats so you can decide how you want the list of Avalon attractions on Mark's flyer to look. First, you must reopen the page you were working on in Session 4.1.

To reopen the Avalon page in Composer:

1. Restart Communicator. You do not have to initiate an Internet connection nor load your home page.

2. Click **File**, then click **Open Page**.

3. Click the **Choose File** button, click the **Look in** list arrow, and then locate and select the drive containing your Student Disk.

4. Open the **Tutorial.04** folder, click **Avalon.htm**, then click the **Open** button.

5. Click the **Composer** option button in the Open Page dialog box.

6. Click the **Open** button. Your Avalon Books page opens in the Composer window.

Creating a Numbered List

You decide to enter the list of Avalon attractions first as a numbered list using the Numbered List style. This style has its own toolbar button that you use instead of the Paragraph style list.

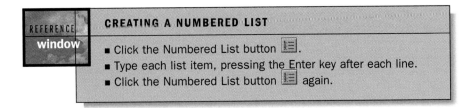

REFERENCE window	CREATING A NUMBERED LIST
	▪ Click the Numbered List button ▤.
	▪ Type each list item, pressing the Enter key after each line.
	▪ Click the Numbered List button ▤ again.

To create a numbered list:

1. Click the end of the **Come to Avalon Books for...** heading, then press **Enter**.

2. Click the **Numbered List** button 📄 on the Formatting toolbar. The pound symbol (#) appears—you'll see what this means in a moment.

3. Type **The largest selection of books in the Midwest**, and then press **Enter**.

4. Continue entering the following items in the list, each on its own line:

   Comfortable reading rooms

   Coffee, wines, and delicious desserts as you read

   A computer lab for kids with the best educational software titles

   The Avalon Books page should now appear as shown in Figure 4-13.

   TROUBLE? If you pressed Enter after the last item in the list, press the Backspace key to remove the extra blank line.

Figure 4-13 ◄
Entering a
numbered list

numbered list ──────

symbol indicates
numbers will appear
in browser

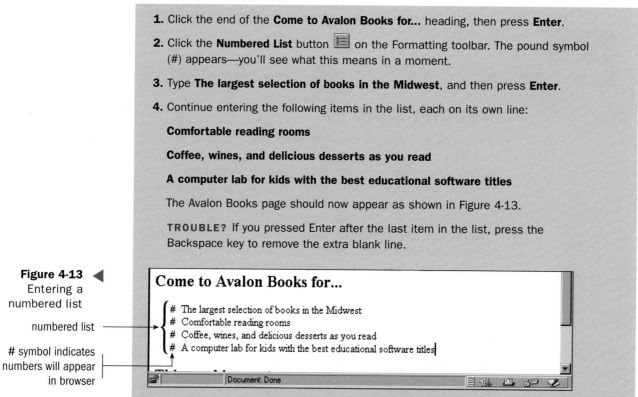

Viewing Your List in the Browser

Up until now, Composer has shown your page just as it will appear to anyone accessing it from Navigator. However, this is not always the case. For example, when you create a numbered list, Composer does not display the numbers in the ordered list. Instead the numbers are represented by the pound sign (#). To see how these numbers will appear to someone accessing the page in a browser, you must actually view the page in the Navigator window. You can switch from Composer to Navigator to view how the browser automatically replaces the # with numbers.

To view the numbered list in the Netscape browser window:

1. Click the **Save** button 🖫 to save your changes to the page.

2. Click the **Preview** button 📄 on the Composition toolbar. The page appears in Navigator as shown in Figure 4-14 (scroll down to see the entire list). The ordered list now appears with numbers. This is how your page will look to other Navigator users, although different browsers might display it differently.

Figure 4-14 ◄
Previewing
page in browser

symbol appears as
numbers in browser

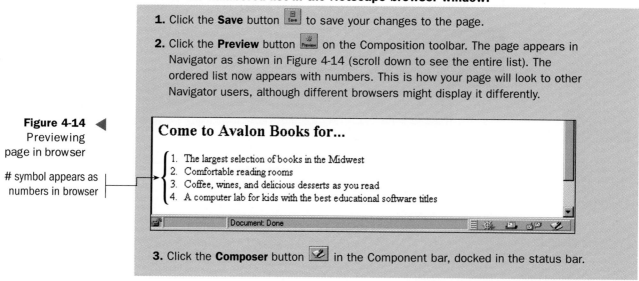

3. Click the **Composer** button 🖉 in the Component bar, docked in the status bar.

Creating a Bulleted List

A bulleted list uses bullets instead of numbers. Like the numbered list, you apply it using one of the toolbar buttons on the Formatting toolbar. You decide to format your list as a bulleted list to see how it appears.

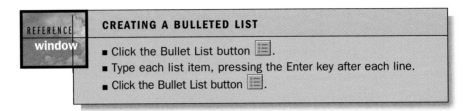

REFERENCE window

CREATING A BULLETED LIST

- Click the Bullet List button .
- Type each list item, pressing the Enter key after each line.
- Click the Bullet List button .

To format a list as a bulleted list:

1. Select the list of attractions by dragging the mouse over all the items in the list.

2. Click the **Bullet List** button on the Formatting toolbar and then click outside the list to deselect it. The list changes to a bulleted list of items as shown in Figure 4-15. Unlike a numbered list, you do not have to view the list in the Navigator browser in order to see the bulleted text.

Figure 4-15
Creating a
bulleted list

bullets appear
instead of numbers

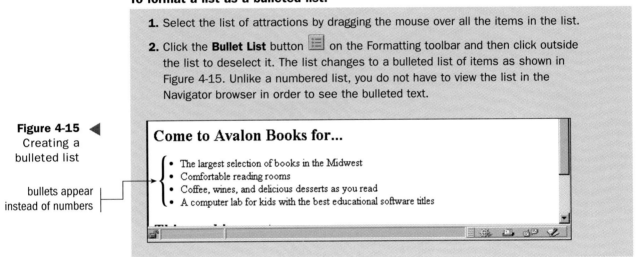

You decide to leave the list as a bulleted list, since it is not in any particular order.

Modifying the Appearance of a List

Composer allows you to choose a different symbol for bulleted lists or a different numbering format for numbered lists. The bullet symbol is one of the properties of the bulleted list style. Some properties, such as the alignment property, can be accessed with toolbar buttons, but not all properties have corresponding toolbar buttons. You access those properties by clicking the selected text with the right mouse button and choosing the appropriate properties option from the menu that opens.

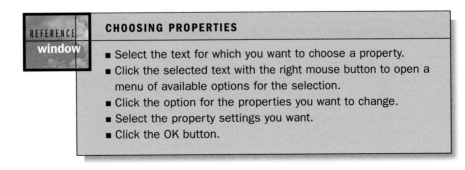

REFERENCE window

CHOOSING PROPERTIES

- Select the text for which you want to choose a property.
- Click the selected text with the right mouse button to open a menu of available options for the selection.
- Click the option for the properties you want to change.
- Select the property settings you want.
- Click the OK button.

Netscape
Communicator

You decide to replace the bullet symbol in your list of attractions with a symbol that more closely approximates the square bullet symbol used in Mark's flyer.

To change the bullet symbol:

1. Select the bulleted list, and right-click the selection.

2. Click **Paragraph/List Properties** from the menu that opens.

3. If necessary, click the **Paragraph** tab.

4. Click the **Bullet Style** list arrow, then click **Solid Square** from the Bullet Style list. See Figure 4-16.

Figure 4-16 ◀
Changing bullet
style

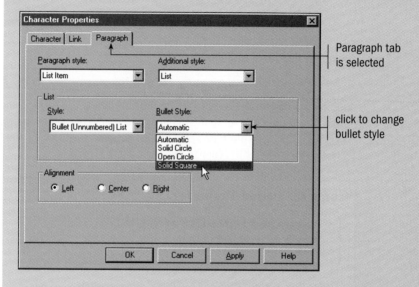

Paragraph tab
is selected

click to change
bullet style

5. Click the **OK** button. The items in the list are now preceded by the new bullet style.

You like the way the bulleted list looks. You're now ready to start entering upcoming events.

Indenting Text

If you want to offset text from the left edge of the page, you can do so by indenting the text using the Indent buttons ⬅▤ and ▤➡ on the toolbar.

Based on Mark's flyer you decide to indent the descriptions of the upcoming events. First you enter the text describing the upcoming events.

To enter the week's events and indent the descriptions:

1. Click the end of the heading **This week's events**, then press **Enter**.

   TROUBLE? If you can't see this heading, scroll down the document window.

2. Verify that the Normal style is applied by checking the Paragraph style list box.

   TROUBLE? If the style does not appear as Normal, select the Norma! style from the Paragraph style list box.

3. Type **Monday, 10/7**, then press **Enter**.

4. Type the following, then press **Enter**:

   Isaac Anderson discusses humor and science fiction and will sign copies of his new book, The Time Traveler's Bar and Grill

5. Continue typing the following information into the document window, pressing **Enter** after each line (Don't press Enter after the word "Deconstructing;" instead, press Enter after "Beethoven").

Wednesday, 10/9
The Avalon Reading Club will discuss Maureen Dawson's book, Deconstructing Beethoven
Friday, 10/11
Soft Jazz by Burns, Sutton, and Davis

6. Select the line or lines describing the Isaac Anderson discussion and book signing (do not include the date).

7. Click the **Increase Indent** button [icon] to shift the line to the right.

8. Indent the rest of the event descriptions in the list, leaving the dates unindented. Your page should look like Figure 4-17.

Figure 4-17 ◀
Indenting text

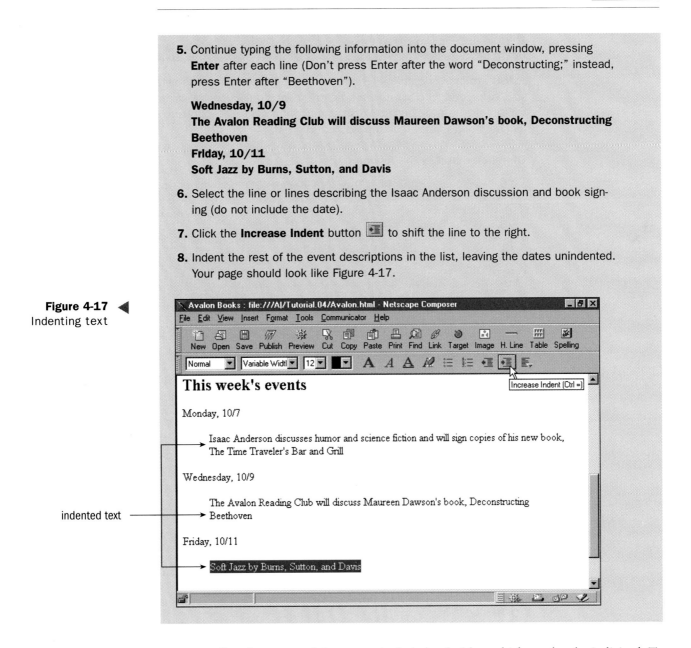

indented text ⟶

You realize that some of the events include book titles, which need to be italicized. To do this, you need to work with character tags.

Applying Character Tags

While you can't change the definition of a style like "Heading 1," you can alter the appearance of individual characters. The HTML formats that you can apply to characters are called **character tags**. Composer allows you to use character tags to italicize your text, bold it, change its font type and size, or display it in a different color.

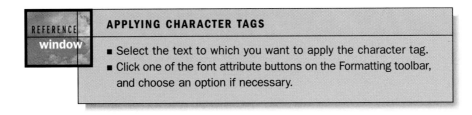

REFERENCE window	**APPLYING CHARACTER TAGS**
	■ Select the text to which you want to apply the character tag. ■ Click one of the font attribute buttons on the Formatting toolbar, and choose an option if necessary.

Changing Font Attributes

A **font attribute** is a characteristic of a font that you can change, including its font type, size, color, and whether it is in bold or italics. Font attributes are represented in Composer by toolbar buttons on the Formatting toolbar. The descriptions of the upcoming events include book names that should be italicized.

To italicize text in the Avalon page:

1. Select the text **The Time Traveler's Bar and Grill** from the description of the Isaac Anderson discussion.

2. Click the **Italic** button [A] on the Formatting toolbar.

3. Select the text **Deconstructing Beethoven** from the description of the Reading Club event.

4. Click [A].

To help the dates stand out better on the page, you decide to bold the day of the event by applying the bold character tag.

To bold text in the Avalon page:

1. Select the text **Monday** from the list of events.

2. Click the **Bold** button [A] on the Formatting toolbar.

3. Repeat steps 1 and 2 to bold **Wednesday** and **Friday**. The updated page should appear as shown in Figure 4-18.

Figure 4-18 ◀
Applying
character tags

days are bolded ——

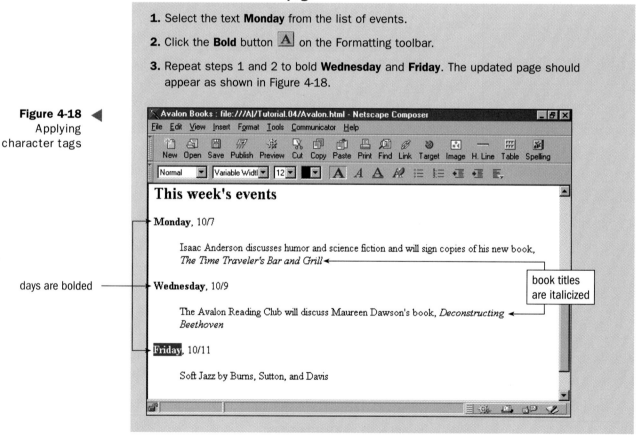

Changing Font Type Size

The type of font and its size are additional font attributes you can change. You have already seen how to change the font size of an entire paragraph by applying one of the heading styles, and individual browsers might change font types based on those headings. To change the font size or type of individual characters, not necessarily entire lines or paragraphs, you use the Font and Font Size lists on the Formatting toolbars.

Looking at your page, you decide to increase the size of the Avalon Books heading. At present it is formatted with the Heading 1 tag. The font size for the Heading 1 tag, as you can see if you click the Heading 1 tag and then look at the value in the Font Size list box, is 24 points. You would like the text to be larger, but there isn't another heading tag that will display the text in a larger font, so you will change its font size attribute. You decide not to change the font type, because you don't want your page design to rely on a font that other browsers might not support.

To increase the size of the Avalon Books heading:

1. Scroll to the top of your Web page, then select the text **Avalon Books** in the first line of your page.

2. Click the **Font Size** list arrow on the Formatting toolbar, and then click 36. The font size is increased accordingly. Figure 4-19 shows the updated page heading.

Figure 4-19 ◀
Increasing
font size

font size is 36 —

The heading looks better, but you'd like to emphasize it further by using color.

Changing Font Color

Another way of adding emphasis and interest to the text on your page is to use different colors by applying the Color character tag to selected text. Netscape allows you to choose colors from a palette of colors. The default color of text in your Web document is black.

You decide to change the color of the first two lines of the page to red to give them greater emphasis.

To change the text color:

1. Select the first two headings on the page.

2. Click the **Font Color** list arrow on the Formatting toolbar.

3. Click the red color shown in Figure 4-20.

Figure 4-20 ◀
Changing font
color

Font Color list arrow ——

click this color ——

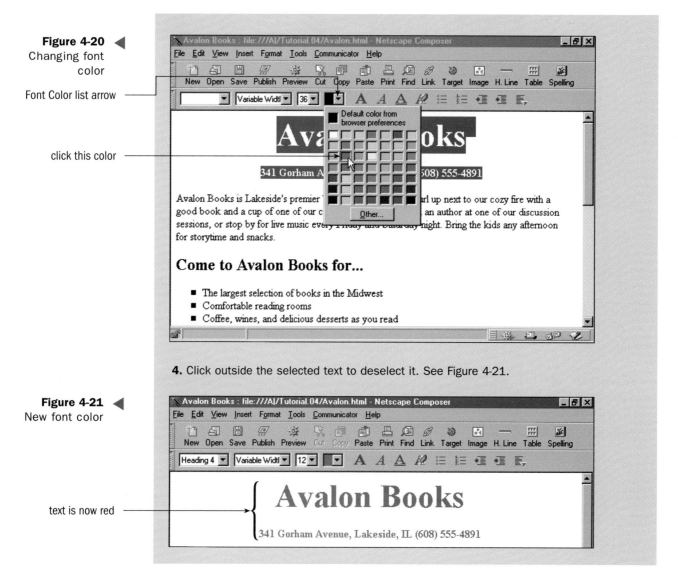

4. Click outside the selected text to deselect it. See Figure 4-21.

Figure 4-21 ◀
New font color

text is now red ——

The first two headings now appear in red.

Applying Multiple Character Tags

So far you've been changing one character property at a time using the buttons on the Formatting toolbar. You can apply more than one character tag at a time using the Character Properties dialog box. You open this dialog box the way you open any properties dialog box: by right-clicking the selected text and choosing the appropriate properties option from the menu that appears. You then make the selections you want in the property sheets, and apply them all at once by clicking the OK button.

Mark stops by and looks at the work you've done. He's pleased with the use of color on the page and would like you to change the color for the two other headings. He thinks they should be italicized as well. You can change the font style, size, and color properties all at the same time.

To apply multiple character tags using the Character Properties sheet:

1. Select the line **Come to Avalon Books for...** .

2. Right-click the selection, then click **Character Properties** from the menu that appears.

3. In the Character Properties dialog box, click the **Italic** check box.

4. Click the **Use Color** button, and then click the fifth blue color from the top in the sixth column, shown in Figure 4-22.

Figure 4-22 ◀
Setting
character
properties

text will be italicized ——

new blue
color

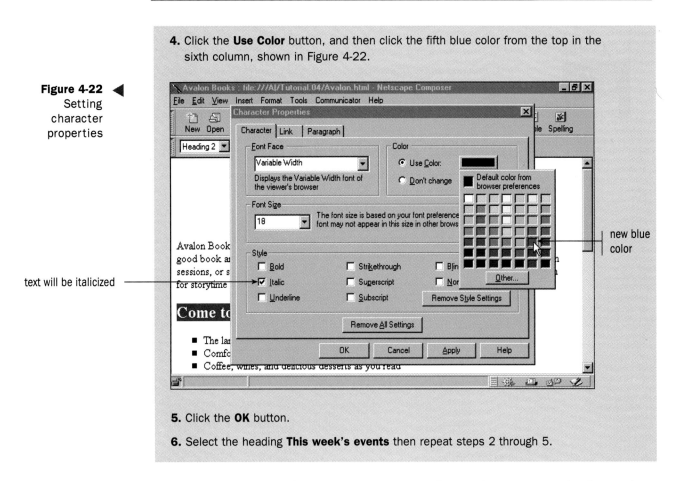

5. Click the **OK** button.

6. Select the heading **This week's events** then repeat steps 2 through 5.

You're finished modifying the text on the Avalon Books page. You decide to take a break. Save your changes to the file and close Communicator. In the next session you'll add graphic elements to the page.

To save your changes and then exit Netscape:

1. Click the **Save** button 🖫.

2. Click **File**, then click **Exit**.

3. Click the **Yes** button to close all Communicator windows. All of your Communicator windows close and your Web page is saved to your Student Disk.

You've finished entering the text of the Avalon Books Web page, and you've formatted it so that the important parts are most noticeable.

Quick Check

1 How are ordered lists displayed by Composer? In the Navigator browser?

2 How do you change the symbol Composer uses in bulleted lists?

3 Name three font attributes you can change in Composer.

4 Why might you decide not to specify a different font, such as Century Gothic, for a heading?

5 How would you change the font size, font color, and appearance for a section of text without opening several dialog boxes?

6 How would you change the color of text on your page to green?

SESSION

4.3

In this session you learn how to insert graphic elements on your page, including graphical lines, images, and a background. You will also learn how to modify the properties of these graphical elements. Finally, you'll learn how to spell-check your Web page.

Inserting a Horizontal Line

Part of the popularity of the Web is due to the ability of browsers like Navigator to display graphic objects within the Web page. Graphic objects lend interest to the page and allow Web authors to share visual information. However, because graphic objects require more time than normal text for a browser to access, you should use graphic objects sparingly.

To give shape to your page, consider adding horizontal lines. Horizontal lines divide the Web page into sections for easy viewing.

REFERENCE window	**INSERTING A HORIZONTAL LINE**
	■ Click the end of the paragraph below which you want to insert the line. ■ Click the H. Line button on the Formatting toolbar. ■ To change the line's appearance, right-click the horizontal line and click Horizontal Line Properties from the menu that appears. Make any changes you want, then click the OK button.

Mark's flyer includes horizontal lines, and he would like his Web page to feature them as well. You decide to add a horizontal line separating the name and address of the bookstore from the rest of the page.

To insert a horizontal line:

1. Restart Communicator and open the Avalon Books page into the Composer window.

   TROUBLE? Make sure the Composer option button is selected in the Open Page dialog box. Review the steps at the beginning of Session 4.2 if you aren't sure how to open your page.

2. Click the end of the heading containing address information for Avalon Books.

3. Click the **H. Line** button H. Line on the Composition toolbar. A horizontal line appears on the page.

You can use the Horizontal Line Properties dialog box to change your line's width, height, alignment, and appearance. Figure 4-23 describes the properties you can change.

Figure 4-23
Line properties

Property	Description
Width	The width of the line is expressed either as a percentage of the window or in the number of pixels, where a pixel is a single dot or point on your monitor's screen. Therefore setting the line width to 100% means the line will stretch the full width of the document window. If you want the line to always stretch across the document window, you should use the percent of window option. If you are trying to define the line width so that it is the same for all browsers, you should use the pixels option.
Height	The height of the line is always expressed in pixels, with a default height of two pixels.
Alignment	Lines can be left-aligned, centered, or right-aligned on the page.
3-D Effect	A line can appear with or without a 3-D effect, which gives the line an illusion of depth.

Figure 4-24 shows several examples of lines whose appearance varies depending on the properties they use.

Figure 4-24
Examples of
line styles

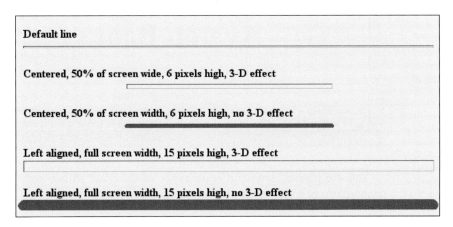

Default line

Centered, 50% of screen wide, 6 pixels high, 3-D effect

Centered, 50% of screen width, 6 pixels high, no 3-D effect

Left aligned, full screen width, 15 pixels high, 3-D effect

Left aligned, full screen width, 15 pixels high, no 3-D effect

You decide to modify the appearance of the line you just created so it looks more like the one in Mark's flyer.

You might find that your line settings already match these; if that is the case, read the steps without performing them.

To change the properties of a horizontal line:

1. Right-click the horizontal line, then click **Horizontal Line Properties**.

2. Type **3** in the Height box to set the line's height to three pixels.

3. Type **325** in the Width box and select **pixels** for the width type.

4. Verify that the **Center** alignment option button is selected.

5. Deselect the **3-D shading** check box. The completed Horizontal Line Properties dialog box should appear as shown in Figure 4-25.

Netscape
Communicator

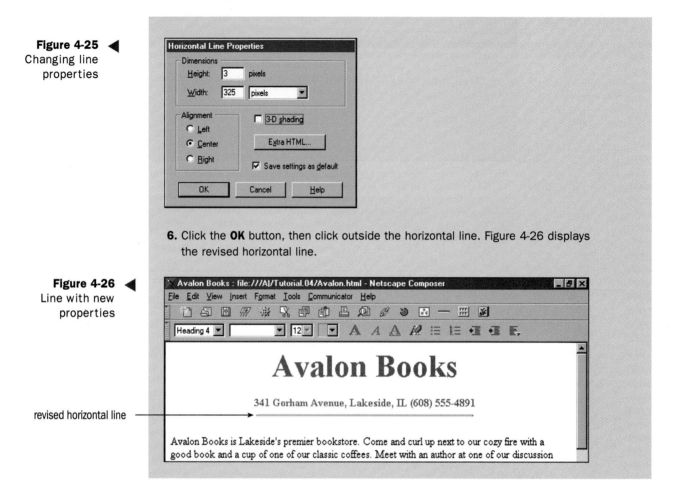

Figure 4-25 ◀
Changing line
properties

Figure 4-26 ◀
Line with new
properties

revised horizontal line

6. Click the **OK** button, then click outside the horizontal line. Figure 4-26 displays the revised horizontal line.

You are pleased with the appearance of the page so far, and are now ready to add a graphic image to the page so that it matches Mark's flyer.

Adding Graphic Images to a Web Page

Most Web browsers can display two types of graphics: inline images and external images. An **inline image** appears directly on the Web page your browser has accessed. To ensure that your inline image is displayable by most browsers, you should use either the GIF or JPEG graphics file formats. If you have a graphic in a different format, you should convert it to a GIF or a JPEG file to ensure that most browsers can display it.

An **external image** is not displayed on the Web page itself. Instead, a link—either a textual or graphical link—appears on the page that represents the image. Figure 4-27 shows the difference between inline and external images.

Figure 4-27
Inline vs.
external
graphic image

inline image appears
on Web page

external image opens
in separate software

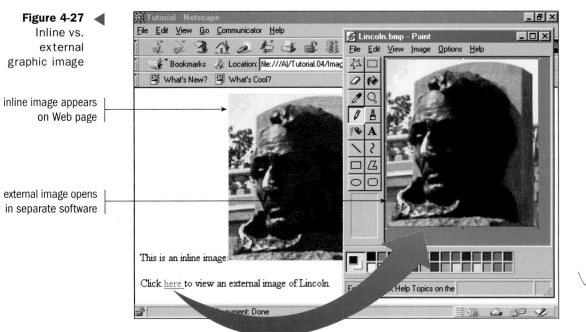

If you have used an external image on your page, a browser accessing that page must load the correct software to display the image. Thus external images have the disadvantage of requiring extra software, and someone reading your page must activate an icon to view the image. But external images are not limited to the GIF or JPEG formats.

GIF File Formats

GIF files come in two formats: interlaced or noninterlaced. When you create your GIF file in your graphics program, you'll need to decide which format you want to use. The difference between the two formats lies in how your browser displays the graphic as it loads the page. With a **noninterlaced** GIF, the image appears one line at a time, starting from the top of the image and working down to the bottom. Figure 4-28 shows this effect. If the graphic is a large one, it might take several minutes for the entire image to appear. People who access your page might find this annoying if the part of the graphic they are interested in is located at the bottom.

Figure 4-28
Noninterlaced
image as
browser
retrieves it

top appears first

image appears one
line at a time

entire image is
retrieved

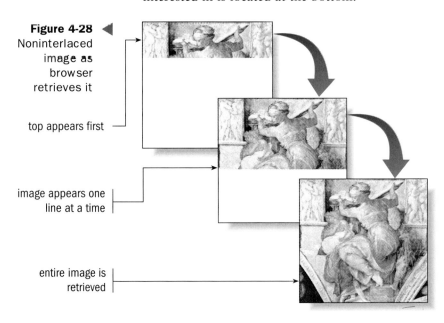

With an **interlaced** GIF, the image appears "stepwise." For example, every fifth line might appear first, followed by every sixth line, and so forth through the remaining rows. As shown in Figure 4-29, the effect of interlacing is that the graphic starts out as a blurry representation of the final image, only gradually coming into focus.

Figure 4-29 ◀
Interlaced image as browser retrieves it

a rough image appears first

image starts to show more detail

final image is crisp and detailed

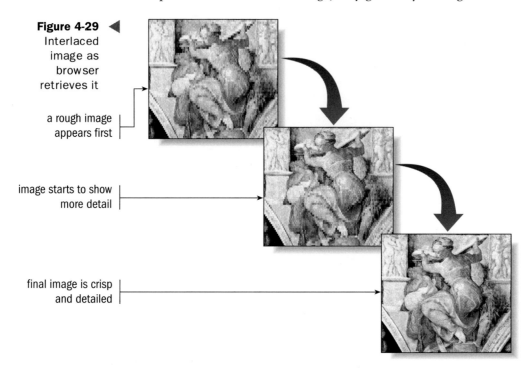

A noninterlaced graphic is always sharp but incomplete while the browser retrieves it. Interlacing is an effective format if you have a large image and want to give users a preview of the final image. They get an idea of what it looks like and can decide whether they want to wait for it to "come into focus." If you are using a graphics package to create GIF images for your Web page, you should determine whether it allows you to save the image as an interlaced GIF.

Inserting an Inline Image

Mark has given you the image file he used in the Avalon Books flyer. You have converted it to a GIF file with one of your graphics programs. You are now ready to insert the graphic into the Avalon Books Web page.

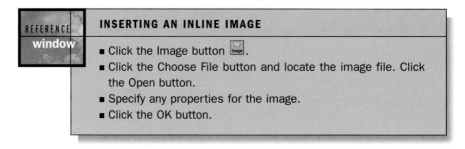

REFERENCE window

INSERTING AN INLINE IMAGE

- Click the Image button [Image].
- Click the Choose File button and locate the image file. Click the Open button.
- Specify any properties for the image.
- Click the OK button.

You want to place Mark's graphic to the left of the introductory paragraph.

To insert an inline image:

1. Click the beginning of the opening paragraph describing the bookstore to place the insertion point.

2. Click the **Image** button 🖼 on the Formatting toolbar. The Image Properties dialog box opens to the Image tab.

3. Click the **Choose File** button next to the Image location box, then locate and select the **Book.gif** file located in the Tutorial.04 folder on your Student Disk.

4. Click the **Open** button, then click the **OK** button. The book graphic is inserted onto the page as shown in Figure 4-30.

Figure 4-30 ◀
Inserted
graphic

graphic ————————▶

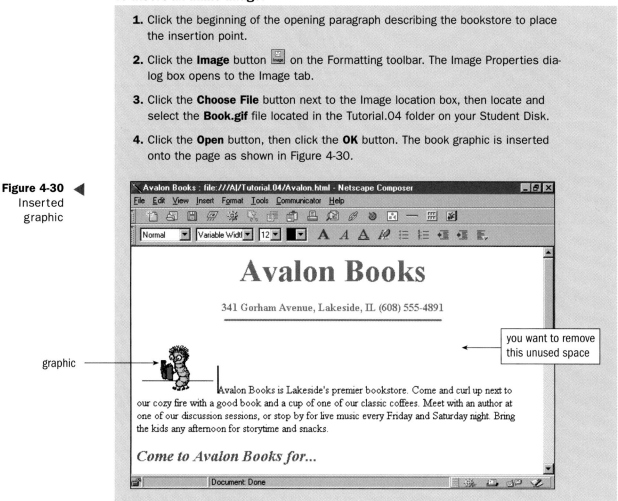

You notice there is a large amount of white space above the paragraph and you decide to solve that problem.

Setting Image Properties

Composer gives you some control over how the image appears on your page. You can change the size of the image, add a border, change the distance between the graphic and surrounding text, and modify how the graphic is aligned relative to surrounding text.

Figure 4-31 shows the options Composer provides for aligning the graphic and the text. You can align the text surrounding the graphic with the graphic's top, center, or bottom. You can also wrap surrounding text to the left or the right of the image.

Figure 4-31 ◀
Examples of
aligned text

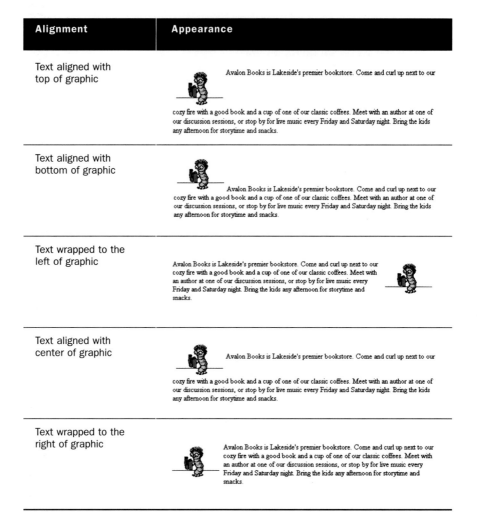

Alignment	Appearance
Text aligned with top of graphic	Avalon Books is Lakeside's premier bookstore. Come and curl up next to our cozy fire with a good book and a cup of one of our classic coffees. Meet with an author at one of our discussion sessions, or stop by for live music every Friday and Saturday night. Bring the kids any afternoon for storytime and snacks.
Text aligned with bottom of graphic	Avalon Books is Lakeside's premier bookstore. Come and curl up next to our cozy fire with a good book and a cup of one of our classic coffees. Meet with an author at one of our discussion sessions, or stop by for live music every Friday and Saturday night. Bring the kids any afternoon for storytime and snacks.
Text wrapped to the left of graphic	Avalon Books is Lakeside's premier bookstore. Come and curl up next to our cozy fire with a good book and a cup of one of our classic coffees. Meet with an author at one of our discussion sessions, or stop by for live music every Friday and Saturday night. Bring the kids any afternoon for storytime and snacks.
Text aligned with center of graphic	Avalon Books is Lakeside's premier bookstore. Come and curl up next to our cozy fire with a good book and a cup of one of our classic coffees. Meet with an author at one of our discussion sessions, or stop by for live music every Friday and Saturday night. Bring the kids any afternoon for storytime and snacks.
Text wrapped to the right of graphic	Avalon Books is Lakeside's premier bookstore. Come and curl up next to our cozy fire with a good book and a cup of one of our classic coffees. Meet with an author at one of our discussion sessions, or stop by for live music every Friday and Saturday night. Bring the kids any afternoon for storytime and snacks.

For large graphics you can use Composer to specify alternative images for the graphic. An **alternative image** is an image that gives users something to look at as they wait for the browser to finish retrieving the larger image from the Web server. You can also specify that text will appear as a browser retrieves a graphic image. This is useful for users who are accessing your page with a text browser incapable of displaying the image. In those cases, they can still read your text description.

Another option to consider for your graphic is the space between the graphic and the surrounding text. As shown in Figure 4-32 you can set up your page to have the text closely hugging the graphic or you can add extra space between the image and the text.

Figure 4-32 ◀
Spacing
between image
and text

less space between
graphic and text

more space between
graphic and text

Avalon Books is Lakeside's premier bookstore. Come and curl up next to our cozy fire with a good book and a cup of one of our classic coffees. Meet with an author at one of our discussion sessions, or stop by for live music every Friday and Saturday night. Bring the kids any afternoon for storytime and snacks.

Avalon Books is Lakeside's premier bookstore. Come and curl up next to our cozy fire with a good book and a cup of one of our classic coffees. Meet with an author at one of our discussion sessions, or stop by for live music every Friday and Saturday night. Bring the kids any afternoon for storytime and snacks.

Considering these various options for your graphic, you decide to wrap the paragraph to the right of the graphic you just inserted. This will remove much of the blank space between the horizontal line and the start of the paragraph. You also decide to add space between the graphic and the text in the paragraph. Finally, since the graphic is already small, you feel you do not need to have an alternative representation, but you will include a text description for users who have text browsers.

To modify the properties of an inline image:

1. Right-click the inline image and then click **Image Properties**.

2. Click the **Alt. Text / LowRes** button and type **Come to Avalon Books!** in the Alternate text box. Click the **OK** button.

3. In the Text alignment section, click the button that wraps text to the right 🔲.

4. In the Space around image area, type **5** in the Left and right box to increase the space around the image to five pixels. The completed dialog box should look like Figure 4-33.

Figure 4-33 ◀
Modifying inline
image
properties

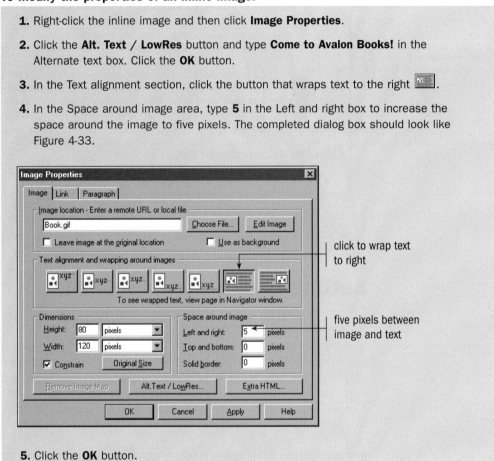

5. Click the **OK** button.

You can't see the effect of wrapping text around an image in Composer—instead you must view the page with the Navigator browser. You decide to save your changes to the page and view it there.

To view your changes in the browser:

1. Click the **Save** button 🔲 on the Composition toolbar.

2. Click the **Preview** button 🔲 on the Composition toolbar. Figure 4-34 displays the revised Avalon page.

Figure 4-34
Inline image
in browser

text is wrapped to
right, five pixels
from graphic

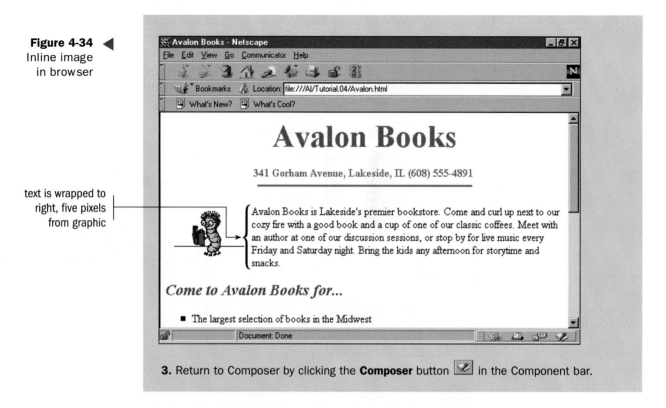

3. Return to Composer by clicking the **Composer** button in the Component bar.

Setting Background Properties

Composer allows you to specify a particular color for your background or a particular background image. When you use a graphic as your background, it appears over and over in a pattern across the document window. Many Web pages employ interesting background images to great effect. You should, however, be careful to minimize the size of the graphic image you use. A large graphic image will cause your page to take much longer to load, causing some users to cancel the page before even getting a chance to view it. Generally the size of a graphic used for a page background should not exceed 20 kilobytes. You should also be careful not to let the background image overwhelm the text.

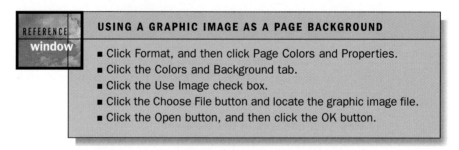

REFERENCE
window

USING A GRAPHIC IMAGE AS A PAGE BACKGROUND

- Click Format, and then click Page Colors and Properties.
- Click the Colors and Background tab.
- Click the Use Image check box.
- Click the Choose File button and locate the graphic image file.
- Click the Open button, and then click the OK button.

You've created an image for the Avalon Books background using the store logo. You've been careful to make the image small and unobtrusive.

To change the background of your Web page:

1. Click **Format** and then click **Page Colors and Properties**.

2. Click the **Colors and Background** tab.

3. Click the **Use Image** check box.

4. Click the **Choose File** button and locate the file **AB.gif** in the Tutorial.04 folder on your Student Disk.

5. Click the **Open** button, then click the **OK** button.

The image background appears throughout the background. You'll take a look at the final page in the browser momentarily, but first you want to check the page's spelling before you finish your work.

Checking Spelling

Like most word processors, Composer provides a spell-checker that checks the spelling of your Web page. Whenever it locates a word its dictionary does not recognize, it lists suggestions that you can double-click to replace the misspelled word. If the spelling of the word is correct, you can click the Ignore button. The spell checker often identifies proper names, such as Avalon, as words whose spelling you should check.

To check your page's spelling:

1. Click the **Spelling** button [Spelling] on the Composition toolbar. The spell checker will most likely not recognize Avalon as a word in its dictionary, so it marks it and suggests replacement words. See Figure 4-35.

Figure 4-35 ◀
Spell-checking
your Web page

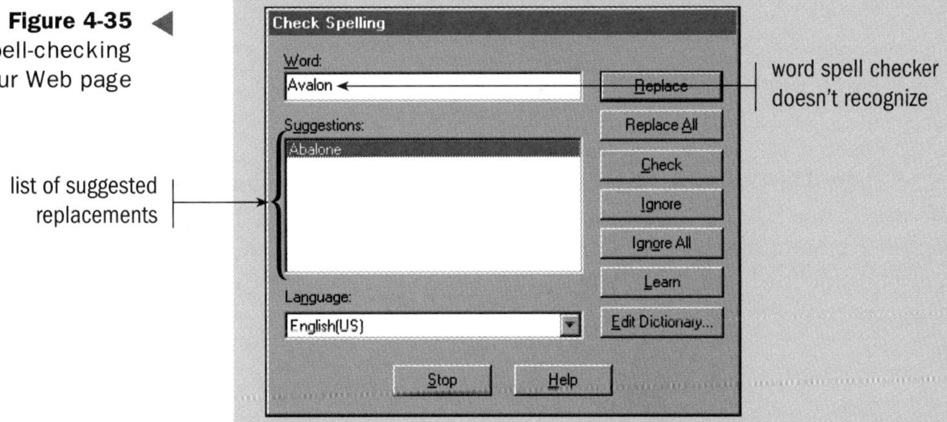

list of suggested
replacements

word spell checker
doesn't recognize

2. Click the **Ignore All** button if Avalon is spelled correctly; the spell checker will no longer ask you about the spelling of that word. If it is not spelled correctly, type the correct spelling in the Word box and then click the **Replace** button.

3. Continue through the spell check, clicking **Ignore** for words spelled correctly. If the spell checker locates a word that truly is misspelled, check the Suggestions box, and if the proper spelling is there, double-click it. Otherwise correct it manually in the Word box.

4. Click the **Done** button when you are done with the spell check.

The page is finished. Save the page to your Student Disk and view the final version in the Navigator browser.

To view the final version of your work:

1. Click the **Save** button [Save].

2. Click the **Preview** button [Preview] to return to the Navigator browser. Figure 4-36 displays the final version of the page.

Figure 4-36 ◀
Final Avalon
Books page
in browser
window

background graphic
displayed in pattern

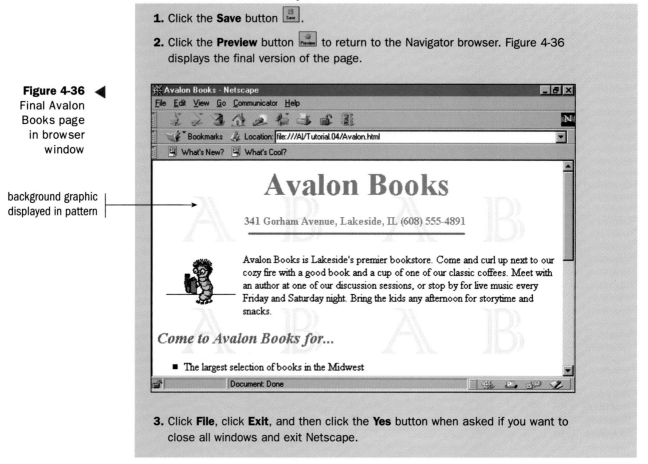

3. Click **File**, click **Exit**, and then click the **Yes** button when asked if you want to close all windows and exit Netscape.

You show Mark the final version of the page. He's pleased with the work you've done and will contact his Internet service provider about posting this page on the store's Internet account. Since you've done such a good job creating this page, he asks that you be responsible for keeping the page up to date. Since creating the page was so easy with Composer, you quickly agree.

Quick Check

1 Explain the difference between expressing line width in percent of window vs. pixels.

2 What is the difference between an inline graphic and an external graphic?

3 Name two file formats you can use for inline graphics.

4 If you want to use a Windows Bitmap image (file extension bmp) as an inline image on your Web page, what should you do to it first?

5 What is the difference between an interlaced graphic and a noninterlaced graphic?

6 How would you set up a horizontal line so that it is centered on a page and covers 25% of the width of the document window?

7 What should you watch out for when using a graphic image for your page background?

8 If you display a picture on your Web page, why might you want to enter a text description of that picture?

9 True or False: the Composer spell-checker only highlights misspelled words.

Tutorial Assignments

It's been a week since you created the Avalon Books Web page. Mark approaches you with a list of things he wants to add and change on the page. In the upcoming week, the bookstore will host the following events:

Monday, 10/14
    A lecture given by Professor Patricia Fuller on *The Art of Maurice Sendak*

Thursday, 10/17
    Peter Daynes will sign copies of his new book, *Glencoe Memories*

Friday, 10/18
    Classical music by the Lakeside Quartet

Mark asks you to add these events to the page and remove the old event list. He also wants you to include a new item in the bulleted list of Avalon Books attractions: "An impressive collection of used and out-of-print books."

As for the appearance of the page, he wants you to change the color of the activity days so that they match the blue color of the section heading. He also has a new graphic image that he wants you to use in place of the bookworm image. He has the image stored in a file called "Book2.gif." When inserting the image he wants you to increase the space between the graphic image and the text in the surrounding paragraph. Finally you should replace the background image with the new Avalon Books logo, found in the "AB2.gif" file. The final version of this page should appear as shown in Figure 4-37.

Figure 4-37 ◄

Avalon Books

341 Gorham Avenue, Lakeside, IL (608) 555-4891

Avalon Books is Lakeside's premier bookstore. Come and curl up next to our cozy fire with a good book and a cup of one of our classic coffees. Meet with an author at one of our discussion sessions, or stop by for live music every Friday and Saturday night. Bring the kids any afternoon for storytime and snacks.

Come to Avalon Books for...

- The largest selection of books in the Midwest
- Comfortable reading rooms
- Coffe, wines and delicious desserts as you read
- A computer lab for kids with the best educational software titles
- An impressive collection of used and out-of-print books

This week's events

Monday, 10/14

A lecture given by Professor Patricia Fuller on *The Art of Maurice Sendak*

Thursday, 10/17

Peter Daynes will sign copies of his new book, *Glencoe Memories*

Friday 10/18

Classical music by the Lakeside Quartet

To complete this tutorial assignment:

1. Open the "Avalon.htm" file that you created in this tutorial in Composer.

2. Save the page as "Avalon2" to the TAssign folder on your Student Disk.

3. Change the title located on the General tab in the Page Properties dialog box to "Avalon Books 2." Change the description box to read "This is the revised version of the Avalon Books home page."

4. Add the item, "An impressive collection of used and out-of-print books" to the end of the bulleted list.

5. Delete the outdated events list and replace it with the new events list. Use the same indentation.

6. Change the color of the day to match the color of the section heading.

7. Replace the "Book.gif" graphic with the "Book2.gif" graphic found in the TAssign folder of the Tutorial.04 folder on your Student Disk.

8. Change the left/right spacing around the graphic to 9 pixels but continue to wrap the paragraph to the right around the graphic. If the bulleted list wraps to the right of the graphic, add a blank line above the list. Then the list will no longer wrap around the graphic and will be properly aligned to the left margin.

9. Replace the "AB.gif" background graphic with the "AB2.gif" graphic in the TAssign folder of the Tutorial.04 folder on your Student Disk.

10. Spell-check the Web page.

11. Save the Web page.

12. View the revised page in the Netscape browser.

13. Print a copy of the page for your instructor.

14. Close Communicator.

Case Problems

1. Creating a Web Page for the River Bar Seafood Restaurant You work as a manager at the River Bar Seafood Restaurant in Woolworth, Missouri. The owner, Gwen Foucoult, has asked you to create a Web page listing the weekly specials at the restaurant. She shows you a printout of what she wants on the page, shown in Figure 4-38.

Figure 4-38 ◀

The River Bar Seafood Restaurant
211 West State St., Woolworth, 555-4532

Stop by the River Bar for the best in seafood, or call us today and order one of our delicious dishes for carryout!

This Week's Specials

Grilled Norwegian Salmon
Grilled salmon topped with Dijon mustard sauce, served with vegetables and roasted red potatoes. $15.95

Grilled Yellowfin Tuna
Grilled and topped with cilantro-lime salsa. Served with roasted red potatoes and vegetables. $15.95

Scallops with Linguine
Jumbo scallops with mushroom and herbs in lemon cream sauce. $14.95

Butterflied Shrimp
Tender shrimp lightly breaded and fried, served with vegetable and rice pilaf. $15.25

Grilled Halibut
Atlantic halibut steak seasoned with lemon and pepper and grilled, served with vegetables and roasted potatoes. $14.95

Using Figure 4-38 as a guide, create the River Bar page.
To complete this case problem:

1. Open Composer to a blank page.

2. Enter properties for your document, giving the page the title "River Bar Specials".

3. Enter your name as the page author.

4. Type "Weekly specials at the River Bar seafood restaurant" in the Description box.

5. Save the page as "Seafood.htm" to the Cases folder in the Tutorial.04 folder on your Student Disk.

6. Enter the text shown in Figure 4-38.

7. Format the main heading using the Heading 2 style. Then apply an interesting, applicable font to it. Center the heading.

8. Format the restaurant address using the Heading 5 style. Center the address.

9. Insert a horizontal line after the restaurant address. Use the default line style.

10. Enter a brief description of the restaurant in the Normal style.

11. Format the heading "This Week's Specials" with the Heading 3 style. Center the heading.

12. Format the name of each dish with the Heading 4 style.

13. Indent the description of each dish.

14. Use the graphic file "Fish.gif," located in the Cases folder of the Tutorial.04 folder on your Student Disk, as a background for your page.

15. Save your changes to the page and spell-check the page.

16. Print the page for your instructor. On the back of the printed page, write the name of the font you used to format the main heading in step 7.

17. Close Communicator.

2. Displaying a Lecture Outline   You are the teaching assistant for history professor Clifford Foote. Starting this semester, he is putting his lecture outlines on the Web for students to view. He wants you to create the lecture outline for his September 22 lecture on Abraham Lincoln's life prior to the Civil War.

To create such a page you will have to use numbered lists. With Composer you specify the symbol used for the list items. You can use Roman Numerals (I, II, III, IV...), capital letters (A, B, C...), numbers (1, 2, 3...), and so forth. For Professor Foote's lecture outline, you will format major points with the Roman Numerals format. You will also indent minor points, listing them with capital letters.

The professor also has a photo from the Lincoln mausoleum that he wants you to place on the page. The photo has been saved to the file "Lincoln.gif."

The page should include a heading for the history course, the professor's name, and the date of the lecture. The professor also wants you to place the text on a solid blue background. The complete Web page should look like Figure 4-39.

Figure 4-39 ◀

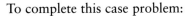

U.S. History 1722 - 1872

Professor: Clifford Foote

Lecture outline from September 22

Life of Lincoln

I. Early Life
    A. Born 1809 in Hodgenville, KY
    B. Moved to Spencer County, IN in 1811
    C. Settled in Macon County, IL in 1831
    D. Worked as a rail splitter and grocery store
       clerk
    E. Captain in Black Hawk war in 1832
II. Politician and Lawyer
    A. Defeated in run for state legislature in 1832
    B. Elected to state legislature in 1834 as a Whig
    C. Admitted to the bar in 1837 and joined law
       partnership
    D. Served in U.S. Congress from 1846-1848
III. Rise to national prominence
    A. Campaigned for newly-formed Republican party in 1856
    B. Lincoln-Douglas debates in 1858
    C. House Divided Speech in 1858
    D. Republican presidential nominee in 1860
    E. Elected president in 1860

To complete this case problem:

1. Open a blank document in Composer.

2. On the General tab of the Page Properties dialog box, type "September 22 lecture" in the Title box.

3. Type your name in the Properties Author box.

4. Type "The outline of the 9/22 lecture in U.S. history" in the Description box.

5. Set the page background color to blue. To do this, use the Colors and Background tab on the Page Properties dialog box, click the Background button, and select a light blue shade.

6. Save the page as "Lincoln.htm" to the Cases folder in the Tutorial.04 folder on your Student Disk.

7. Type the main heading "U.S. History 1722-1872", formatted with the Heading 1 style and centered on the page.

8. Change the color of the main heading to red (third row, second column in the list of basic colors).

9. Type the secondary heading "Professor: Clifford Foote", formatted with the Normal style and centered.

10. Bold the title of Professor.

11. Type "Lecture outline from September 22", formatted with the Normal style, italicized, and left-aligned.

12. Type "Life of Lincoln", formatted with the Heading 3 style and left-aligned.

13. Enter the three main outline heads as an ordered list, and use the Roman Numeral style for the list items. You can change ordered list styles on the Paragraph tab of the Character Properties dialog box. Click the Number Style list arrow.

14. Within each main point, enter the subpoints as an ordered list.

15. Indent the subpoints, apply the List Item style to the subpoints, and use the Capital Letter style for each group of subpoints.

16. At the beginning of the line reading "Life of Lincoln" insert the "Lincoln.gif" image, available in the Cases folder of the Tutorial.04 folder on your Student Disk.

17. Format the image so that text will wrap around the image on the left.

18. Add a 2 pixel width border to the image.

19. Save and spell-check your completed page.

20. View the page in the Netscape browser and print the page.

21. Hand in the printout to your instructor.

22. Close Communicator.

3. Using Preformatted Text on the Weber State Weather Page You are in charge of a weather page at Weber State University. You use a program that creates temperature charts like the one shown in Figure 4-40.

Figure 4-40 ◀

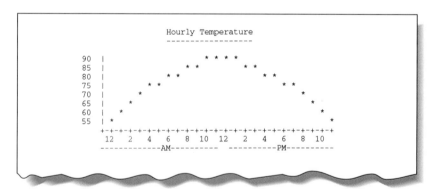

This chart uses a monospace font that allots the same amount of space to each character. Because it is monospace font, the characters in the chart are perfectly aligned. However, the normal font used by most Web browsers is not monospaced. Using the normal font would result in a chart that is out of alignment. You can solve this problem by using another of the styles provided with Composer called "Formatted." The Formatted tag displays text in a monospace font. The temperature chart has been placed in the file "Temp.txt" in the Cases folder of the Tutorial.04 folder on your Student Disk. By copying the temperature chart from the Temp.txt file and pasting it into Composer, try to create a Web page detailing the previous day's temperature variations.

To complete this case problem:

1. Open Composer to a blank page.

2. Open the Page Properties dialog box to the General tab.

3. Type "Weber State Weather Page" as the title of the page.

4. Enter your name in the Author box.

5. Type "This page displays a temperature chart from the previous day" in the Description box.

6. Save the page as "Temp" in the Cases folder in the Tutorial.04 folder on your Student Disk.

7. Return to the document window and type the text "Yesterday's Temperature Chart" at the top of the page.

8. Format the heading with the Heading 1 style and center it on the page.

9. Beneath the heading, type yesterday's date.

10. Center the date and format it with the Heading 5 style.

11. Insert a horizontal line beneath the date.

12. Start Notepad (click the Start button, point to Programs, point to Accessories, and then click Notepad). Open the file "Temp.txt" in the Cases folder of the Tutorial.04 folder on your Student Disk.

13. Copy the temperature chart (click Edit, click Select All, click Edit again, and then click Copy) and then close Notepad.

14. Return to the Temp page.

15. Insert a new paragraph underneath the horizontal line and format it with the Formatted tag on the Paragraph style list.

16. Click the Left Align button to align any Formatted text with the left edge of the window.

17. Paste the temperature chart into the new line (click Edit and then click Paste).

18. Save the changes you made to the Temp page.

19. View the page in the Netscape browser.

20. Print the page and hand in the printout to your instructor.

21. Close Communicator.

4. Creating a Realty Listing You work as a realty agent for TK Realty. Just recently your company has started putting listings on the World Wide Web. You're responsible for creating your own listing. One of the houses you want to create a Web page for is a lakefront house located at 22 Northshore Drive. The owners have given you this description that they want on the page:

"This is a must see. Large waterfront home overlooking Lake Mills. It comes complete with 3 bedrooms, a huge master bedroom, hot tub, family room, large office, and three-car garage. Wood boat ramp. Great condition."

The main points about the house are:

- 2300 sq. feet

- 15 years old

- Updated electrical and heat

- Asking price: $230,000

You also have a photo of the house, saved as "House.jpg" in the Cases folder on the Tutorial.04 folder on your Student Disk. Using this information, create a page describing the house to interested house-hunters. You may choose any design for the page, but it must include the following elements:

1. a title, description, and your name in the Page Properties dialog box

2. a main heading

3. the photo of the house

4. a bulleted list describing the features of the house

5. a paragraph containing the owner's description

6. information on how to contact you, in italics

Save the page you create in the Cases folder of the Tutorial.04 folder on your Student Disk with the name "Realty".

Creating a Hypertext Document

Creating a Web Presentation

OBJECTIVES

In this tutorial you will:

- Create targets for links

- Create hypertext links to targets on the same page

- Learn the principles of structuring a Web presentation

- Create hypertext links to other pages on the same computer

- Create links to specific items on other pages

- Create links to other Web pages on the Internet

- Create links to e-mail addresses

- Publish a page on the Web

CASE

The Findlay Farmhouse Bed and Breakfast

Prince Edward Island in Canada is a popular summer vacation spot. The island is known for its natural beauty and peaceful setting. Visitors to the island can choose their lodging from several attractive inns and picturesque bed and breakfasts. One of the most popular bed and breakfasts on the island is the Findlay Farmhouse outside the town of Summerside. The proprietors, Ian and Fiona Findlay, have owned the inn for many years. Several years ago they bought a computer to help manage their business, and recently set up an Internet connection. The Findlays want to advertise their bed and breakfast on the Internet in hopes that it will generate new business. Fiona has started creating a page for the Findlay Farmhouse, and hopes you can help her finish it.

Fiona explains that she has organized information about the Findlay Farmhouse and its surroundings into five topics, each with a Heading 2 style heading, with the following titles:

- Your home on Prince Edward Island

- What are they saying about us?

- Area attractions

- How do I get there?

- For more information

Fiona tells you that she has also created two supplementary Web pages, Bio and Events, that contain information on the Findlay family and area events. She would like users to be able to access the Bio and Events pages from the Findlay Farmhouse page, jump to other pages on Prince Edward Island from the Findlay Farmhouse page, and be able to send her e-mail messages. You tell her she can accomplish all this with hypertext links. Then you suggest that she could make her page, which is rather long, more user-friendly by adding links that help users move around the page more easily. Fiona agrees that would be a good idea, so the two of you get to work.

SESSION

5.1

In this session you will learn how to create targets within a Web document and to create hypertext links to those targets.

Setting Targets

As you've seen by browsing the Web, Web pages contain hypertext, or links that you can select, usually by clicking the mouse, to jump instantly to another location. In addition to making access to other documents easy, hypertext links provide some important organizational benefits.

For example, when your Web page is too long to fit on a single screen, you can help users quickly locate the information they need by providing hypertext links to important points within the page. A typical screen can display only a small section of a long page, and this could be a problem for users in a hurry. Because many Web users glance at a page and then move on, you should make your page's topics as accessible as possible. You can do this by placing links at the beginning that point to the main topics on the page. When readers click the link, they jump to that section of the document.

To create links that jump to a specific point on a Web page, you must first insert a target at the destination location. A **target**, also called an **anchor**, is a reference point that identifies a specific location on the page. Once you insert a target, you can then refer to that particular location. You create the link and indicate the target to which the link points. Figure 5-1 illustrates how the target you create will work as a reference point for a link.

Figure 5-1 ◀
Link pointing
to target
within the
same Web
document

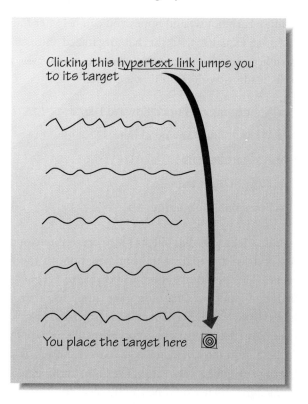

Clicking this hypertext link jumps you
to its target

You place the target here

Targets do not appear in the browser, but you can view them in Composer. Targets don't have to just be text. You can also designate inline images to act as targets.

For the Findlay Web page, you decide to create five targets—one target at each of the five section headings of the document. You can then create links at the beginning of the page that point to each of the five targets. A user can click one of the links to jump to its target without having to scroll through the page to reach it. Figure 5-2 shows the location of the five targets you will create on the Findlay Web page.

Figure 5-2
Targets in
the Findlay
Web page

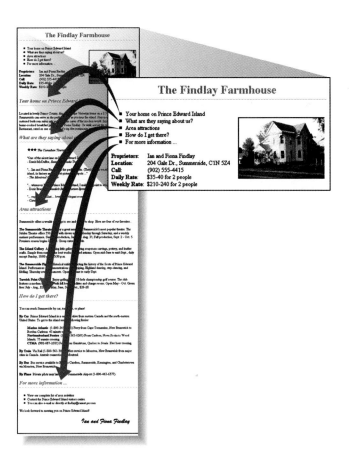

Fiona stored her page as Findlay.htm. You'll open the file and save it with a new name, Findlay2.htm, so you can work with the original later if you want.

To open the Findlay.htm file in Composer and save it with a new name:

1. Launch Communicator and insert your Student Disk in the drive.

2. If your computer tries to initiate an Internet connection, click the **Cancel** button. You do not need an Internet connection to use Composer.

3. If the Navigator browser tries to load a home page, click the **Stop** button [Stop].

4. Click **File**, then click **Open Page**.

5. Click the **Choose File** button, locate the **Findlay** file from the Tutorial.05 folder on your Student Disk, and then click the **Open** button.

6. Click the **Composer** option button, and then click the **Open** button.

7. Click **File**, then click **Save As**.

8. Type **Findlay2** in the File name box, then click the **Save** button.

9. Scroll down the entire page to view the location of the five section headings.

First you will create the five targets. Composer makes it easy for you to create a target. The first target you create will be for the heading "Your home on Prince Edward Island."

To set a target in your Web page:

1. Scroll the page to the first section heading, "Your home on Prince Edward Island." Make sure you are viewing the section heading, not the bulleted list.

2. Click at the start of the section heading to place the blinking insertion point at the beginning of the line.

   TROUBLE? If you click too far to the left of the section heading, you highlight the heading. Make sure the blinking insertion point is just to the left of the heading.

3. Click the **Target** button 🔲 on the Composition toolbar.

   TROUBLE? If the Composer toolbars aren't visible, click View, and then click Show Composition Toolbar. Then click View and click Show Formatting Toolbar.

4. Type **Your home** in the target name text box as shown in Figure 5-3.

Figure 5-3 ◀
Setting a target

click here to
insert target

target name

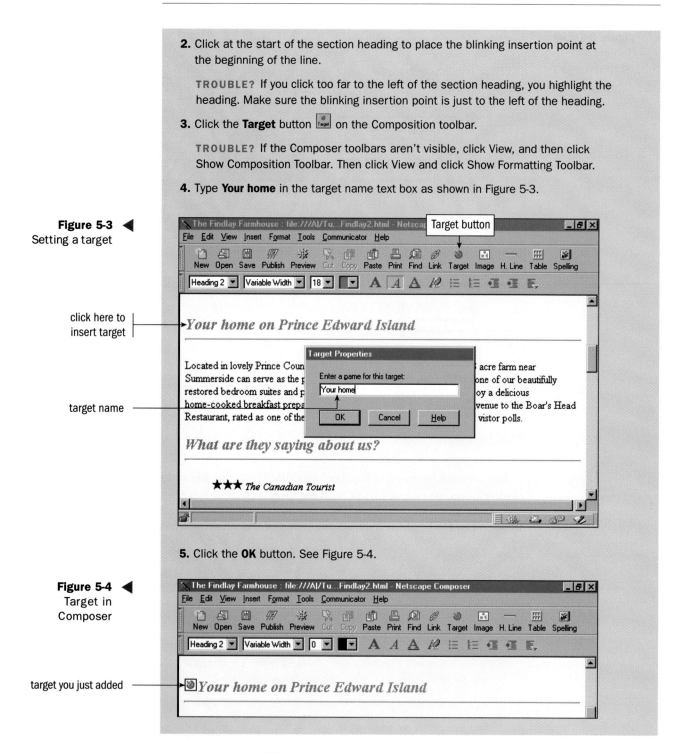

5. Click the **OK** button. See Figure 5-4.

Figure 5-4 ◀
Target in
Composer

target you just added

The target icon 🔲 indicates the presence of a target on a Web page. This icon appears only in Composer—not in the browser. If you ever forget the name you gave the target, you can pass your mouse pointer over the target icon and its name appears in a yellow box.

You're ready to add the rest of the targets, one for each section heading. You can type in any characters or blanks spaces into the target name. Be sure you pay attention to case. A target named "home" is different from one named "HOME."

To add your other hypertext targets:

1. Scroll down to the heading, "What are they saying about us?" then click the left side of the heading.

2. Click the **Target** button and type **Reviews**, then click the **OK** button.

3. Scroll down to the heading, "Area attractions," then click the left side of the heading.

4. Add a target named **Attractions**.

5. Scroll down to the heading, "How do I get there?" then add a target named **Travel**.

6. Scroll down to the heading, "For more information," then add a target named **More Info**.

Now all five targets are in place. You are ready to create hypertext links to the targets.

Hypertext Links

With Composer you can insert links into a Web page either by turning existing text into a hypertext link or by inserting linked text directly into the page.

Changing Existing Text to Hypertext

You can change existing text to a hypertext link simply by selecting the text, then clicking the Link button and indicating the target to which you want the link to point. The Findlay Farmhouse page begins with a bulleted list that corresponds to the five section headings. By changing the items in this list to hypertext links, you enable users to jump directly to a target. You begin by creating the link to the first section heading, which has a target named Your home.

To change the list item to a hypertext link:

1. Scroll to the top of the page.

2. Select **Your home on Prince Edward Island** from the bulleted list.

3. Click the **Link** button on the Composition toolbar.

4. If necessary, click the Link tab.

5. Click **Your home** from the list of named targets in the current document. Figure 5-5 shows the completed dialog box.

Figure 5-5 ◀
Selecting a
target for a
hypertext link

text will be converted
to hypertext link

# indicates a target

target list

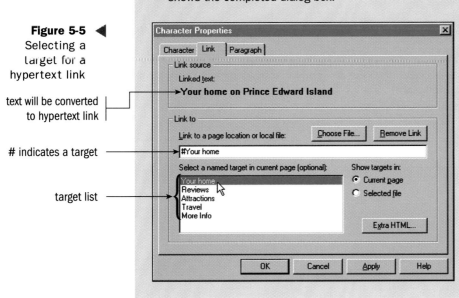

6. Click the **OK** button, then click the page to deselect the link. The text, "Your home on Prince Edward Island," is now underlined and in a different color as shown in Figure 5-6, indicating that it is a hypertext link.

Figure 5-6 ◀
Hypertext link
you just added

hypertext link

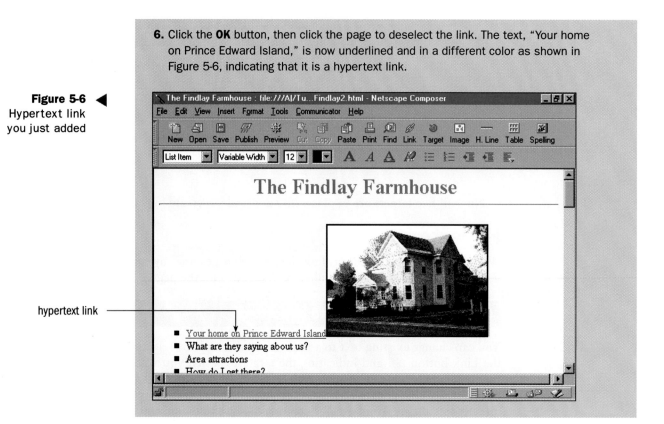

You can confirm the location of a hypertext link in Composer by moving your mouse pointer over the linked text. The link's target appears in the status bar. Note that the name of the target is prefaced by a pound sign (#). All target names are prefaced by this symbol to differentiate them from other names such as file names or document locations.

Using the same technique you just learned, turn the other items in the bulleted list to hypertext links.

To convert the rest of the list to hypertext links:

1. Select the list item, **What are they saying about us?** then link the text to the **Reviews** target.

2. Select the list item, **Area attractions**, then link the text to the **Attractions** target.

3. Select the list item, **How do I get there?** then link the text to the **Travel** target.

4. Select the list item, **For more information...**, then link the text to the **More Info** target. Figure 5-7 shows the completed list of hypertext links.

Netscape Communicator

Figure 5-7 ◀
Inserted links

new links →

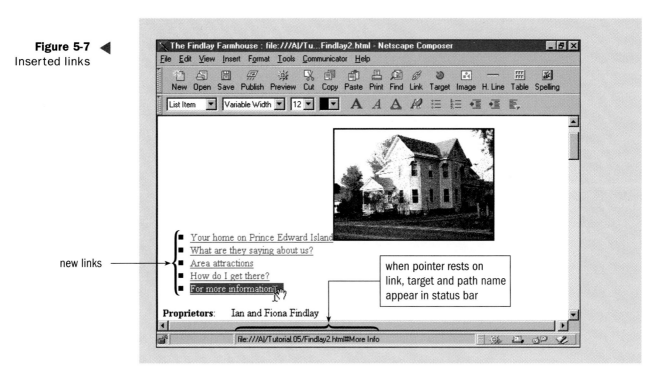

Users can now use the bulleted list to jump to any heading on the Findlay page.

Inserting New Hypertext Links

Although the Findlay Farmhouse page had a bulleted list of topics ready for you to convert to hypertext, often you'll want to create a new link from scratch. For example, you notice that there is no easy way of returning to the top of the Findlay Farmhouse page, aside from scrolling. You realize that it might be helpful to include a hypertext link pointing to the top of the page. This is a common feature of long pages. To create this hypertext link, you first must create a target at the top of the page.

To add a target to the top of the page:

1. If necessary, scroll to the top of the document, then click to the left of the main heading, **The Findlay Farmhouse.**

2. Click the **Target** button.

3. Type **Top** in the target name box, then click the **OK** button.

Now you create a new hypertext link at the bottom of the document that points to the target you just created at the top of the page. You can enter the link text directly from the Link Properties dialog box.

To insert hypertext into the document:

1. Scroll down to the bottom of the page.

2. Click at the end of the line: **We look forward to meeting you on Prince Edward Island!** then press **Enter**.

3. Click the **Link** button 🖉.

4. Click **Top** from the list of targets.

5. Click the **Enter text to display for a new link** box, then type **Return to the top of the page**. See Figure 5-8.

Figure 5-8 ◀
Entering text
for a new link

text will appear as
a hypertext link

target

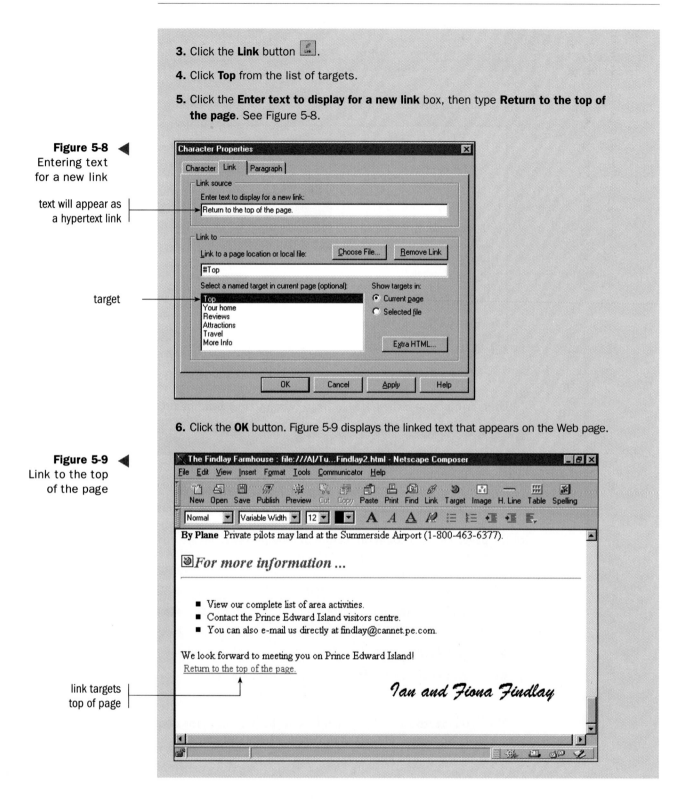

6. Click the **OK** button. Figure 5-9 displays the linked text that appears on the Web page.

Figure 5-9 ◀
Link to the top
of the page

link targets
top of page

You are finished adding links that help users navigate the Findlay page.

Testing Links

Once you have entered links into a hypertext document, you should test them in the Navigator browser to make sure they jump to the correct targets.

To test the links in the Netscape browser:

1. Click the **Save** button and then click the **Preview** button on the Composition toolbar. You can now verify that your hypertext links are working correctly.

2. Move the mouse pointer over the list item, **Your home on Prince Edward Island**. Note that the mouse pointer changes to 🖑 and the status bar shows the name of the file, drive, and folder in which the file is located, followed by a pound sign (#) and the name of the target, Your home. See Figure 5-10.

Figure 5-10 ◀
Testing a link

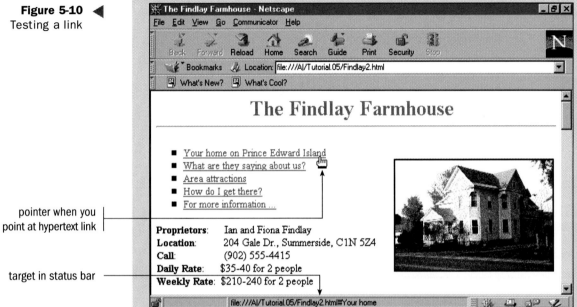

pointer when you point at hypertext link

target in status bar

3. Click the **Your home on Prince Edward Island** link. The browser jumps to the Your home target and displays the Your home on Prince Edward Island heading. See Figure 5-11.

Figure 5-11 ◀
Jumping to a link's destination

location of Your home target; target icon doesn't appear in browser

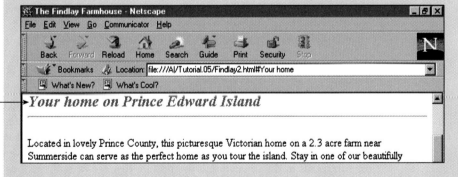

4. Repeat steps 2-4 with the other links on the page to verify that they are all working properly.

   TROUBLE? If you discover a link that is not working properly, go back to Composer by clicking the Composer button 🖉. Right-click the link in Composer, click Link Properties, click the Link tab, click the correct target, and then click the OK button.

You're finished adding hypertext links to the Findlay Web page. Users can now efficiently navigate to different locations on the page. You decide to take a break.

To close all the Netscape windows:

1. Click **File**, then click **Exit**.

2. Click the **Yes** button to close all windows and exit Netscape.

Quick Check

1. What is a target? When is it necessary?

2. How do you create a target with Composer?

3. Are target names case sensitive or case insensitive?

4. How do you convert existing text to hypertext with Composer?

5. How is the presence of a target indicated in a URL?

6. How do you create new hypertext with Composer?

7. Where do you test links?

SESSION 5.2

In this session you will create a Web presentation that consists of several documents connected together with hypertext links. You'll learn how to control the development of such multidocument structures through the technique of storyboarding.

Principles of Storyboarding

When you are developing a Web page, one of the first things you must ask yourself is whether you intend to develop and include additional pages on related topics. A structure that contains the primary Web page, additional related pages, and the hypertext links that allow users to move among the pages, is known as a **Web presentation**. Web presentations are usually created by the same person or group, and the pages within a Web presentation usually have the same look and feel.

When you plan your Web presentation, you should determine exactly how you want to relate the pages using hypertext links. Charting the relationship between all the pages in your Web presentation is a technique known as **storyboarding**. Storyboarding your Web pages before you create links helps you determine which structure will work best for the type of information you're presenting and helps you avoid some common problems. You want to make sure readers can navigate easily from page to page without getting lost.

Fiona reminds you that she has developed two other pages for the Findlay Farmhouse Web presentation: Bio, a directory of people on the island; and Events, a list of activities and organizations in the area. Fiona would like readers who access her page to be able to reach either of these pages from the main Findlay Farmhouse page, as shown in Figure 5-12.

Figure 5-12 ◀
Findlay
Farmhouse
Web
presentation

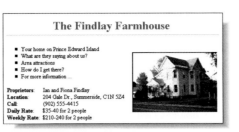

Findlay Farmhouse page

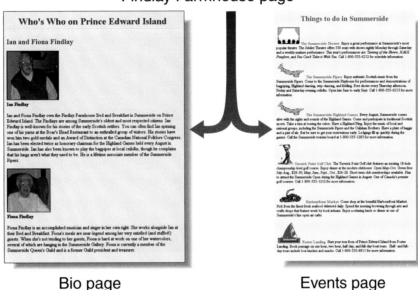

Bio page   Events page

You tell Fiona she should think about the basic principles of structuring Web presentations to decide how to link the three pages together.

Linear Structures

Web presentations can be structured in a number of ways. Examining basic structures can help you decide how to design your Web presentation. Figure 5-13 shows a storyboard for one common structure, the **linear structure**, in which each page is linked to the next and previous pages in an ordered chain of pages.

Figure 5-13 ◀
Linear
structure

in this structure you
can jump only from
one page to the next
or previous page

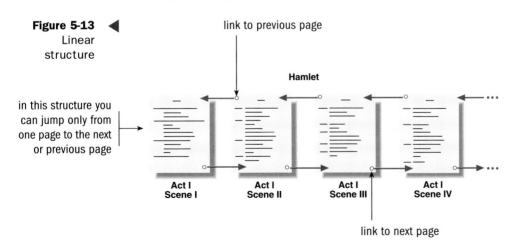

You might use this type of structure in Web pages that have a well-defined order. For example, if you are trying to create a Web presentation of Shakespeare's Hamlet, you could create a single Web page for each scene from the play. By using a linear structure, you make it easy for users to progress back and forth through the play. Each hypertext link takes them to either the previous scene or the next scene.

You might, however, want to make it easier for users to return immediately to the opening scene rather than backtrack through several scenes. Figure 5-14 shows how you could include a link in each page that jumps directly back to the first page.

Figure 5-14 ◀
Augmented
linear
structure

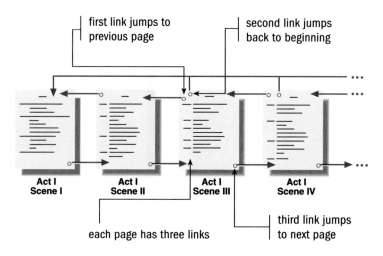

Hierarchical Structures

Another popular structure is the hierarchical structure of Web pages shown in Figure 5-15. A **hierarchical structure** starts with a general topic that includes links to more specific topics. Each specific topic includes links to yet more specialized topics, and so on. In a hierarchical structure, users can move easily from the general to the specific and back again.

Figure 5-15 ◀
Hierarchical
structure

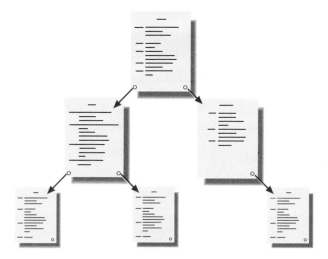

As with the linear structure, including a link to the top of the structure on each page gives users an easy way back to the hierarchy tree. Figure 5-16 shows a storyboard for this kind of Web presentation.

Figure 5-16 ◀
Augmented
hierarchical
structure

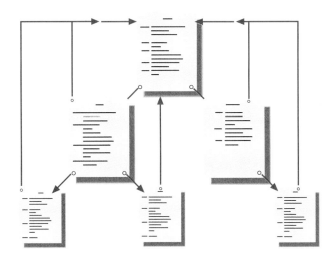

Mixed Structures

You can also combine structures. Figure 5-17 shows a hierarchical structure in which each page level is related in a linear structure. You might use this system for the Hamlet Web site to let the user move from scene to scene linearly or from a specific scene to the general act to the overall play.

Figure 5-17 ◀
Combination
of linear and
hierarchical
structures

overall structure
is hierarchical

the scenes

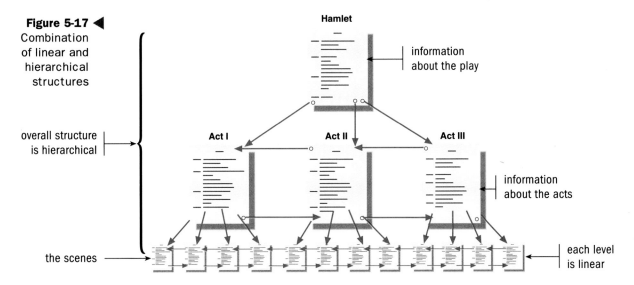

Hamlet

information
about the play

Act I   Act II   Act III

information
about the acts

each level
is linear

As these examples show, a little foresight can go a long way in making your Web pages easier to use. The best time to organize a structure is when you first start creating multiple pages and those pages are small and easy to manage. If you're not careful, you might end up with a structure like the one shown in Figure 5-18.

Figure 5-18 ◀
Web
presentation
with no
coherent
structure

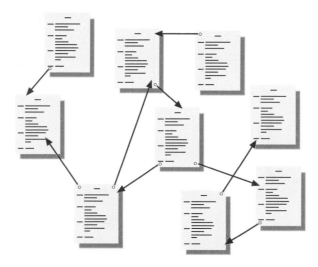

Many of the pages in this Web presentation are isolated from one another, and there is no clear path from one document to another. A user won't know what content to expect when jumping from one link to another. Nor will users ever be sure if they have viewed all possible pages.

Creating Links to Other Documents

You and Fiona discuss the type of structure that will work best for the Findlay Farmhouse Web presentation. Fiona wants users to access the Findlay Farmhouse page first, and then both the Bio page and the Events page from the Findlay Farmhouse page. To make navigation easy, she wants hypertext links on both the Bio and Events pages that jump back to the Findlay Farmhouse page. Fiona doesn't see a need to include a hypertext link between the Bio page and the Events page. Based on her recommendations, you draw the storyboard shown in Figure 5-19. Fiona looks it over and agrees that this is what she had in mind.

Figure 5-19 ◀
Structure of
the Findlay
Farmhouse Web
presentation

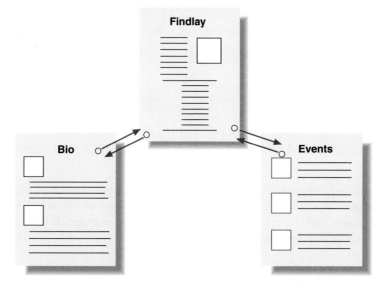

Opening Multiple Documents

Fiona's Web presentation has three pages, and you'd like to be able to work with all of them at once. When you want to open multiple documents in Communicator, a new Composer window opens for each document. The Windows taskbar will then show multiple Composer buttons with the page's title showing on the button. If there are many buttons on the taskbar and the titles aren't visible, you can identify which button corresponds to which Web page by pointing at a button in the taskbar and examining the button name that appears. You need to open Findlay2 (the page you were working on in Session 5.1), Bio, and Events, and then you need to save Bio as Bio2 and Events as Events2, so you don't alter the original files.

To open and rename the files in different Composer windows:

1. Start Communicator. You do not have to connect to the Internet or load your home page.

2. Click **File**, then click **Open Page**.

3. Locate and open **Findlay2.htm** in the Tutorial.05 folder on your Student Disk. Make sure you open the page in Composer.

4. Click **File**, then click **Open Page**, then locate and open **Bio.htm** from the Tutorial.05 folder.

5. Click **File**, then click **Save As**.

6. Type **Bio2** in the File name box, then click the **Save** button.

7. Click **File**, then click **Open Page**, then locate and open **Events.htm** from the Tutorial.05 folder.

8. Click **File**, then click **Save As**. Type **Events2** in the File name box, then click the **Save** button.

9. Point at one of the Composer buttons in the taskbar. Figure 5-20 shows the Events2 page as the active document. If you were to click the button corresponding to the Findlay Farmhouse page, that window would then be the active document.

Figure 5-20 ◀
Opening
multiple Web
documents

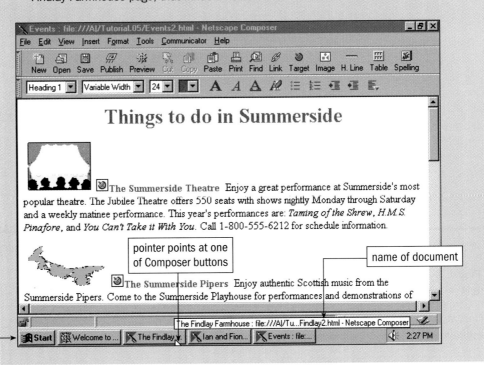

Creating a Hypertext Link Between Two Documents

You create a link between two documents in the same way you created a link to a target within the same document—using the Link button 🔗. However, instead of clicking a target, you use the Choose File button to indicate the filename of the page that is the destination of the link.

Fiona's three pages are all open in separate Composer windows. You are ready to create links between the pages. You decide to start by linking the Findlay2 page to the Bio2 page.

To create a hypertext link to the Bio2 page:

1. Click the **Composer** button on the taskbar that corresponds to the Findlay2 page.

   TROUBLE? Point at the Composer buttons on the taskbar until you see one that says The Findlay Farmhouse (the page's title). Refer back to Figure 5-20 to see this button.

2. Locate the Proprietor information just below the bulleted list at the top of the page.

3. Select the text **Ian and Fiona Findlay**.

4. Click the **Link** button 🔗.

5. Click the **Choose File** button.

6. Click **Bio2**, then click the **Open** button. See Figure 5-21.

Figure 5-21 ◀
Creating a link
to another
document

linked text in
document

target filename

click to locate file

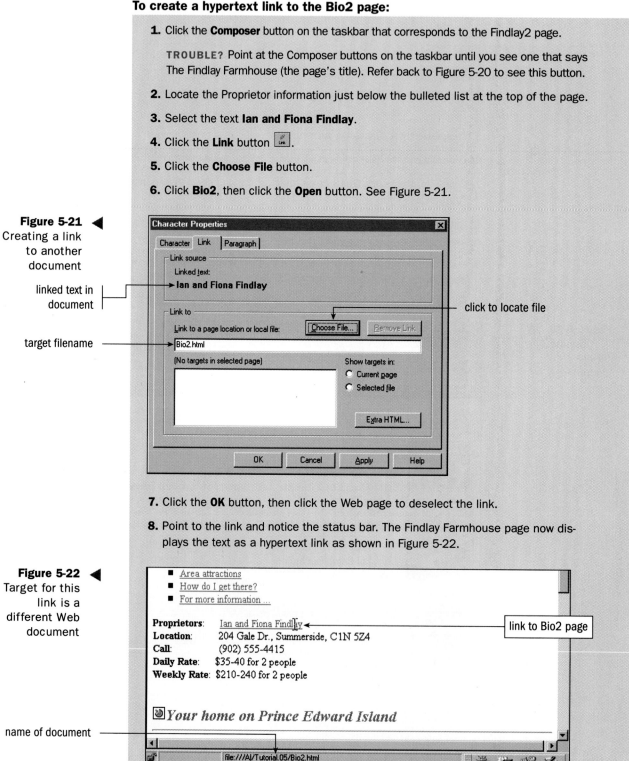

7. Click the **OK** button, then click the Web page to deselect the link.

8. Point to the link and notice the status bar. The Findlay Farmhouse page now displays the text as a hypertext link as shown in Figure 5-22.

Figure 5-22 ◀
Target for this
link is a
different Web
document

name of document

Clicking the link shown in Figure 5-22 will jump you to the Bio2 page. You'll test this link later. Now you are ready to create a hypertext link to the Events2 page.

To create a hypertext link to the Events2 page:

1. Scroll down the document window to the **For more information...** section.

2. Select the text **View our complete list of area activities**.

3. Click the **Link** button 🔗.

4. Click the **Choose File** button, click **Events2**, then click the **Open** button.

5. Click the **OK** button. The text referring to area activities should now be converted to hypertext as is displayed in Figure 5-23.

Figure 5-23 ◀
New hypertext
link

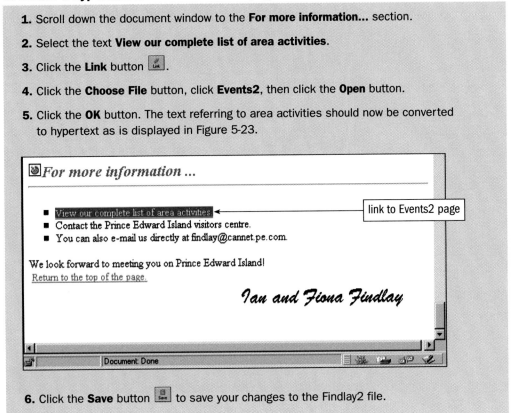

6. Click the **Save** button 💾 to save your changes to the Findlay2 file.

Now insert links in the Bio2 and Events2 pages that point back to the Findlay2 page. Start with the Bio2 page first.

To create a hypertext link from the Bio2 page to the Findlay2 page:

1. Click the **Ian and Fiona Findlay** button for the Bio2 page.

2. Select the text **Findlay Farmhouse Bed and Breakfast** located in the paragraph below the picture of Ian Findlay.

3. Click the **Link** button 🔗.

4. Click the **Choose File** button, select the **Findlay2** file, click **Open**, then click the **OK** button.

5. Click the **Save** button 💾.

Finally, you need to create the hypertext link from the Events2 page back to the Findlay2 page. Since there is no text on the Events2 page that specifically references the Findlays or their bed and breakfast, you will have to insert a hypertext link.

To create a hypertext link from the Events2 page to the Findlay2 page:

1. Click the **Events** button for the Events2 page.

2. Scroll to the bottom of the document window and click to the right of the description of Foster Landing, then press **Enter** twice.

3. Click the **Link** button 🔗.

4. Click the **Choose File** button, select **Findlay2**, then click the **Open** button.

5. Click the **Enter text to display for a new link** box.

6. Type **Go to the Findlay Farmhouse page.**

7. Click the **OK** button. Figure 5-24 shows the page with the newly-inserted hypertext link.

Figure 5-24 ◀
Link to Findlay
Farmhouse
page

location of link
to Findlay
Farmhouse page

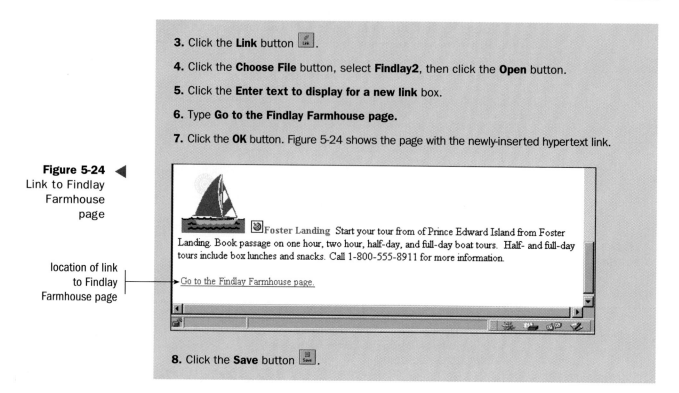

8. Click the **Save** button 💾.

The hypertext links between the pages in the Findlay Farmhouse Web presentation are now in place.

Testing Your Hypertext Links

Now that the hypertext links are in place, you should return to the Findlay2 page in the browser and then test the links among the three pages to verify that they are working properly.

To test your links:

1. Click **The Findlay Farmhouse** button for the Findlay2 page.

2. Click the **Preview** button 🔆. The page opens in the Navigator browser.

3. Click the hypertext link **Ian and Fiona Findlay**. The Bio2 page opens in the browser.

4. Scroll down the document window and click the hypertext link, **Findlay Farmhouse Bed and Breakfast**. You return to the Findlay Farmhouse page.

5. Click the **For More Information...** hypertext link to jump down the Findlay Farmhouse page to that heading.

6. Click the hypertext link, **View our complete list of area activities**. The Events2 page is displayed in the browser.

7. Scroll to the bottom of the document window and click the hypertext link, **Go to the Findlay Farmhouse page**. You return to the Findlay Farmhouse page.

8. Click **File**, then click **Close** to close the browser.

The links are working properly.

Linking to Targets Within Other Documents

You can create links not just to other documents, but also to specific points within documents. The destination point must have a target, and the hypertext link you insert must point to that target. You already know how to link to targets within the same document, but now you'll see how to link to targets in a different document.

You and Fiona discuss creating links from the individual items on the Findlay Farmhouse page that correspond to events on the Events2 page. You both agree that it would be a good idea. To save you time, the Events2 page already contains targets for theatre, bagpiping, golf, and so on. Using those targets, you decide to add links from activities mentioned on the Findlay2 page to the corresponding activity on the Events2 page.

To insert a link to an event on the Events2 page:

1. Be sure the **Findlay2** page is active in Composer.

2. Scroll to the **Area attractions** section.

3. Select the text **The Summerside Theatre**, then click the **Link** button.

4. Click the **Choose File** button, click **Events2**, then click **Open**. A list of targets on the Events2 page appears in the target box. See Figure 5-25.

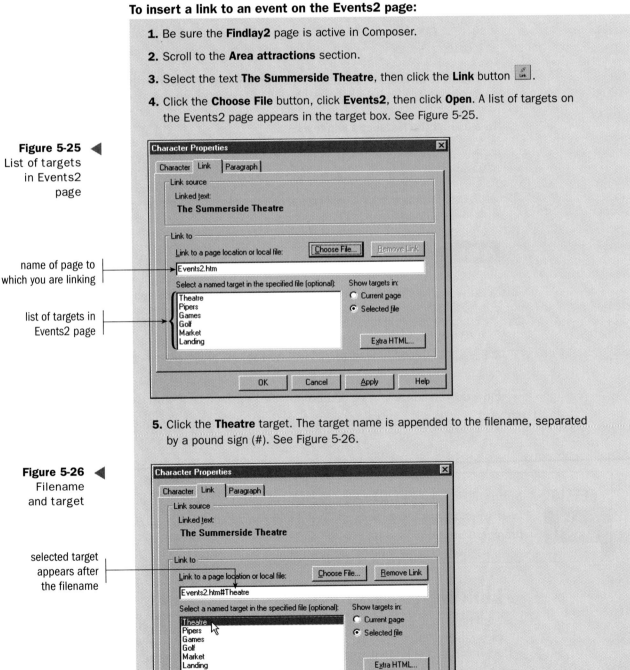

Figure 5-25
List of targets
in Events2
page

name of page to
which you are linking

list of targets in
Events2 page

5. Click the **Theatre** target. The target name is appended to the filename, separated by a pound sign (#). See Figure 5-26.

Figure 5-26
Filename
and target

selected target
appears after
the filename

6. Click the **OK** button.

7. In a similar manner, link **The Summerside Pipers** to the **Pipers** target and **Turwick Point Golf Club** to the **Golf** target.

8. Save the changes to the Findlay Farmhouse page, then click the **Preview** button.

9. Scroll to and then test each of the three links and verify that you jump to the appropriate targets in the Events2 page. Click the **Back** button each time you test a link to return to the Findlay Farmhouse page.

TROUBLE? If a link does not jump to the correct place, open the Findlay2 page in Composer, right-click the link, click Link Properties, then verify that the correct target is specified. If it isn't, correct the link as necessary to correct the link target.

10. Click **File**, then click **Close** to close the browser.

You have now inserted links to the Findlay's Web page that make it easy for users to navigate through the presentation. You decide to take a break.

To close all the Netscape windows:

1. Click any one of Composer buttons on the taskbar.

2. Click **File** and then click **Exit**.

3. Click the **Yes** button to close all windows and exit Netscape.

Quick Check

1. What is storyboarding? Why is it important in creating a Web page presentation?

2. What is a linear structure? Draw a diagram of a linear structure and give an example of how to use it.

3. What is a hierarchical structure? Draw a diagram of a hierarchical structure and give an example how to use it.

4. How do you create a hypertext link to another document with Composer?

5. How do you create a hypertext link to a target in another document with Composer?

SESSION 5.3

In this session you will learn how to create hypertext links to Web pages on the Internet and to an e-mail address. You'll also learn how to publish your Web presentation.

Linking to Web Pages

Until now you've worked with files all located on the same computer. However, you make use of the real power of the Web when you start linking your document with Web pages on other computers located anywhere from across the hall to across the world. The technique for creating a hypertext link to a Web page on a different computer is very similar to the technique you use to link to documents on your computer, except that instead of specifying the page's filename, you have to specify the page's URL.

As you have seen, a URL is the address of a page on the World Wide Web. If the URL you are targeting includes additional targets within the page, you can add that target to the URL so the link points to a specific location in the document. For example, the URL you might enter for a section of a page on majors at MidWest University might be:

http://www.mwu.edu/course/info.html#majors

Figure 5-27 dissects the structure of the fictional MidWest University URL about majors.

Figure 5-27 ◄
Parts of a URL

Parts of URL	Interpretation
http	The communications protocol. Between the protocol and the Internet host name you type a separator, usually a colon followed by a double slash (://).
www.mwu.edu	The Internet host name for the computer storing the Web document.
course	The folder containing the Web document.
info.html	The filename of the Web document.
#majors	The target in the document, preceded by a pound sign (#).

Some Web page URLs, such as http://www.microsoft.com/, do not include the filename section. In cases where the filename is missing, the name of the file is assumed to be index.html, but you don't need to specify that in the URL you enter on your page.

Inserting a Hypertext Link to a Web Page

Fiona would like the Findlay Farmhouse page to include a link that points to a Prince Edward Island information page. The URL for this page is http://www.gov.pe.ca. The text for this link is already in place at the bottom of the page.

To insert a link to a page on another computer:

1. Open **Findlay2** from the Tutorial.05 folder in Composer.

2. Scroll down to the **For More Information...** section at the bottom of the page.

3. Select the text **Contact the Prince Edward Island visitors centre**.

4. Click the **Link** button 🔗.

5. Type **http://www.gov.pe.ca** in the Link to box as shown in Figure 5-28.

Figure 5-28 ◀
Specifying a
URL as the
link target

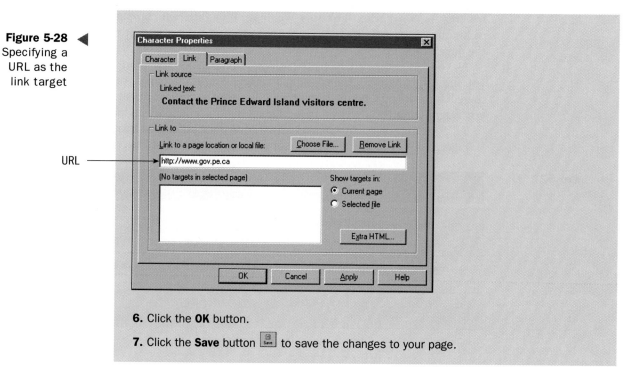

URL ────────▶

6. Click the **OK** button.

7. Click the **Save** button 🖫 to save the changes to your page.

As usual, you should test your link. To test a link on another computer, you will need to connect to the Internet.

To test this hypertext link:

1. Connect to the Internet, if necessary.

2. Return to Composer, if necessary.

3. Click the **Preview** button 🔆.

4. Scroll to the bottom and then click the **Contact the Prince Edward Island visitors centre** hypertext link. The information page appears as shown in Figure 5-29.

TROUBLE? If the page does not appear, it could be because you are not connected to the Internet or that the Web server that is storing this page is not working. If the page looks different from the one shown in the figure, it could be because the page has changed since the time this tutorial was written. Ask your instructor if you should create a different link. To edit the link, right-click the link in Composer, and then click Link Properties. Make changes to the link's target as necessary, and then click the OK button.

Figure 5-29 ◀
Prince Edward
Island page

Web page might
look different

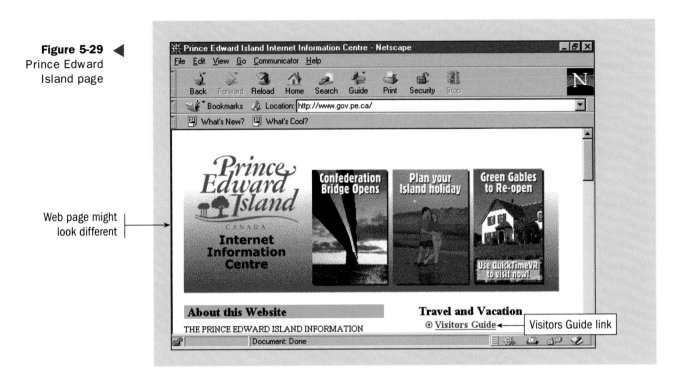

Users of the Findlay page will now be able to access Prince Edward Island information directly.

Creating a Link Using Drag and Drop

Composer offers an even easier way to add links to your Web page. The **drag and drop** technique involves dragging a hypertext link from the Navigator browser window and dropping it into Composer window. This useful technique helps you avoid typing errors, because you don't have to type long and complicated URLs. The Findlays would like a link to a page featuring attractions on the island. The information page that you just accessed includes a link to a visitors guide. You decide to view that page and then locate a link to area attractions. You can drag the link to that page directly into your document.

To create a link through dragging and dropping:

1. Click the **Visitors Guide** link shown in Figure 5-29.

   TROUBLE? If you don't see a Visitors Guide link, scroll the page or select a different link.

2. Resize the Visitors Guide Navigator window and The Findlay Farmhouse Composer window so that you can see both on your desktop.

   TROUBLE? To resize windows, you must first click the Restore button 🗗 on each of the windows. Then drag the lower-right corner until the two windows are about the same size. Drag the title bars to move the windows into place.

3. Click within the Composer window to make it the active window.

4. Add a new list item in the Composer window by clicking the end of the item, "Contact the Prince Edward Island visitors centre" at the bottom of the page and pressing **Enter**. See Figure 5-30.

   TROUBLE? Don't worry if your Visitors Guide page looks different or if the URL is different. The page is updated periodically.

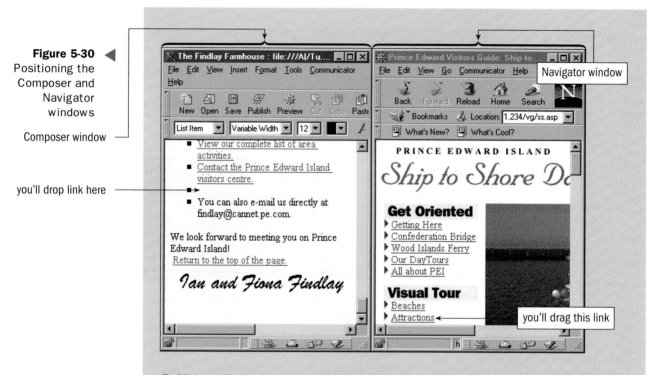

Figure 5-30 ◀
Positioning the
Composer and
Navigator
windows

Composer window

5. Click the Navigator browser window to activate it.

6. Point to the **Attractions** link on the tourism page within the Navigator window. Then, with the mouse button held down, drag the pointer across to Composer window as shown in Figure 5-31.

> **TROUBLE?** If you don't see an Attractions link such as the one in Figure 5-31, scroll to locate it, or choose a different link.

> **TROUBLE?** If you click the Attractions link by mistake, click the Back button [Back], then repeat step 5.

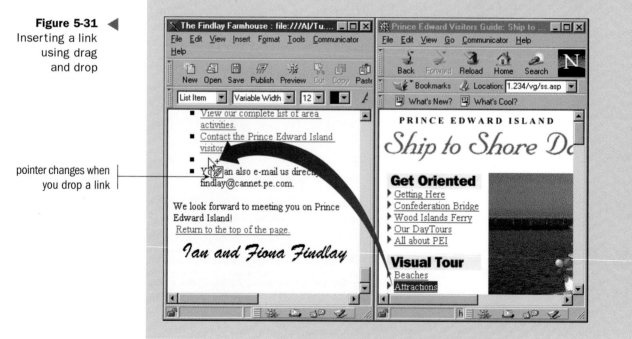

Figure 5-31 ◀
Inserting a link
using drag
and drop

pointer changes when
you drop a link

7. Release the mouse button, dropping the link into the space for the new list item you created.

8. Maximize the Composer window. Figure 5-32 shows the new hypertext link in the list of items.

> **TROUBLE?** If a space appears before the Attractions link in the Composer window, delete the space.

Figure 5-32 ◀
Inserted link

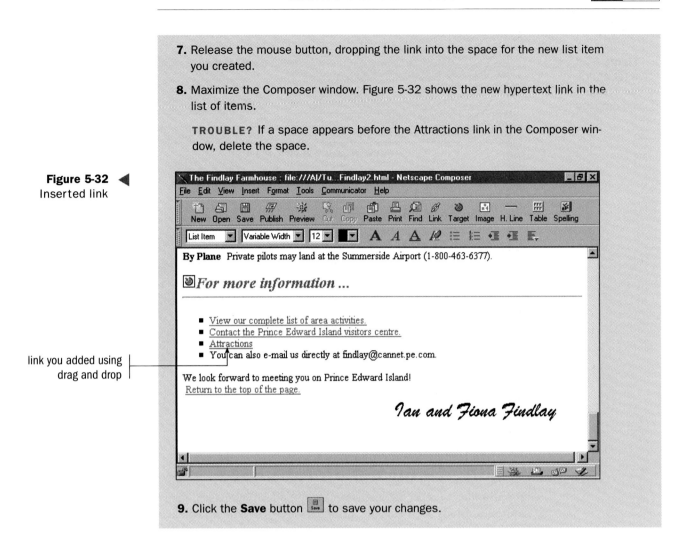

link you added using
drag and drop

9. Click the **Save** button to save your changes.

As usual, you should confirm that the link you just created works.

To check your new hypertext link:

1. Click the **Preview** button. Scroll to the bottom of the page, then click the **Attractions** link. The Attractions page appears as shown in Figure 5-33.

> **TROUBLE?** If the page that appears looks different, don't worry. The links and pages at this site might have changed since this book was published.

Figure 5-33 ◀
Target of link
you dragged
and dropped

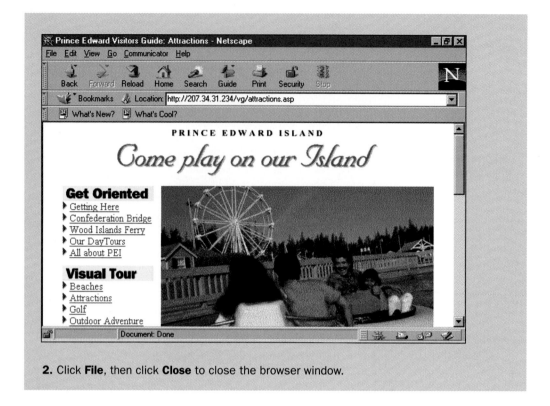

2. Click **File**, then click **Close** to close the browser window.

You return to the Composer window.

Linking to an E-mail Address

You can link to other Internet resources besides Web pages, such as FTP servers or e-mail addresses. Many Web authors include their e-mail address on their Web pages so that they can receive direct feedback from people who use the page. The URL for an e-mail address is:

> mailto:*e-mail_address*

where *e-mail_address* is the Internet e-mail address of the user. For example, if a user's e-mail address is davis@mwu.edu, the URL for this address is mailto:davis.mwu.edu. When someone reading the page clicks this e-mail address link, the browser starts an e-mail program from which the user can create and send an e-mail message. Not all browsers can work with the e-mail hypertext link.

In order to make it easy for people to contact them, the Findlays have included their e-mail address on their Web page. You suggest that they make this a hypertext link.

To create a link to an e-mail address:

1. In the Composer window, if necessary, scroll to the bottom of the page. Select the text **findlay@cannet.pe.com** from the For more information... section.

2. Click the **Link** button 🔗.

3. Type **mailto:findlay@cannet.pe.com** in the Link to box as shown in Figure 5-34.

Figure 5-34 ◀
Creating an
e-mail link

e-mail link ————→

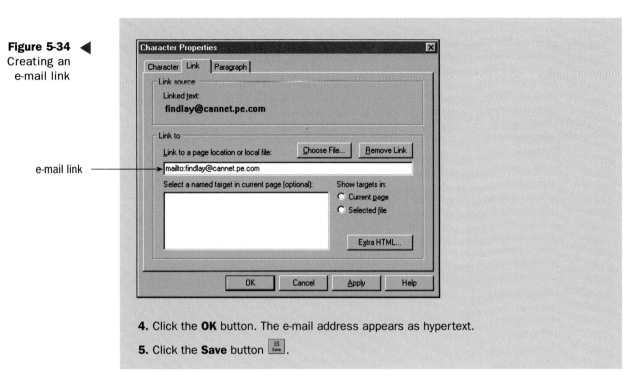

4. Click the **OK** button. The e-mail address appears as hypertext.

5. Click the **Save** button.

Now you should test this link to verify that it works properly. When you click an e-mail link, Communicator automatically opens the Composition window: the same one you used with Messenger.

To test your e-mail address link:

1. Click the **Preview** button.

2. Scroll to the bottom of the page and click **findlay@cannet.pe.com**. The Composition window opens and the address you clicked automatically appears in the To box as shown in Figure 5-35. At this point you could enter a message and send it off. For now, you should simply exit without sending anything (the e-mail address is fictional).

Figure 5-35 ◀
Composition
window

Findlay e-mail
address automatically
inserted

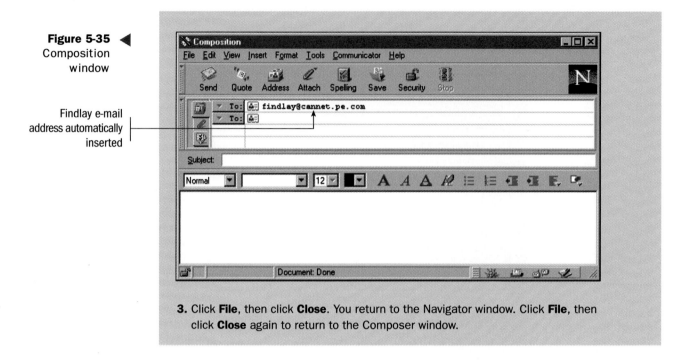

3. Click **File**, then click **Close**. You return to the Navigator window. Click **File**, then click **Close** again to return to the Composer window.

The Findlay Farmhouse home page is now complete.

Publishing a Web Page

Ian and Fiona are pleased with the final appearance of the Findlay Farmhouse home page. They are ready to publish it on their Web site so that the general public can access it. To publish a page on the Web, you must first have space on a Web server. Your Internet Service Provider (ISP)—the entity through which you have Internet access—usually has a Web server available for your use. Since each ISP has a different procedure for storing Web pages, you should contact your ISP to learn its policies and procedures. Generally, you should be prepared to do the following:

■ Make sure your HTML documents have the four-letter extension "HTML." Composer automatically saves files with the four-letter extension.

■ Make sure the filenames of your documents have correct case. For example, if your page refers to "Ian.gif" make sure the filename is Ian.gif, not ian.gif.

■ Find out from your ISP the name of the folder into which you'll be placing your HTML documents.

■ Work with your ISP to select a name for your site on the Web (such as http://www.findlays.com). Choose a name that will be easy for customers and interested parties to remember and return to.

- If you select a special name for your Web site, register it at http://www.internic.net. Registration is necessary to ensure that any name you give to your site is unique and not already in use by another party.

- Add your site to the indexes of search pages on the Web. This is not required, but will make it easier for people to find your site. Each search facility has different policies regarding adding information about Web sites to their index. Be aware that some will charge a fee to include your Web site in their list.

The Findlays have already worked with their ISP to acquire and register the name www.findlays.com. They are ready to publish their page on the Web. Their home page includes not just the Findlay Farmhouse page, but the biography and events pages, as well as numerous gif image files. You'll want to include all those files. Often the easiest way to do this is place all the files associated with the page in a single folder. Your files are all in the Tutorial.05 folder, but there are additional files there too, so you'll need to select only the files you need when you publish your pages.

You will only be able to perform the next sets of steps if you have space on a Web server.

To publish a Web page:

1. With the Findlay2 page open in the Composer window, click the **Publish** button [Publish]. The Publish window opens.

2. Type the http or ftp location to which you want to publish in the HTTP or FTP Location box. This address must begin with http:// or ftp://. The Findlays type ftp://ftp.findlays.com/findlay/web/ but you will type something different.

   TROUBLE? If you aren't sure what you should enter, check your default publishing location in the Preferences dialog box. Click Edit, click Preferences, and then click Publishing under the Composer category. Your ftp or http site appear, as well as the http browsing address that users will use to locate your page.

3. Press **Tab** and type your username in the User name box. Often the username and password for your Web page is different than for your email.

   TROUBLE? If you don't know your username and password, check with your ISP.

4. Press **Tab** and type your password in the Password box. Now you'll select the files you want to include.

5. Click the **All files in page's folder** option button. All the files in the Tutorial.05 folder appear. You can click the ones you don't need to deselect them. In this case, you've been working with the Findlay2, Bio2, and Events2 pages, so click **Bio.htm**, **Events.htm**, and **Findlay.htm** to deselect them. The rest of the files are gif files that you should include. See Figure 5-36.

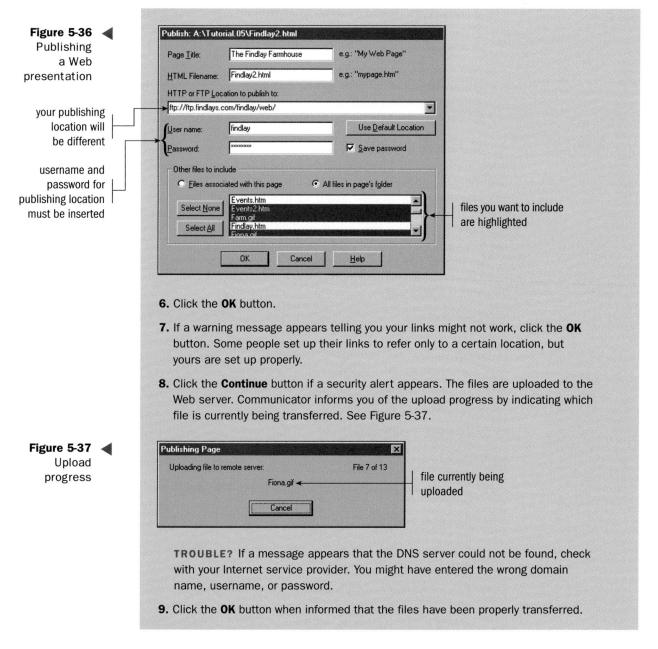

Figure 5-36
Publishing
a Web
presentation

your publishing
location will
be different

username and
password for
publishing location
must be inserted

files you want to include
are highlighted

6. Click the **OK** button.

7. If a warning message appears telling you your links might not work, click the **OK** button. Some people set up their links to refer only to a certain location, but yours are set up properly.

8. Click the **Continue** button if a security alert appears. The files are uploaded to the Web server. Communicator informs you of the upload progress by indicating which file is currently being transferred. See Figure 5-37.

Figure 5-37
Upload
progress

file currently being
uploaded

TROUBLE? If a message appears that the DNS server could not be found, check with your Internet service provider. You might have entered the wrong domain name, username, or password.

9. Click the **OK** button when informed that the files have been properly transferred.

Once you have published your Web page, you should connect to it on the Web to make sure the graphics appear correctly and the links all work.

To test your Web page:

1. Click the **Navigator** button in the Component bar.

2. Type the URL of the Web page you just published in the Location box and then press **Enter**.

3. Test all the links by clicking them and using the navigation buttons. See Figure 5-38.

Figure 5-38 ◀
Findlay page
on the Web

Findlay's Web site ——

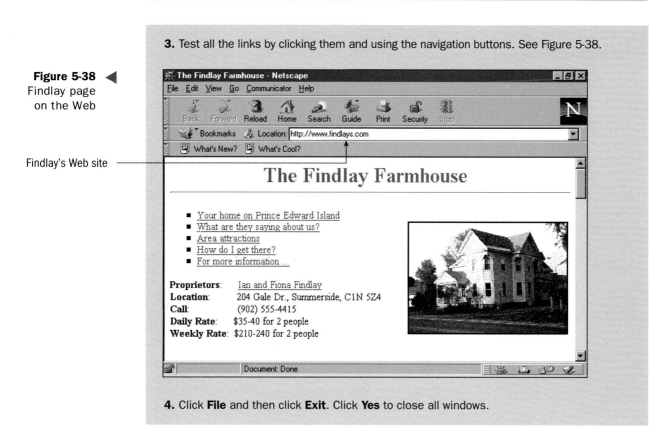

4. Click **File** and then click **Exit**. Click **Yes** to close all windows.

Ian and Fiona thank you for your help. They decide to work with the page for a few days and get customer feedback. Then they'll let you know if they need any more help.

Quick Check

1. What is the URL for a target named petunia in a file named info.htm located in the /flowers/inventory folder of the Web server whose host name is www.ftd.com?

2. If you are connecting to the URL http://www.cinemagreats.com, what is the name of the html file that the browser will open?

3. If you are connected to a page containing a link that you'd like to include on your page, how can you easily create such a link?

4. What is the advantage of using drag and drop to add a link to your page?

5. If you want to include a link to your e-mail address, what URL should you enter?

6. If you have just published your Web page but when you test it you notice a graphic doesn't appear properly, what might you suspect? Give two possibilities.

7. True or false: Adding your Web page to Web indexes is always free.

Tutorial Assignments

Ian and Fiona have had a chance to work with the page you created. They would like you to make the following changes:

- Add a link to the Events2 page that takes the user from the bottom of the page to the top.

- On the Events2 page, include a note that Ian Findlay is honorary chairman of the Highland Games. Include a link to the Bio2 page.

- Include a link on the Events2 page that points to the official Prince Edward Island list of events and attractions located at http://www.gov.pe.ca/vg/attractions.asp

To complete this tutorial assignment:

1. Open the Events2.htm file in Composer.

2. Insert a target named "Top" at the beginning of the main heading.

3. Scroll to the bottom of the page and add a new line, "Return to the top of the page."

4. Link the text to the target named "Top" that you just created.

5. Scroll up to the description of the Summerside Highland Games. Add the following text to the end of the paragraph:

   "You can also contact Ian Findlay, this year's honorary chairman, care of the Findlay Farmhouse Bed and Breakfast."

6. Select the text "Ian Findlay" from the sentence you just entered and link it to the Bio2 page in the Tutorial.05 folder.

7. Scroll down to the bottom of the page and add a new line:

   "For more events and attractions, go to the Prince Edward Island list of current attractions".

   Note: Make sure you do not make the line you add a continuation of the existing link when you press Enter. If your new line does continue the link, highlight the new line, then choose Remove Links from the Edit menu.

8. Select the text "Prince Edward Island list of current attractions" and link it to the URL http://www.gov.pe.ca/vg/attractions.asp.

9. Save your changes to the "Events2.htm" file.

10. Preview the Events2 page in the browser to confirm that the links are working properly. If the attractions URL is not available, ask your instructor if you should use a different URL.

11. Print the page.

12. If you are able, publish the Events2 page. You might be prompted to replace the existing page on your Web site. Check that all links are still working properly.

13. Hand in the printout to your instructor.

14. Close Communicator.

Case Problems

1. The Author Series at Avalon Books Avalon Books is adding a new set of pages to their home page that will include biographical information for authors making appearances at the bookstore. They've asked you to set up the hypertext links between the bookstore's home page and the biographical pages.

To complete this case problem:

1. Start Composer and open the file "Avalon3.htm," located in the Cases folder in the Tutorial.05 folder on your Student Disk.

2. Save the file as "Avalon4" in the Cases folder.

3. Scroll down to the list of the coming week's events.

4. Select the text "Sandy Davis" and create a hypertext link to the file "Sd.htm," located in the Cases folder in the Tutorial.05 folder on your Student Disk.

5. Select the text "John Sheridan" and create a hypertext link to the file "Js.htm" in the Cases folder in the Tutorial.05 folder on your Student Disk.

6. Save your changes to the Avalon4 file.

7. Preview the file in the Navigator browser and confirm that the links are working correctly.

8. Print the Avalon4 page.

9. Hand in the printout to your instructor.

10. Close Communicator.

2. Creating a List of Movie Reviewers You want to create a Web page for the Film School that lists pages containing reviews and synopses of major movies. You've received a list of existing pages and their URLs from your instructor. See Figure 5-39.

Figure 5-39 ◀

Page Name	URL
America Cinema	http://www.geocities.com/Hollywood/2171/
Washington Post Reviews	http://www.washingtonpost.com/wp-srv/searches/movies.htm
All-Movie Guide	http://www.allmovie.com/amg/movie_Root.html
Roger Ebert on Movies	http://www.suntimes.com/ebert/ebert.html
The A-List Movie Reviews	http://www.geocities.com/Hollywood/Hills/1197/a-list.html
The Best Video Guide	http://www.tbvg.com/
BoxOffice Online	http://www.boxoff.com/

Create a Web page of this list. Format the list as a bulleted list with a solid square bullet. Make each page name a hypertext link to the appropriate Web page. Add the title "Movie Review Pages" at the top of the Web page, and then publish the page when you are finished.

To complete this case problem:

1. Open a blank document in Composer.

2. In the Page Properties dialog box, on the General tab, type "Movie Review Pages" in the Title box.

3. Type your name in the Author box, and type "A list of useful movie review Web pages" in the Description box.

4. Save the page as "Movie.htm" in the Cases folder in the Tutorial.05 folder on your Student Disk.

5. Type the main heading "Movie Review Pages," formatted with the Heading 1 style and centered on the page.

6. Create a left-aligned bulleted list of the page names and URLs shown in Figure 5-39.

7. Select the bulleted list and using the Properties dialog box, choose the solid square symbol for the bullets.

8. Select each URL in the list and link the URL text in the item to the URL specified in Figure 5-39.

9. Save your changes to the file.

10. Preview the file in the Netscape browser and confirm that each link is working correctly.

11. Create a printout of your Web page.

EXPLORE

12. If possible, publish your page and ensure that you can connect to it once it is published.

13. Hand in the printout to your instructor.

14. Close Communicator.

3. Personnel Pages at First City Bank The systems manager at First City Bank is creating Web pages listing company employees and their positions. Figure 5-40 shows one such page that details the bank's loan officers.

Figure 5-40 ◄

First City Bank

Loan Officers

Loan Officer, Linda Keller

Loan Officer, Laura Flint

Assistant Loan Officer, Mary Taylor

Each photo on the page is linked to another page that gives more detail about the employee. The three employee pages are located on your Student Disk in the Cases folder in the Tutorial.05 folder with the filenames Keller.htm, Flint.htm, and Taylor.htm. Create the page shown in Figure 5-40, including the hypertext links to these three files.

To complete this case problem:

1. Open a blank document in Composer.

2. In the Page Properties dialog box on the General tab, type "First City Bank Loan Officers" in the Title box.

3. Type your name in the Author box, then type "Loan officers at First City Bank" in the Description box.

4. Save the page as "Bank.htm" in the Cases folder in the Tutorial.05 folder on your Student Disk.

5. Type the main heading "First City Bank," formatted with the Heading 1 style and centered on the page.

6. Insert a horizontal line after the main heading that covers the width of the page.

7. On a new line, type the title "Loan Officers," formatted with the Heading 2 style and left-aligned on the page.

8. Insert the graphic image file "Keller.gif" on the first line below the Loan Officers heading.

9. Type "Loan Officer, Linda Keller" to the right of her photo.

10. Insert the graphic image file "Flint.gif" on the next line.

11. Type "Loan Officer, Laura Flint" to the right of her photo.

12. Insert the graphic image file "Taylor.gif" on the next line.

13. Type "Assistant Loan Officer, Mary Taylor" to the right of her photo.

 14. Select each of the three photos, and using the Link button, link the photos to the files Keller.htm, Flint.htm, and Taylor.htm.

15. Save your changes to the file.

16. Open the "Bank.htm" file in the Navigator browser and verify that the links are working properly.

 17. If possible, publish the page and verify that the links are functioning.

18. Print a copy of your page.

19. Hand in your printout to your instructor.

20. Close Communicator.

4. Create Your Own Web Presentation Create a Web presentation about yourself. There should be three pages in the presentation. The first page should deal with your interests. Include an ordered list of your top-ten favorite Web pages. The second page should deal with your coursework. Include a bulleted list detailing your previous courses. The third page should be a resume page that you could submit to an employer. Include short summaries of your work experience and educational background. Create hypertext links between the three pages including links to specific points within each page using targets. The appearance of the page is up to you. Use whatever colors, page backgrounds, or inline images that you think are appropriate. Publish the page on your Web server when you are finished and provide the URL of your page to your instructor.

Answers to Quick Check Questions

SESSION 4.1

1 "What you see is what you get"—allows you to see how the final document will appear as you develop your page

2 when you don't need to be connected to the Internet, such as when you are developing a Web page

3 so that users will be able to find your page more easily

4 HTML

5 A markup tag is an HTML label within angle brackets. A style is a name assigned by Composer to a tag that appears in a list on the Formatting toolbar.

6 Not all browsers will be able to view it.

7 It allows only options supported by HTML.

8 Normal

SESSION 4.2

1 In Navigator they appear numbered; in Composer with a pound sign #.

2 Select the list items and right-click the selection. Click Paragraph/List Properties and then select the bullet from the Bullet Style list. Click OK.

3 Italics, bold, font type, font size, font color.

4 Not all browsers will be able to display the font.

5 Select the text, right-click the selection, click Character Properties, change the properties, and then click OK.

6 Select the text, click the Font Color list arrow, and then click green.

SESSION 4.3

1 Percent of window indicates what percentage of the window the line will extend across; pixels indicates the number of pixels the line will occupy.

2 Browser displays inline graphic on the page while a separate application must start to display an external graphic.

3 GIF and JPEG

4 Convert it to GIF or JPEG format.

5 A non-interlaced graphic appears one line at a time, starting from the top of the image and working down. In an interlaced graphic, the image appears stepwise with the image coming gradually into focus.

6 Right-click the line, click Horizontal Line Properties, enter 25 in the Width box and choose % of window as the width option. Click OK.

7 That the graphic is not so large that it makes the page take longer to display and that it is not too distracting from the main text on the page.

8 So users know the picture's content without having to view the image itself.

9 False. It highlights words it doesn't recognize; they are not necessarily misspelled.

SESSION 5.1

1   A target is a reference point on a page that identifies a specific location; it is necessary when you want to link to that location.

2   Click where you want the target or highlight the text you want to use as the target, then click the Target button.

3   Case sensitive.

4   Select the text, click the Link button, and specify the location to link to.

5   With a pound sign #.

6   Click the Link button, enter the text you want to use as hypertext, enter the link's target, then click OK.

7   Navigator.

SESSION 5.2

1   Storyboarding is the technique of creating a graphical representation of the pages and links in a Web presentation. Storyboarding is important in creating a coherent and user-friendly structure.

2   A linear structure is one in which Web pages are linked from one to another in a direct chain. Users can go to the previous page or next page in the chain, but not to a page in a different section of the chain.

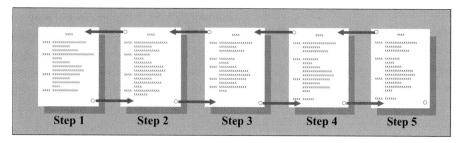

You could use a linear structure in a Web page presentation that included a series of steps that the user must follow, such as in a recipe or instructions to complete a task.

3   A hierarchical structure is one in which Web pages are linked from general to specific topics. Users can move up and down the hierarchy tree.

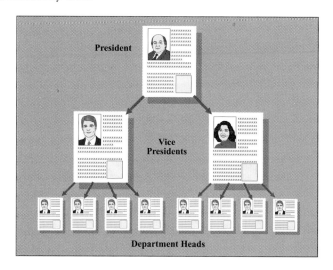

A company might use such a structure to describe the management organization.

4   Click the Link button, click the Browse button, and select the file you want to link to.

5   Click the Link button, click the Browse button, select the file, and then click the target in that file you want to link to.

SESSION 5.3

1   http://www.ftd.com/flowers/inventory/info.htm#petunia

2   index.html

3   drag the link onto your Web page

4   You are less likely to make a typographical error.

5   mailto:*e-mail address* where *e-mail address* is the Internet e-mail address of the user

6   The graphic filename might have the wrong case or might be in the wrong folder.

7   False.

Downloading and Installing a New Version of Netscape Communicator

Downloading the Communicator Software

You can download the Communicator software, upgrade to the Communicator software, or any other software available through Netscape Communications Corporation, from Netscape's Web site. You first connect to the Web site and then locate the download software page. Netscape constantly updates their Web site, and the download instructions might change. If you use these steps as a general guide and you read the Netscape pages for information, you should be able to download the software successfully.

You need to download the executable file that contains the Setup program that will install Communicator on your computer. You need to decide where you want to store this file. Many users store program files in a temporary directory they have created for the purpose of storing downloaded software, or in the Windows Program Files directory.

To download the Communicator Setup program:

1. Start your browser.

2. Enter **http://home.netscape.com** in the Location box and then press **Enter.**

3. Click the download link, which appears somewhere on the Netscape home page, depending on what software is currently available. This button might appear at the bottom of the page, and it might be labeled Download Software or Get Software or something similar. The Software Download page opens.

   TROUBLE? If you have a version of Communicator already loaded, Netscape might recognize that fact and prompt you to upgrade to the current version. If that is the case, follow the directions as they appear on the screen.

4. Click the link for the version of Communicator you want, and then click **Next** if necessary. You should see a set of list arrows from which you choose the software and options you want. Figure A-1 shows downloading the Communicator Standard edition, version 4.0.

Figure A-1 ◀
Selecting
version to
download

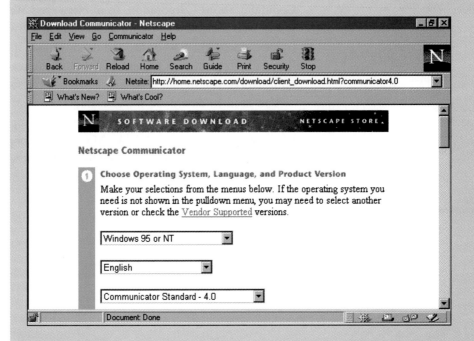

5. Once you have scrolled through the page and filled in the applicable options, click a button such as **Download for Free** or **Buy Now.**

6. If a Security Information dialog box opens, click the **Continue** button.

7. When the Save As dialog box opens, select a folder into which you want to place the program you are downloading.

8. Click the **Save** button. The Saving Location dialog box appears, shown in Figure A-2. Note the Saving line, which shows the folder into which you are downloading the software. This dialog box informs you of the download progress. When the download finishes, the dialog box will close.

   TROUBLE? If the Saving Location dialog box does not appear, there might be a delay in connecting to the server. After waiting a reasonable amount of time, you might need to repeat Steps 5-8.

Figure A-2 ◀
Downloading
program file

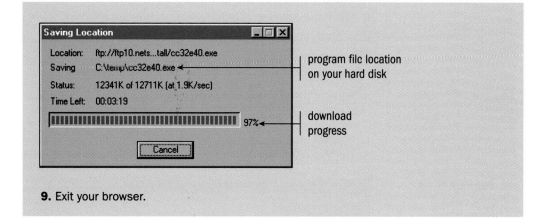

program file location
on your hard disk

download
progress

9. Exit your browser.

Once the Saving Location dialog box closes, the download is complete and the Communicator setup program file is stored on your hard disk.

Installing Communicator

Once you have downloaded the Communicator Setup program, you are ready to install Communicator. When you run the program, it first uses a self-extraction program to extract the Setup files. Then the Setup program starts automatically and completes the installation process.

Depending on the version of Communicator you are installing, it is possible these steps will vary somewhat. If that is the case, read through the steps because they are likely to be similar to what you see on your screen. Then proceed through the installation process and read the Setup windows carefully. They should guide you through a smooth installation.

To initialize the Setup program:

1. Close all open windows and programs.

2. Click the **Start** button and then click **Run**.

3. Type the path of the file you just downloaded, shown in Figure A-2. Figure A-3 shows the Run dialog box for a computer whose program file was saved in a temp directory on drive C.

Figure A-3 ◀
Running the
installation
program

4. Click the **OK** button.

5. Click the **Yes** button to continue. First the Setup files are extracted. See Figure A-4.

Figure A-4 ◀
Initializing the
Setup program

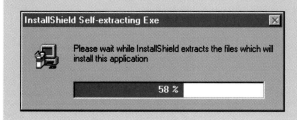

6. Next Setup initializes. Click the **Next** button to continue.

7. Click the **Yes** button to accept the terms of the licensing agreement. The Setup Type dialog box opens, with Typical selected. The Destination Directory box shows the path where Communicator will be installed. See Figure A-5.

TROUBLE? If you want to change this location click the Browse button and then click a new location.

TROUBLE? If you want to choose the options you want to install, click the Custom option button, but only use this option if you are an advanced user.

Figure A-5 ◀
Selecting Setup
preferences

Once Setup is initialized you are ready to install Communicator. The Setup program guides you through the process with a set of easy-to-read dialog boxes.

To install Communicator with the Setup program:

1. Click the **Next** button. The Select Program Folder dialog box opens, identifying Netscape Communicator as the name of the Program Folder that will be installed.

2. Click the **Next** button. The Start Copying Files dialog box opens for you to review your setup information. See Figure A-6.

Figure A-6 ◀
Verifying Setup
settings

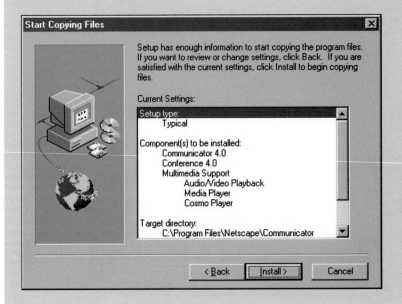

Netscape Communicator

TROUBLE? If you want to change setup information, click the Back button until you reach the dialog box that displays the information you want to change. Make the changes, and then click the Next button until you reach the Start Copying Files dialog box again.

3. Click the **Install** button. Setup installs the program and informs you of the setup progress. When setup is 100% finished, it asks if you want to view the README file, which informs you of licensing and release note issues.

4. Click the **Yes** button to view the README file. When you are finished reading it, click the **Close** button ☒. You are informed that Setup is complete.

5. Click the **OK** button. You are informed that Setup must restart your computer. Click the **Yes** option button, unless you have other programs running, in which case you must restart your computer later to run Communicator.

6. Click the **OK** button.

TROUBLE? If your computer doesn't restart, you might have to restart manually. Exit Windows and then turn the computer off and then on again.

Your computer restarts. You are now ready to launch Communicator. Proceed to the first tutorial in this book. You can read the next two sections in this appendix for information on adding components to your version of Communicator or adding plug-in software.

Adding Components with SmartUpdate

Netscape makes new components available periodically that you might want to add to your Communicator software. One such component is the Netcaster component. Depending on your installation you might already have this component, but if you don't, or you want new components that have recently been made available, you can use the Netscape SmartUpdate feature. **SmartUpdate** helps you download a component of Communicator without having to download the entire Communicator package. It analyzes your system and installs the correct software with ease.

These steps show you how to use SmartUpdate to download Netcaster, but you can also use it to download other components or plug-ins that enhance your version of Communicator.

To use SmartUpdate to download Netcaster:

1. Launch Navigator, connect to **http://home.netscape.com**, the Netscape Communications Corporation home page, and then link to the **Netscape Products** page.

   TROUBLE? The Netscape Products page is usually available via a button at the top of the page, such as Company & Products.

2. Click **Communicator**.

3. Scroll through the Communicator overview to locate the SmartUpdate link.

4. Click **SmartUpdate** and then scroll down to the installation options section.

5. Click the **Netcaster** option button. See Figure A-7.

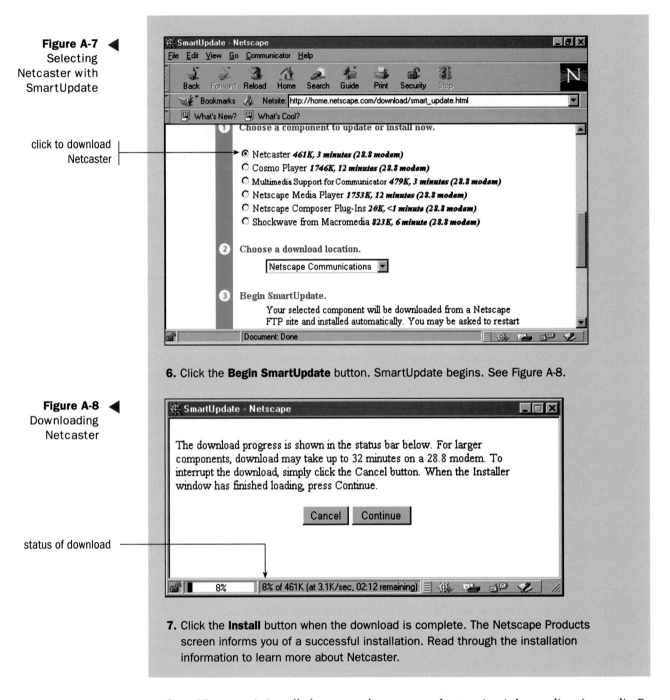

Figure A-7 ◄
Selecting
Netcaster with
SmartUpdate

click to download
Netcaster

Figure A-8 ◄
Downloading
Netcaster

status of download

6. Click the **Begin SmartUpdate** button. SmartUpdate begins. See Figure A-8.

7. Click the **Install** button when the download is complete. The Netscape Products screen informs you of a successful installation. Read through the installation information to learn more about Netcaster.

Once Netcaster is installed, you can learn more about using it by reading Appendix B.

Reviewing Communicator Plug-ins

Communicator **plug-ins** are software programs that extend the capabilities of Communicator and its components. Media Player, for example, is a plug-in that allows you to play sound files. Third-party (non-Netscape) companies develop plug-ins and make them available through the Netscape Web site. You can often download trial versions of plug-ins for free.

Figure A-9 shows the plug-in categories Netscape maintains. It's possible that Netscape has added or removed plug-in categories since this book was printed.

Figure A-9 ◀
Plug-in
categories

Category	Description
3D and Animation	Software that allows you to experience 3D pages and play animated files.
Business and Utilities	Business or computer-related software related to office uses, such as address books, scheduling, remote computer operation, and so on.
Presentations	Presentation software that allows you to enhance your Web presentations.
Plug-in Extras	Extensions of plug-ins that enhance their functionality.
Audio/Video	Software that plays media files.
Image Viewers	Graphic image viewers that allow you to open graphic images with non-standard file types.
What's New	Page of new and interesting plug-ins.
What's Cool	Page of unusual plug-ins.

To view a list of available plug-ins:

1. Connect to **http://home.netscape.com** and then connect to the Communicator page.

2. Scroll to the bottom, if necessary, and locate and click the link similar to **Plug-ins & Extras**. The Inline Plug-ins page opens. See Figure A-10.

Figure A-10 ◀
Connecting to
the plug-in page

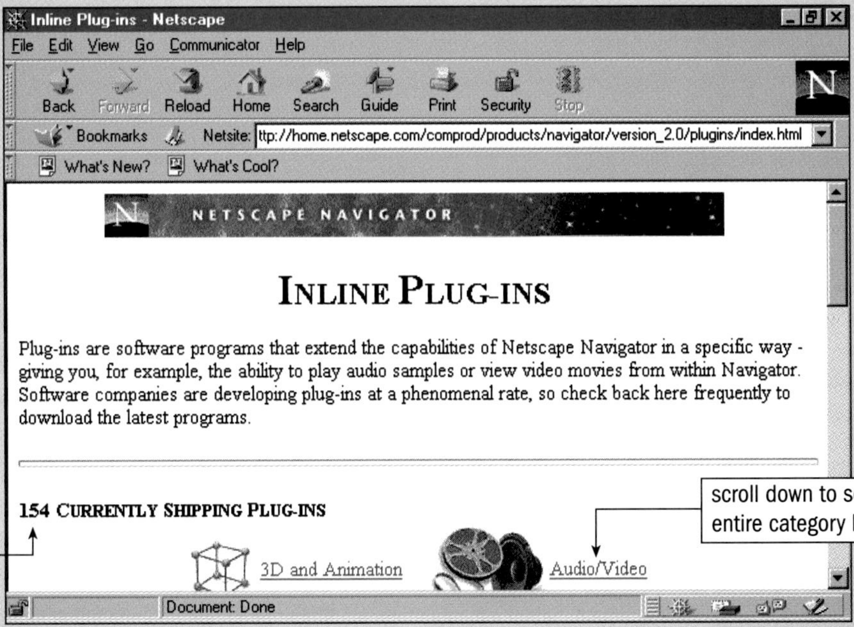

number of currently
available plug-ins;
your number will
probably be different

scroll down to see
entire category list

3. Click the category link you are interested in.

4. Click the plug-in you want to download and follow the instructions that appear on the screen.

5. You might need to restart Communicator to enable the plug-in you just downloaded.

You might not notice the plug-in has been installed until you have a reason to use it. Media Player, for example, doesn't run until you click a media file.

Receiving Information Automatically with Netcaster

OBJECTIVES

In this tutorial you will learn to:

- Understand push technology

- Start Netcaster and preview a channel

- Subsribe to and open a channel

- Change the default channel

- Delete a channel

When you use Navigator to find information on the Web, you search for information and then "pull" the information from the Web onto your computer. Recent Web technology, however, has made it possible for you to request that information be delivered automatically, just as a newspaper is delivered to your front doorstep, without requiring you to go search for it. Users indicate the type of information they want and how often they want it delivered. Special software will go onto the Web, locate the information, and "push" it to the user's computer. Figure B-1 illustrates the difference between the pulling and pushing of information.

Figure B-1 ◀
Pulling vs.
pushing

Pull technology

Web server

with Navigator, you pull information
to your computer

Push technology

Channel

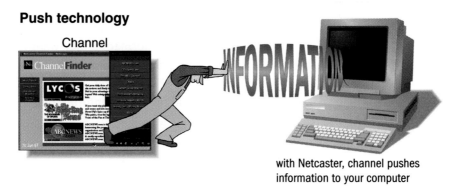

with Netcaster, channel pushes
information to your computer

With **push technology**, providers of information broadcast their content to Web users who have requested it. You subscribe to a **channel**, or a Web site that offers push technology, whose information can be delivered automatically to a desktop. You can indicate how often you want to receive the updated information. An organization such as CNN or Newsweek might maintain a Web channel to push late-breaking news to subscribers. They can then simply check their desktops at regular intervals to get a quick look at the news. As push technology becomes more common it is likely that channels will increase in frequency just as Web pages have done.

Previewing a Channel

Although channels are constructed similarly to Web pages in that they use HTML and other Web authoring tools, you access them differently. With Navigator you navigated to a Web page, but with Netcaster you preview a channel and then decide whether you want to subscribe to it so it will push you information automatically.

When you first start Netcaster, the Netcaster window appears on the right. The Netcaster window features **Channel Finder,** a ready-made list of interesting channels chosen by Netscape. It also allows you to preview channels not included in Channel Finder.

In order to receive pushed information, you must be connected to the Internet, but it is unlikely that in a student lab you will be logged in long enough to take advantage of push technology. It's also likely that your lab managers have disabled this feature because students often don't have the rights to receive information on the hard drive. For this reason, you might only be able to read these steps. Moreover, the Netcaster software is relatively new and is undergoing rapid development, so you might have a different version of Netcaster than the one shown here. If that is the case, the steps might differ somewhat.

These steps demonstrate how to preview the Wired channel.

To start Netcaster and preview a channel:

1. Click **Communicator** and then click **Netcaster**. The Netcaster window appears on the right side of your screen. See Figure B-2. If this is the first time you've started Netcaster, it might take some time to load (5 minutes or more).

   TROUBLE? If you see only a small bar with the Netscape logo and an arrow on your screen, your Netcaster window is minimized. Click the arrow, shown in Figure B-2, to display the entire Netcaster window.

Figure B-2 ◀
Netcaster
window

Netcaster window ——

Channel Finder bar ——

if Netcaster window
doesn't appear, click
this arrow

2. If necessary, you might need to click the **Channel Finder** bar to open the Channel Finder channels list.

3. Click the **More Channels** bar in the Channel Finder list. Channel Finder opens, displaying a list of channels and their descriptions. Each channel includes an Add button **+ ADD CHANNEL** that you can click to preview the channel. See Figure B-3.

   TROUBLE? If More Channels doesn't appear, click one of the channels listed in the Channel finder.

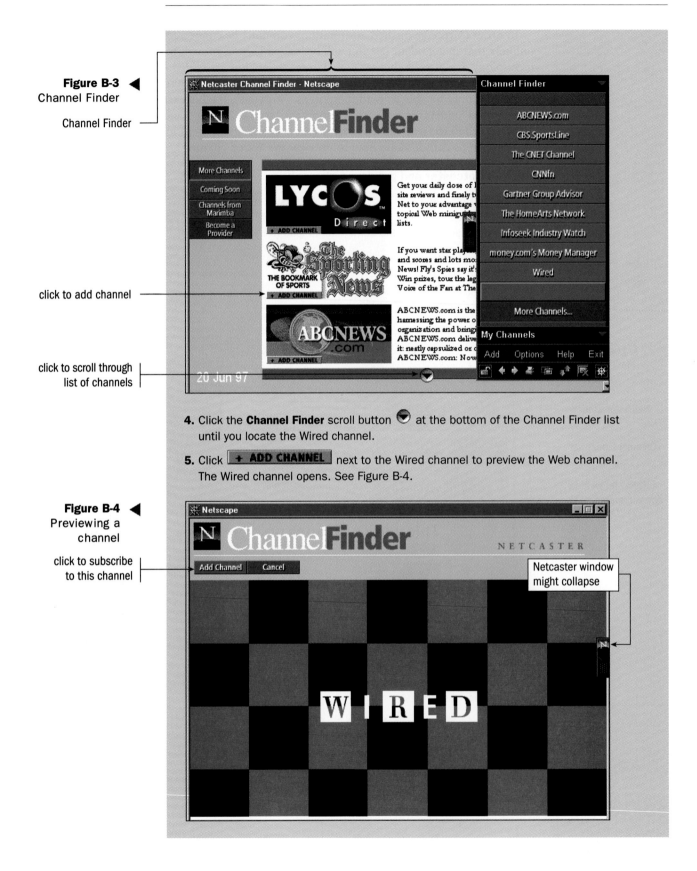

Figure B-3
Channel Finder

Channel Finder

click to add channel

click to scroll through
list of channels

4. Click the **Channel Finder** scroll button at the bottom of the Channel Finder list
until you locate the Wired channel.

5. Click **+ ADD CHANNEL** next to the Wired channel to preview the Web channel.
The Wired channel opens. See Figure B-4.

Figure B-4
Previewing a
channel

click to subscribe
to this channel

Netcaster window
might collapse

You can preview a channel without actually having subscribed to it, but information will not be pushed from that channel until you have subscribed to the channel.

Subscribing to a Channel

If you find a channel you like, you might want to subscribe to it so that its information is sent to you regularly. Netcaster offers two ways to subscribe to a channel:

- Preview the channel first and then click the channel's Add button. The Channel Properties dialog box opens, which automatically inserts the channel's location.

- If you want to add a channel that you haven't previewed, you can click the add button in the Netcaster window. The Channel Properties dialog box opens, and you enter the channel's location.

When you subscribe to a channel, you have two information delivery options. The information can either be sent to a Netcaster window, in which case you must open Netcaster and open that particular channel in order to view the updated information, or you can specify that the channel be saved as a webtop. A **webtop** is a channel that appears in place of your computer's desktop. For example, if you use the Windows 95 operating system, the default desktop is green and there are icons representing objects such as the Recycle Bin and the My Computer window. With a webtop, that desktop is hidden under the channel to which you are subscribed. A user on a corporate intranet, for example, might replace her desktop with the company's webtop, because she then has instantaneous access to her company's updates. Netscape's online NetHelp system can help you learn more about webtops.

You also will need to decide how often you want the channel to update. You might want some channels, such as news channels, you update every 30 minutes. For other channels, a daily update might be sufficient.

You also need to specify how much of the channel you want to download. Each channel is made up of **levels** that represent a Web site's page structure. The first level is that site's home page, and the second level consists of pages that are targets of links on the first level, and so on. By default, Netcaster downloads a site's first two levels so that any link you click on the first level will function without requiring you to connect to the Internet to view your channel.

You decide to subscribe to the Wired channel you just opened and specify that it update every morning.

To subscribe to a channel you are previewing:

1. Click the **Add Channel** button that appears at the top of the channel window. The Channel Properties dialog box opens, with that channel's location already filled in for you.

   TROUBLE? If you are in a computer lab, an error message might appear warning you that you cannot subscribe to channels. Click the OK button, exit Netscape Communicator, and then read the rest of this section.

2. Click the **Update this channel or site every** check box and then click **day**. Change the time, if necessary. See Figure B-5.

Figure B-5 ◄
Setting channel
properties

click to schedule
updates

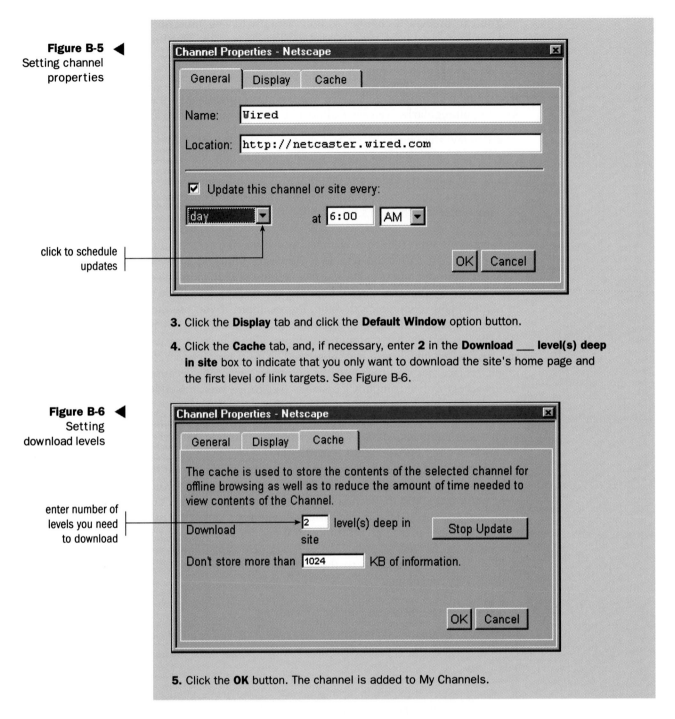

3. Click the **Display** tab and click the **Default Window** option button.

4. Click the **Cache** tab, and, if necessary, enter **2** in the **Download ___ level(s) deep in site** box to indicate that you only want to download the site's home page and the first level of link targets. See Figure B-6.

Figure B-6 ◄
Setting
download levels

enter number of
levels you need
to download

5. Click the **OK** button. The channel is added to My Channels.

When you subscribe to a channel, it is added to the My Channels list, the list of channels to which you are subscribed. Information from this channel will now be sent to Netcaster daily. If you check the Netcaster window tomorrow, new information from this channel will have appeared if you were connected to the Internet at the specified time.

Once you have subscribed to a channel, you can open it from My Channels.

To open a channel from My Channels:

1. Open the Netcaster window.

2. Click the **My Channels** bar. The list of channels to which you have subscribed opens. See Figure B-7.

Figure B-7 ◀
Viewing My
Channels

My Channels bar ──

your subscription
channels (your list
might be different)

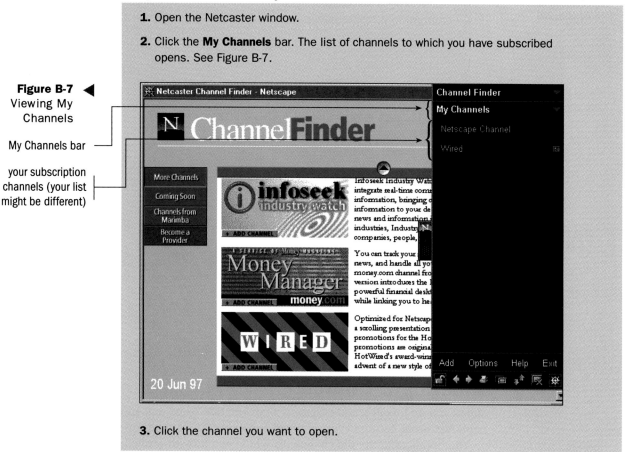

3. Click the channel you want to open.

Changing the Default Channel

By default, the Netcaster channel opens when you start Netcaster. If you want a different channel to appear, such as a daily news channel, you can specify that channel as the default channel. You can also specify that no channel appear when you start Netcaster.

To specify a channel as the default channel:

1. Click the **Options** button in the Netcaster window.

2. Click the **Layout** tab.

3. Click the **Set default to** list arrow, and then click the channel you want to use as the default. See Figure B-8.

Figure B-8 ◄
Changing
default channel

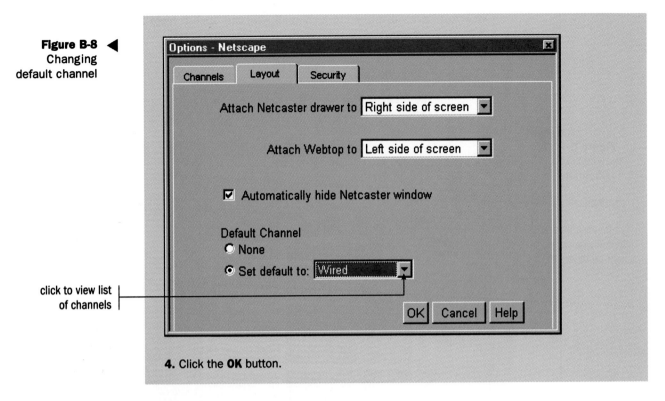

click to view list
of channels

4. Click the **OK** button.

The channel you chose will now appear automatically when you next start Netcaster.

Deleting a Channel

When you no longer want a channel's information to be sent to you, you should delete it from Netcaster, because every channel you subscribe to takes up your system's resources. You decide to delete the channel to which you just subscribed.

To delete a channel:

1. Make sure the Netcaster window is open.

2. Click **Options**, and then click the **Channels** tab.

3. Click the channel you want to delete.

4. Click the **Delete** button, and then click the **OK** button twice.

5. Click the **Exit** button to close Netcaster.

The channel you deleted will no longer send you updated information.

The Internet Using Netscape Communicator **Index**

If you are using this text as part of our Custom Edition Program, you will find entries in the Index and Task Reference that do not apply to your custom tutorials.

The Internet Using Netscape Communicator
Task Reference

TASK	PAGE #	RECOMMENDED METHOD
Address Book entries, delete	NC 3.26	Click Communicator, click Address Book, click entry you want to delete, press 🗑️
Address Book, add entry to	NC 3.11	See "Adding an Entry to the Address Book"
Address Book, create list	NC 3.12	Click Communicator, click Address Book, click 📇, type name, enter addresses, click OK
Address Book, use address from	NC 3.14	Click Communicator, click Address Book, click 📝, click 📇, click recipient, click To:, click OK
Attached file, view	NC 3.15	See "Viewing an Attached File"
Audio clip, play	NC 2.5	Click audio file link; playback device starts automatically
Background, set	NC 4.34	See "Using a Graphic Image as a Page Background"
Bookmark file, create	NC 2.16	See "Using Bookmarks"
Bookmark folder, create	NC 2.16	See "Creating a Bookmark Folder"
Bookmark, access	NC 2.16	Click Bookmarks button, if necessary point to folder, click bookmark you want to access
Bookmark, add	NC 2.15	Click Bookmarks button, click Add Bookmark, or, to add bookmark in a folder, click File Bookmark and then click folder
Bookmark, delete	NC 2.19	See "Deleting a Bookmark"
Bullet symbol, change	NC 4.18	Select the bulleted list, right-click the selection, click Paragraph/List Properties, click Bullet Style list arrow, click style, click OK
Bulleted list, create	NC 4.17	See "Creating a Bulleted List"
Component bar, dock or show	NC 1.14	Click Communicator, click Dock or Show Component Bar
Composer, start	NC 4.5	See "Starting Composer"
Document properties, set	NC 4.6	In Composer, click Format, click Page Colors and Properties, click General tab, enter properties, click OK
E-mail folder, delete	NC 3.26	In Messenger, click 📂 to open Message Center, right-click folder, click Delete Folder
E-mail message folder, create	NC 3.18	See "Creating a Message Folder"
E-mail with attached file, see Attached file		
E-mail, check for messages	NC 3.7	Click 📧, type password, or click 📥
E-mail, configure preferences	NC 3.2	Click Edit, click Preferences, click Mail & Groups
E-mail, delete	NC 3.25	Right-click message in Messenger message list, click Delete Message

The Internet Using Netscape Communicator
Task Reference

TASK	PAGE #	RECOMMENDED METHOD
E-mail, file	NC 3.19	See "Filing a Message"
E-mail, forward	NC 3.25	Click message in Messenger message list, click [Forward]
E-mail, print	NC 3.10	Click message in Messenger message list, click File, click Print, click OK
E-mail, read	NC 3.8	Double-click message in Messenger message list
E-mail, reply to	NC 3.9	Click message in Messenger message list, click [Reply], click Reply to Sender, enter message, click [Send]
E-mail, save to a text file	NC 3.24	Right-click message in Messenger message list, click Save Message, enter location, click Save
E-mail, send	NC 3.4	See "Sending an E-mail Message"
File associations, check	NC 2.3	Click Edit, click Preferences, click Applications, click file type
File, attach to e-mail message	NC 3.22	See "Attaching a File to an E-mail Message"
File, download	NC 2.31	Right-click link to file, click Save Link As, enter a location, click Save
Font size, change	NC 4.21	In Composer, select text, click Font Size button, click size
Help, access	NC 1.33	Click Help, click Help Contents
History list, navigate using [Back] and [Forward]	NC 2.12	See "Searching the Back and Forward History Lists"
History list, open	NC 2.9	Click Go
History window, open	NC 2.11	Click Communicator, click History
Image, insert inline	NC 4.28	See "Inserting an Inline Image"
Image, modify properties	NC 4.31	Right-click image, click Image Properties, change properties, click OK
Image, save from a Web page	NC 2.30	See "Saving an Image from a Web Page"
Images, load automatically	NC 1.29	See "Viewing Images on Demand"
Infoseek, search using	NC 2.25	Click [Search], click Infoseek, type query, click Seek
Line, change properties	NC 4.25	Right-click horizontal line, click Horizontal Line Properties, change properties, click OK
Line, insert	NC 4.24	See "Inserting a Horizontal Line"
Link, abort	NC 1.20	Click [Stop]
Link, activate	NC 1.17	Click the link
Link, create from existing text to target	NC 5.5	Select text, click [Link], click target, click OK

The Internet Using Netscape Communicator
Task Reference

TASK	PAGE #	RECOMMENDED METHOD
Link, create new to target	NC 5.7	Click [icon], click target, type text in Enter text to display for a new link box, click OK
Link, create to e-mail address	NC 5.26	Click [icon], type mailto:*e-mail address*, where *e-mail address* is address you are linking to, click OK
Link, create to file	NC 5.16	Click [icon], click Choose File, click file, click Open, click OK
Link, create to Web page	NC 5.21	Click [icon], type URL in Link to box, click OK
Link, create using drag and drop	NC 5.23	Make sure both Navigator and Composer windows are visible, then drag link from page in Navigator to page in Composer
Navigator, exit	NC 1.23	Click [icon]
Navigator, start	NC 1.11	Connect to Internet account, click [Start], point to Programs, point to Netscape Communicator, click Netscape Navigator
Newsgroup message, post new	NC 3.39	Open newsgroup, click [icon]
Newsgroup message, reply to	NC 3.38	Open message, click [icon], click Reply to Group
Newsgroup messages, download for the first time	NC 3.33	Click [icon], double-click newsgroup whose messages you want to view, click Download
Newsgroup messages, download new	NC 3.37	Open newsgroup, click File, click Get Messages, click New
Newsgroup messages, read	NC 3.36	Click [icon] to view thread, double-click first message, click [icon]
Newsgroup messages, search through	NC 3.40	Open newsgroup, click Edit, click Search Messages, enter criteria, click Search
Newsgroup messages, sort	NC 3.38	Click View, click Sort, click sort option
Newsgroup, search for	NC 3.39	Click [icon], click subscribe, click Search for a Group tab, type keyword, click Search Now
Newsgroup, subscribe to	NC 3.33	In newsgroup list, click newsgroup, click subscribe, click OK
Newsgroup, unsubscribe from	NC 3.41	Right-click newsgroup in Message Center, click Remove Discussion Group
Newsgroup, view list	NC 3.30	Click [icon], click [icon]
Numbered list, create	NC 4.15	See "Creating a Numbered List"
Search, by subject	NC 2.27	Click [icon], click button of search service you want to use, click subject links
Search, conduct a query	NC 2.22	Click [icon], click search service you want to use, type keyword in query box, click Seek or similar button

The Internet Using Netscape Communicator
Task Reference